Hormonageddon

How chemical and electromagnetic influences weakened the human character in three generations

Sacha P. Dobler

This Book is dedicated to my Daughter Ava Sol

Table of content

Chapter 1 Testosterogeddon 19
   1.1. Men lack testosterone, women have too much in gestation, but lack estrogen. 19
      The basics of gonadal hormones (sex hormones) 21
      The history of estrogen treatment for women 22
      Women's common symptoms of low estrogen are: 22
      Estrogen deficiency and mental health 23
   1.2. Biochemistry of the soul 25
      The nuclear family 30

Chapter 2 Overall decline in male testosterone over time 31
   2.1. Rates of Overall decline in testosterone over time 31
      Fertility and testosterone 33
   2.2. Decline in sperm counts 34
      Invitro fertilization is no solution against spermageddon 35
   2.3. Testosterone decline isn't a necessary part of aging 37

Chapter 3 Testosterone alone does not cause aggression 39

Chapter 4 Symptoms of testosterone deficiency 42
   4.1. List of symptoms in men as reported in the literature 42
   4.2. The vicious spiral of disruption of testosterone/ estrogen 45
      Testosterone replacement therapy (TRT) can accelerate the spiral. 46

Chapter 5 Causes 50
   5.1. Endocrine Disrupting Chemicals (EDCs) 50
      The multigenerational death spiral 51
   5.2. Genital malformation is associated with EDC exposure 52
      Genital malformation and EDC exposure in diverse places of the world 52
   5.3. Pesticides 54
      Smoking 60
      Pharmaceutical drugs 61
      Vaccines (Update of 6.2.2022): 61
      The Nanoparticle Pandemic COVID: how the global bio-tech and Insurance Industry predicted a Nanotech Disaster 64

Chapter 6 Electromagnetic fields and testosterone/ estrogen 73
6.1. Endocrine Disrupting Non- Ionizing Radiation (EDNR). 73
6.2. EMF general frequencies (not mobile radiation specific).......... 76
6.3. Wireless/ EMF and testosterone 77
6.4. Mobile phone EMFs and additional hormone disruption 81
Playing hormone roulette.. 81
6.5. Wireless EMF and sperm cells, fertility 82

Chapter 7 Wireless/ EMF exposure: additional cerebral and cognitive effects (not restricted to endocrine disruptors)............. 86
7.1. Mobile phones emit ELF-MFs in the frequency of Alpha brain waves and the first mode Schumann resonance............................. 86
10 Hz frequencies in WLAN (WIFI) affect humans...................... 88
Declining eye sight in children from screen devices..................... 89

Chapter 8 Blurring gender lines 91
8.1. Intersex Variation 92

Chapter 9 Accidental social engineering?..................................... 99
Biochemical and Electromagnetic consolidation of propaganda? 99
Did the chemically assisted reduction in testosterone help reduce wars and interpersonal violence in the post-war era?................. 101
9.2. A global conspiracy?... 102
9.3. Abolishing the nuclear family 103

Chapter 10 Theories and proposals for population control 106
Recent proposals for chemical behavioral control..................... 112

Chapter 11 Solar- and geomagnetic activity 114
11.1. The Glitch 114

Chapter 12 Gonad hormones in solar maximum and minimum 118

Chapter 13 Treatments and attempted treatments for male testosterone deficiency 123
13.1. Testosterone Replacement Therapy 123
13.2. The risks of TRT... 124

Chapter 14 Historic precedents of oikophobia and low ethnocentrism.. 127
14.1. natural variations in testosterone over time, solar cycles and the Pacification Process in the Middle Ages, self-domestication 127

Chapter 15 The Fall of the Roman Empire and EDCs 129
Lead poisoning inhibits endocrine function 132

Chapter 16 Remedies and prevention 138

16.1. Minerals and vitamins 138

Testosterone and COVID 138

EMFs cause mineral and vitamin deficiency 140

Vitamin D deficiency, wireless EMF and virus diseases: closing the circle to testosterone function 141

EMF and zinc (organic) supplementation 143

16.2. Steps to reduce EDC exposure 147

16.3. Steps to reduce wireless/ EMF exposure 148

Notes 152

Preface

Have you been wondering how many people became more docile, defeatist and irritable recently?

Males, for instance, increasingly conduct themselves as if they were suffering from plummeting testosterone levels, including depression, passive aggression and negative attitude to life. And that is what has been happening. Testosterone levels in men were declining about 1% per year for over 50 years and more recently up to 2 % per year.

Measured by testosterone, a man is now "half the man" his grandfather was. And many think: 'thank God.' Likewise, women are not the women their mothers were.

What's more, all other markers of reproductive health - and with them the expected behavioral and social disturbances - are moving in the same direction at roughly the same rate: estrogen levels in women, infertility, miscarriages, cancer of the reproductive organs. Genital malformation in boys is now almost at 3 %.

This factbook will elucidate how all of these biological changes are consistent with the well-established multi-generational effects of endocrine disrupting chemicals and, more recently, electromagnetic fields as used in wireless technology.

The same disruption of sex hormones that is pushing humanity, at the current progression, towards borderline infertility or *a median sperm count of zero by 2045'*, can incidentally also induce people to just not care, to accept increasingly authoritarian government actions and to jump up and insist these actions are not authoritarian at all. People, especially men with normal testosterone, who are happy, healthy and productive for society, are perceived by the mob as dangerous and "toxic". The decline in gonad hormones cannot be an evolutionary effect, as low gonad hormones are concurrent with infertility and a lower desire to have children.

This is a book about testosterone and estrogen that does neither tell men to "man up" or women to act this way or another, nor does it complain about male toxicity - whatever that means. Rather, it aims to have a positive impact on an unprecedented reset event.

The hormonal havoc results in well-meaning, but shortsighted, empathy-driven political decisions that will cause destruction and suffering further down the line.

Most who subscribe to current day extreme progressivism and radical collectivist ideologies, are not just indoctrinated, but they are biologically inclined to it, they truly feel it in their core. So, it is appropriate to try to understand where they are coming from.

None of the political and social problems of these decisive times in history can be solved without a regeneration of healthy hormone balances especially in gonadal (sex) hormones.

In this updated version, I point out the recent incites on how the Covld vaccine has accelerated the collapse in sex hormones, infertility and the process of Hormonageddon at a mindboggling speed.

We'll also discuss precautions to prevent endocrine disrupting chemicals and sources of radiation to improve mental and physical health for those who will rebuild civilization.

Introduction

When people read the title of the Forbes story: *'You are not the man your father was'*, [1] a few years ago, many affected men thought with regards to themselves and women thought with regards to men: 'Thank God (or rather, thank heavens).' What they don't know is testosterone alone does not cause aggression in men, rather to the contrary.
So, what does this really mean, when measured by testosterone levels, an average man is now ¾ the man his father was and half the man his grandfather was? Compared to our grandfathers and everyone before, we are technically chemically half-castrated. And what does this mean when likewise, women are not the women their mothers were? Aren't we all just more peaceful and tolerant now and everyone sings kumbaya? No.

Testosterone levels have declined from 1999 to 2016 in adolescent and young adult men (AYA), according to results presented at the 2020 American Urological Association. Mean total testosterone decreased from 605.39 ng/dL in 2000 to 451.22 ng/dL in 2016. [2] **A decline of 25 % in 16 years, or 1.5 % per year.**
65-year-old finish men in 2012 had 37% less serum testosterone than 65-year-old finish men in 1983. [3] **A decrease of 1.27% per year].**
Meanwhile, sperm concentration and total sperm count declined between 1973 and 2011 by **50–60%** in Western countries. [4] At the current trajectory, males will have a median sperm count of 0 by 2045. [5]

In all of this, it is important to note that foetal (in utero) testosterone is more decisive for male and female development and the integrity of a society than are the effects of ongoing testosterone reducing agents in adulthood. The latter effects are partly reversible, the in-utero effects are not. Rather, they are accumulating over generations. Preventing endocrine disrupting effects in pregnancy has the biggest positive impact on the well-being of a human being.
A study by Stefano Parmigiani et al, 2003 concluded that "exposure to very low doses of endocrine disrupting chemicals during fetal life permanently alters brain development and behavior in animals and humans". [6]

We are now an epigenetically modified species, biologically and behaviorally different from those who built the infrastructure we live on. It will take more than a generation to reverse the process.

Our personalities and all our opinions are influenced by this multi-generational hormone disruption.

In all of this, it must be considered that artificial administration of hormones or administration of hormone releasing pharmaceuticals do not involve the full natural activation mechanism, they don't generate healthy and sustainable hormone balances and mostly soon have a counterproductive effect. A homeostatic effect might set in that can further shut down natural hormone release. See below how testosterone replacement therapy can even accelerate the process of *'Hormonageddon'*.

Endocrine Disrupting Chemicals can cause a progressive decrease in sperm counts over multiple generations—a phenomenon that environmental scientist Pete Myers refers to as a **"male fertility death spiral."** [7]

Studies on the causes for declining testosterone levels in men are conducted prevailingly in non-western countries, again along the line of the vicious cycles of already low testosterone inhibiting the drive to find out what is going wrong with the instincts to create prosperity and a future for their own family.

Dr. Shanna Swan insists the decline in sperm counts is serious: even though she does not speak of a direct path to extinction:

"If you follow the curve from the 2017 sperm-decline meta-analysis, it predicts that by 2045 we will have a median sperm count of zero. It is speculative to extrapolate, but there is also no evidence that it is tapering off. This means that most couples may have to use assisted reproduction." [8]

Well, invitro fertilization can only help in cases of loss of sperm mobility and numbers: it will mean kicking the can down the road, but only for a short time, because of higher rates of birth defects in IVF babies (see page 35).

Men lack testosterone, women lack estrogen. **Women behave more like men, but that does not make them feel better:**

Common symptoms of low estrogen in women include: fatigue, depression and mood swings.

Coincidently, by many objective measures the lives of women in the United States have improved over the past 35 years, "yet measures of subjective well-being indicate that women's happiness and self-reported well-being have declined both absolutely and relative to men." This paradox of women's declining relative well-being is pervasive across demographic groups and industrialized countries. "These declines have continued and a new gender gap is emerging - one with higher subjective well-being for men." [9]

A tragic accident?
There are now hundreds of endocrine disrupting chemicals in food, drinking water and household goods, so it is impossible to differentiate what substance did what exactly. But as it happens, we are not only approaching borderline male infertility by 2045, but more dramatic is the fact that all other markers of reproductive health - and with them the expected behavioral and social trends - have been moving in the same direction at about the same rate, around 1% per year, and in the last decade accelerating to up to 2 % per year: Not only falling testosterone levels in men and falling estrogen levels in women but miscarriages, genital malformation - including micropenis – cancer of the reproductive organs, all moving towards a scenario as in the movie "Children of Men".
 A French study showed that sperm count has been decreasing 1.9% per year. And that was up to 2005. [10] We don't even know the current rate.
Coincidentally, the males of this society react to this "selection process" just as it is expected of low testosterone males: by shrugging their (feeble) shoulders in the face of their approaching genetic extinction.
It is a hard pill to swallow, but an undeniable fact, that we have turned out to be very different from previous generations, and this not because of psycho-social adaptation or because 'times change' and societies 'evolve', but mostly due to chemical intervention. Peoples and cultures don't "change", just because they want it so. Individuals sometimes change. No wonder grandparents and adult grandchildren understand each other less than ever in recorded history, they can't. Throughout time, grandparents always had concerns the youth should be more prudent and respectful or foresighted, but after all, they realized they were just the same when they were young.
But now, we are a different breed of humans. As an average human you don't have the same personality you would if you had developed in a pristine, natural environment.
What has happened to our gonadal hormones over 3 generations is now part of our personalities, our opinions, our hopes and dreams.

Gonad hormones literally determine political elections. In the 2012 presidential election season (Obama/ Biden's reelection against Mitt Romney) weakly affiliated Democrats had 19% higher basal testosterone than those who identified strongly with the party. When weakly affiliated Democrats received additional testosterone, the strength of their party fell by 12% (p=.01) and they reported 45% warmer feelings towards Republican candidates for president. "Testosterone induces a **"red shift" among weakly-affiliated Democrats," summarized the paper**. [11]

Leaving out artificial testosterone administrated in the experiment: If a 19% lower basal testosterone level can make a strongly affiliated Democrat as opposed to a weakly affiliated Democrat, then what would this mean for testosterone levels of men 50 years ago, when they were twice as high as today?

By the trajectory the democratic party has shifted to the left in recent years, it is easy to extrapolate, that if people as a whole would not have their gonad hormones artificially compromised, i.e. if man had the testosterone of their grandfathers (twice their current levels), and women had the estrogen levels of their grandmothers, then no one would vote for the current democrat platform. Biden could have received but a few percentages of the votes. Again, people and peoples don't just "evolve" without an interference to biology and times don't just "change".

In recent years, average men have become the open target of social developments of politics, media and corporations.

Men (prevailingly - but not exclusively - in the West) are taught to believe without evidence that they are humanly inferior from birth, "male toxicity, believe all women, systemic sexism, systemic racism, neo-colonialism…".

And the more they are accused without evidence, the more they try to appease their accusers and make concessions that they will help to fight male toxicity and that they will "do better", even if (and especially if) they have never done or said anything racist, sexist or homophobe or malicious in their life.

By the same token, women are indoctrinated to believe all men are somehow morally deficient, and those women who don't go along with it, are then targeted as well and they are told that they are responsible for everyone's and everything's problem in the world.

Most average people are in favor of tolerance and acceptance.

The point here is not whether people accept alternative personal identities, lifestyles and other cultures, this has happened increasingly in the past decades in the West and beyond for the first time in history. The big challenge for humanity is how the scales have flipped so abruptly, how it is possible that average people suddenly are targeted and willing to apologize for simply being straight or 'cisgender.' (See for instance: Government funded feminists suggest banning heterosexual relationships, and no one protests). [12]

While all of the exposure to authoritarian ideology has an obvious influence on normal men and women - especially on susceptible young people - there is an underlying biological foundation to all of this, and I will demonstrate that without drastic bio-chemical, endocrine and cerebral changes, which have accumulated over decades, normal people would never accept the premises of current political and social doctrine.

Feminism does not cause boys getting born with micropenis. Radical progressive indoctrination does not cause underdeveloped testicles at birth that produce low testosterone (hypogonadism). Internet censorship of "politically incorrect" media does not cause various forms of genital malformation (now at 2.7% of newborn boys and girls).

When people are opposed to radical transgender ideologies, when children are indoctrinated at school that being transgender is not just ok, but the norm and that they have to choose their gender, then the proponents often argue that some people are born with an intersex condition, with ambiguous genitals and secondary sexual markers and sometimes even with non-binary genetics (neither 46XX nor 46XY). *"Conditions in which chromosomal sex is inconsistent with phenotypic sex, or in which the phenotype is not classifiable as either male or female", the prevalence of intersex is about 0.018%."* [13] Then opponents of current gender doctrine often argue that these are extremely rare cases and the affected children should be evaluated and helped on their way individually.

All of this is changing rapidly, with about 3 % of boys being born with genital malformation, there are now exponentially increasing numbers of actual intersex persons, affording more validity to the transsexual discussion.

The transformation cannot have happened in terms of genetic evolution in 2 to 3 generations simultaneously in different cultures, neither via natural selection nor by naturally induced epigenetic changes, be it also because variations from hetero-sexuality and 'cisgender' identities result in lower birth rates.

Imagine trying to convince your grandfather that people born today should pay reparations for crimes committed hundreds of years ago, while currently committed crime should be decriminalized, as in California. [14] Or imagine your grandmother being told that women who want to raise children, are just week and abused by the patriarchy.

I remember my great grandfather, a gentle, soft-spoken rock of a man, at almost hundred, in the 1980s, sitting in front of his house, playing his mouth organ after feeding his sheep. If someone had told him his great grandkids had to pay reparations for two hundred years ago and they had to be taught gender reassignment ideology in kindergarten, he would not have had it.

He had gone to defend the Swiss border in two World Wars, his grandparents were of the generation who began instating constitutional governments, democracy, equal rights for all humans, the end of privileges for nobility, separation of state and church, the abolishment of the concept of inherited sin or original sin. Things were far from perfect still at the turn of the millennium, obviously, but they were better than at any other time or place in history.

Even if he had been locked up, tortured and brainwashed in a socialist reeducation camp, he could not have accepted that original sin should be reintroduced.

Whether people like it or not, hormonal and behavioral differences in species and genders have developed over millions of years, and they had good reasons to be the way they used to be a few decades ago. Humans have changed their social behavior and lowered reactive aggression over hundreds of millennia, including the process of "self-domestication". More recently, aggressive, antisocial individuals were removed from the gene pool in the pacification process in the Middle Ages and the Renaissance (by harsh punishment of violent crime), which decreased interpersonal violence and aggression by a factor of up to 50 within 800 years. In nature, major genetic shifts occur every 10,000 years; in modern humans these changes take place every 400 years, and they always go through solid biologicals selection processes insuring sustainable changes.

To allow (either recklessly or intentionally) artificial chemical and radiological influences to alter human biology – even if they make people more mellow and less confrontational for a time – will certainly lead to a fantastic genetic selection event and population reduction in the coming decade(s).

Solar History (2018) pointed out what I call a 'glitch' in the relationship between solar- /geomagnetic activity and human excitability.
In the Modern Grand Solar Maximum, roughly the past century, the pattern of violence and solar activity seems to be interrupted sharply after the 1950s. After two world wars, solar and geomagnetic activity kept increasing to record levels in the 1960s and remained high only to drop off in the late 1990s. But interpersonal violence already leveled off precipitously after the 1950s. On the other side of the spectrum, following the historical pattern, since the early 2000s, we should be seeing an increase not only in peacefulness, but rationality and invention.
In *Solar Behavior* (2020) I had proposed a hypothesis of what could have contributed to this inconsistency, which I defend unaltered to this day. But what I had underestimated is the impact that artificial chemical and electromagnetic influences could have had on hormone balances and thus on human behavior. The present book may provide a missing link in this 'glitch'.

Endocrine disrupting pesticides like atrazine were introduced in the late 1950s, and hundreds of ED chemicals such as DDT have been used proficiently since, such as phthalate plasticizers, flame-retardants, cosmetics etc. with accumulative, multi-generational effects. This was then topped off in the 2000s with the expansion of electromagnetic frequencies in wireless radiation in the microwave spectrum, which now turn out to have endocrine disrupting effects as well, by some unfortunate mishap.
Much great work has been done on the effects of endocrine disrupting chemicals and their detrimental influence on fertility as for instance in the new book '*Countdown*' by Dr. S. Swan. See also '*Spermageddon*' the title of a 2019 book by Niels Christian Geelmuyden. [15] The title Hormonageddon is inspired by the former title. Little will be added from my part to the analysis and solving of the chemically induced fertility part of the problem. As for the causes of this hormonal downward spiral, Swan specializes on Endocrine Disrupting Chemicals, EDCs and does not include electromagnetic contributors. The present book will add a wealth of recent studies on the electromagnetic endocrine disrupting effects (particularly in male testosterone) of mobile phone- and Wi-fi radiation, and of course I will discuss the cerebral and behavioral ramifications of solar and geomagnetic activity.
We will focus on the behavioral and social ramifications of low testosterone in men as well as estrogen disturbances in women, which proceed downwards hand in hand at the same rate as fertility.

So, at the current trajectory, we are facing borderline infertility in 24 years from now on and will then slowly go extinct. In this book, the main objective is to find out why most people just don't care and even celebrate (for the first time in history) their genetic extinction. When you hear, for instance: 'if we don't stop greenhouse gases, then Earth will heat up 2 degrees in a hundred years! Think about the children!" Then you know, these people are either uninformed or haven't thought things through, or they are full of it. For if we don't fix the infertility abyss, then there will be no one around to care for rising sea levels or drowning polar bears. And as nature is going to fix itself, there would be no point worrying about anything in these final hours. And if we don't fix the crisis of sex hormones, there will be no fixing the infertility crises, because there will be no one to even want to have children.
But many of us will not go anywhere, and we have an unprecedented chance to create prosperity and peace for the remaining population, not least also because we are entering a deep solar minimum, which is almost certainly merging into a new Grand Solar Minimum.

In the historic context, we see that the Greek and the Roman empires saw a similar decline of family values, plummeting birth rates, increasing oikophobia (hatred of the homeland), obviously without the thousands of endocrine disrupting chemicals of modern societies. However, the ancient Greeks and Romans elite suffered from lead poisoning [16], and lead is also an endocrine disrupting chemical, disturbing testosterone in men and estrogen in women (see p. 132).

I will postulate that without these endocrine disrupting chemical and radiological influences to human biology, few people would still believe anything a politician or a (social) media mogul has to say.
And I will further propose that it is the same hormonal disruptions, that further push people to react to the before said defensively, to jump up and say these ideologies and government actions are not totalitarian at all, and those who think so, should be censored and punished.

Societies that are still concerned about the recent detrimental influences on their testosterone levels are prevailingly Middle Eastern/ Islamic nations (Saudi Arabia, Iran, Turkey etc.), industrialized, non- western countries, mostly Islamic or Persian. They have growing infertility problems, similar as in the West, but they are behind in the process of feminizing of men and masculinizing of women or the 'coming apart' of the nuclear family. "A steady and significant decline in the fertility rate has been observed in Qatar during the past fifty years." [17] It appears that even though they are facing growing problems in reproductive health as well, the men and women in these regions still have enough gonadal hormones to care about the future of their families and societies (we don't have exact recent data on testosterone levels for every nation, cultural and genetic differences certainly also play a significant role).

Thus, much of the research on the relationship between testosterone and mobile/wireless radiation of the past few years is conducted in institutions in these Middle Eastern regions. If things continue the way they are going, the rest of humanity is going to owe the institutions in these countries a big favor.

The fact that behavioral consequences of Hormonageddon is affecting western societies more than non-western countries is also reflected in that women in poor countries - with lower health index - prefer men with manlier faces more so than women in wealthy countries (see also p. 31).

The nuclear family has always been the backbone of any society in history, even in totalitarian collectivist states, where the extended family was made obsolete.

Today's societies are the first to give up on this most archaic social instinct of having children and investing large amounts of personal resources and energy in raising them.

It would have been every totalitarian collectivist state's dream to dismantle the family completely, and to force women to hand over their anonymous babies, to be raised in state run nursing homes from infancy on. The abolishment of the family was proposed by Marx and Engels, [18] even by Plato. But no communist leader has seriously tried to implement it.

The modern-day inclination to destroy the nuclear family from within, the loss of the instinct to reproduce is unprecedented and it strongly coincides with the biological endocrinal disruption in the population.

A global conspiracy? Not necessarily. Kind of. It might as well be global stupidity. History has shown that well-informed bureaucrats and industrialists are also lazy and careless, much like the rest of us. They often managed to convince themselves to tolerate a certain degree of public health risks, if they "believe it will serve the 'greater good' of society, even when they themselves are exposed to these hazards.

This phenomenon is demonstrated in countless environmental health scandals like asbestos, lead or arsenic pollution, where many of the small bureaucrats were affected just as the rest of us.

More recently, low testosterone in men is also implicated in the virus crisis.
"For men, low testosterone means a higher risk of severe COVID-19."[19] And low zinc levels are associated with low testosterone in men and with severity of Covld infections, and electromagnetic fields can disrupt zinc metabolism. Exposure to an electromagnetic field leads to a significant decrease in zinc levels in lung and liver tissues." Further, Wi-Fi router radiation has caused lung tissue changes in rats. [20]
And now it turns out that the C vaccines contain nanoparticles that also affect the endocrine system and accelerate the progress of Hormonageddon at an unprecedented speed.

The main premise of this book is this: none of the social and political problems of these decisive times in history can be solved without a regeneration of healthy hormone balances especially in gonadal (sex) hormones. No education or rational argument in social discourse will convince the masses of the destructiveness of current authoritarian/ collectivist political tendencies. Most who assign to current day extreme multiculturalism, anti-family sentiments and radical collectivist ideologies, are not just indoctrinated, but they are biologically inclined to it, they truly feel it in every cell of their body. Keep that in mind when you talk to them.
At the end we discuss precautions that can be taken to prevent endocrine disrupting chemicals and radiation in your personal life - especially important for the next generation - in case you are interested in you or your children being involved in rebuilding civilization.

Chapter 1
Testosterogeddon

1.1. Men lack testosterone, women have too much in gestation, but lack estrogen.

What is happening to men's testosterone is simultaneously happening to women's estradiol levels (the main component of estrogen).

The two problems are closely related and have largely the same root causes. We are focusing on testosterone throughout this book for the reason that much more data is available to demonstrate the direct effects men's plummeting testosterone levels have on society. The book could almost be called 'Gonadal-Hormonageddon', which I found didn't sound right, somehow.

On sufficient request, I may write a sequel focusing on the female hormone crisis.

The two problems have many converging effects on individuals and society.

Lack of testosterone makes man tired, irritable and depressed - lack of estradiol, estrogen makes women tired, irritable and depressed and both irregularities can be affected by the same chemical and electromagnetic impulses.

The changes that we are seeing obviously result from complicated and intricate interacting biological processes. For women, both too much or too little testosterone is associated with depression.

"Low as well as high testosterone (T) levels are related to depression and well-being in women, T plasma levels correlate to depression in a parabolic curve: at about 0.4–0.6 ng/ml plasma free T, a minimum of depression is detected." [21]

As Stephan Hammes et al 2019 notes: *"In fact, the concept of "male" and "female" hormones is an oversimplification of a complex developmental and biological network of steroid actions that directly impacts many organs."* [22]

It is sometimes claimed that plummeting male testosterone couldn't be caused by artificial influences, because women's testosterone levels are not lowered. This is demonstrably false, as will be elaborated below, supported by hundreds of peer reviewed scientific papers.

When gonad cells are compromised, there is no reason why a particular chemical agent will not interfere with the individual very different gonad cells of men and women in very different or even contrary ways. It is not only to be expected, but empirically demonstrated that female hormone metabolism is affected differently than male hormone metabolism by the same agents.

What we are witnessing is a multigenerational degradation of gonad cells and gonadal hormone production and regulation.

We will get to known causes of this *Testosterogeddo*n - which goes hand in hand with declining sperm counts - in Chapter 5. One of the well-established causes are endocrine disrupting chemicals (EDCs), whereas we have less long-term data on the effects of non-ionizing radiation from wireless communication. All we know is they have similar effects as the chemicals. I will demonstrate the testosterone- and estrogen disrupting effects of these electromagnetic fields, the ones that are known so far, with the aid of some 50 + specific peer-reviewed animal and human studies.

Studies on rats showed that exposure to mobile radiation for 60 min for 3 months cut their serum testosterone levels in half. [23]

And then there are possible natural, environmental contributors, of our changing solar system, including discrepancies in the relationship between sunspots and the solar radio flux as are witnessed since the turn of the millennium.

Reinsurance companies

The health risks and the associated grave implications for society - of Endocrine Disrupting Chemicals on the one hand and electromagnetic fields on the other - are also grounds of concern for the global insurance industry. However, I take it they are more worried about the massive money losses in reliability claims in the near future than about the ongoing collapse of society.

The world's largest reinsurance company, Swiss RE declared in their 2013 *Emerging risk insights" SONAR report* that out of the 7 highest insurance risk topics, 3 are casualty-related topics and were assessed as having the highest impact within 4 -10 years. These are: **"endocrine disrupting chemicals ", "unforeseen consequences of electromagnetic fields"** and "unforeseen consequences of nanotechnology ". [24]

The former two problems were connected in the first version of this book. As detailed in this updated version, since the Covld vaccines, nanoparticles are also associated in the hormonal and societal turmoil of our generation. These three may be the most important issues for this decisive moment in history and the fate of billions of people, they not only keep insurance moguls up at night, be it for different reasons.

"The topics "prolonged power blackout", "run-away inflation and surging bond yields" and "big data" were assessed as being of highest concern as they could have a high impact on the entire insurance industry and might occur within a short period of time."

"Further topics assessed as potentially having a high impact are three casualty topics; these are characterised by their long latency periods: "endocrine disrupting chemicals", "unforeseen consequences of nanotechnology" and "unforeseen consequences of electromagnetic fields". [25]

The basics of gonadal hormones (sex hormones)

"A gonad, sex gland, or reproductive gland is a mixed gland that produces the gametes (sex cells) and sex hormones of an organism. In the female of the species the reproductive cells are the egg cells, and in the male the reproductive cells are the sperm. The male gonad, the testicle, produces sperm in the form of spermatozoa. The female gonad, the ovary, produces egg cells. Both of these gametes are haploid cells." [26]

Testosterone is not only produced by the gonads (by the Leydig cells in testes in men and by the ovaries in women), but small quantities are also produced by the adrenal glands in both sexes. It is an androgen, meaning that it stimulates the development of male characteristics. [27]

The hypothalamus and pituitary gland control how much testosterone the testes produce and secrete. The hypothalamus sends a signal to the pituitary gland to release gonadotrophic substances (follicle stimulating hormone and luteinizing hormone). [28]

The actual prevalence of hypogonadism (lack of function in testis) has been estimated to be 39% in men aged 45 years or older presenting to primary care offices in the United States. [29]

There is a high incidence of hyperandrogenism in female partners of infertile couples, meaning the affected women have very high levels of plasma testosterone. [30]

Men are more directly feminized by these inputs than women are masculinized. And in both cases, correcting low sex hormone levels with artificial replacement therapies further shuts down natural hormone production/ secretion and can even exacerbate the vicious downward spiral of sex-hormone imbalance (see also p. 46).

The history of estrogen treatment for women

Women's health is influenced by a healthy testosterone balance. L. Carcaillon et al showed there is a relationship between circulating levels of Free Testosterone and frailty in older women. *"This relation seems to be modulated by BMI. The relevance and the nature of the association of FT levels and frailty are sex-specific, suggesting that different biological mechanisms may be involved."*
"They further demonstrated an implication of testosterone in the frailty syndrome in women, confirming the association of testosterone with frailty in men, they suggest a differential association of testosterone with frailty by sex." [31]
Psychologist Cordelia Fine writes in *Testosterone Rex* (winner of the Royal Society's science book prize for 2017) testosterone has been blamed for the financial crash of 2007-08, yet studies show that -although women have lower levels than men - they can have a higher appetite for risk – even when it comes to financial decisions. [32]

These are the basics of the female sex hormone metabolism:
"Estradiol (E2), also spelled oestradiol, is an estrogen steroid hormone and the major female sex hormone. It is involved in the regulation of the estrous and menstrual female reproductive cycles. Estradiol is responsible for the development of female secondary sexual characteristics such as the breasts, widening of the hips, and a female-associated pattern of fat distribution and is important in the development and maintenance of female reproductive tissues such as the mammary glands, uterus, and vagina during puberty, adulthood, and pregnancy. It also has important effects in many other tissues including bone, fat, skin, liver, and the brain." [33]

Women's common symptoms of low estrogen are:

Depression, fatigue, shifts in mood
an increase in urinary tract infection (UTIs) due to a thinning of the urethra
irregular or absent periods
hot flashes
breast tenderness
headaches or accentuation of pre-existing migraines
trouble concentrating
Compare these individual symptoms also to current societal trends.

Estrogen is an active neuroprotectant and is presently investigated as a potential therapy against Alzheimer's disease for women. [34]

Motherly feelings
The birth control pill was introduced 18. August 1960.
It is still believed that the sexual liberation that came with the pill changed life style opportunities of women in such a way that it made it more attractive for women to have casual relationships into their middle ages and thus they were since less likely to get married and have children. But there is a cause-and-effect problem, here too. The way the pill intervenes with normal hormonal cycles, it probably has fostered lower desires to have a family simply by suppressing hormonally modulated motherly feelings.
"Healthy women who use birth control pills are poorer judges of subtle facial expressions than non-users" according to new research. [35]
Hormonal contraceptives suppress oxytocin-induced brain reward responses to the partner's face. [36]
Thus, the birth control pills affect women's taste in men. [37]
"After taking the pill, these synthetic hormones enter the brain and act as endocrine disruptors, interfering with the signaling process that is necessary for ovulation. In particular, they prevent the hypothalamus from signaling to the pituitary gland (which regulates your hormones) to secrete the hormones that cause an egg to be released." [38] It can be observed that young women start taking the pill as they want to have children later. Then it turns out the longer they are on the pill and don't have children, the less they want children, until they are out of birthing age.

As female infertility increases, so do miscarriages. In Swedish women ages 18 to 42, between 2003 and 2012, the incidence of recurring **miscarriages increased by 74%.** That's an increase of 8% per year. The authors called it a "fairly rapid" increase. I call it a VERY RAPID increase! [39] In the first months of 2022, a year into the vaccine, Sweden experiences an even more extreme and historic drop in birthrates. [40]

Estrogen deficiency and mental health

"Poor mental health can result from low estrogen levels. Since estrogen is believed to help with your neurotransmitters, low levels are associated with a risk of psychosis, schizophrenia, and worsened symptoms of bipolar disorder." [41]

"Some women's vulnerability to anxiety and mood disorders may be explained by their estrogen levels, according to new research by Harvard and Emory University neuroscientists."[42]
Estrogen deficiency is implicated in the incidence of schizophrenia. "There is mounting evidence from clinical, epidemiological and basic research that estradiol, the main component of estrogens, exerts protective effects in schizophrenia and related psychoses."[43] Transdermal estradiol significantly reduced psychopathological symptoms in women with schizophrenia and *"may provide a new adjunctive therapeutic option for severe mental illness. "*[44]
Estrogen also has direct effects on neuronal function that may play an important role not only in the preservation of neurons but in repair of neurons damaged by Alzheimer Disease process.[45]

Similarly as for men and testosterone, in Wuhan, China in 2020, women with low estrogen levels tended to have more severe COVID-19 than women with higher levels of the hormone.[46]
Estrogens regulate female social interactions in many ways.
Researchers at the University of St Andrews in Fife, UK, have found that women's facial attractiveness is directly related to their oestrogen levels.[47] and vice versa, "women with higher estradiol (the major female sex hormone) concentrations exhibit stronger preferences for the faces of men with higher testosterone concentrations. Women's testosterone preference and estradiol curves track one another across days of the cycle."[48]
And then there is this: "Feminist activist women are masculinized in terms of digit-ratio (2D:D4) and social dominance." The feminist activist sample had a significantly smaller (i.e., masculinized) 2D:4D digit ratio than the general female samples. The size of this difference corresponds approximately to a 30% difference in prenatal testosterone/estradiol ratio, which was the index found to have the strongest association with 2D:4D.[49]
We'll take a detailed look at prenatal testosterone exposure and the 2D:4D digit ratio below.

The use of estrogen prescriptions and menopausal hormone therapy (MHT) has fluctuated over the decades:
"In 1942, the US Food and Drug Administration (FDA) approved marketing of equine estrogens (CEE) for the treatment of menopausal symptoms."[50]
Menopausal hormone therapy (MHT) has been used mostly in western countries, with about 600 million woman-years of use since 1970.

"Use increased rapidly during the 1990s, halved abruptly in the early 2000s, and stabilized during the 2010s with about 12 million current users. Most users begin MHT at around the time of the menopause and can continue for several years." [51]

Mobile phone and Wi-Fi radiation can disrupt estrogen levels in female rodents in a similar drastic way as it can disrupt testosterone in male rodents. Studies showed long-term exposure to electromagnetic radiation from mobile phones and Wi-Fi devices decreases plasma prolactin, progesterone, and estrogen levels but increases uterine oxidative stress in pregnant rats and their offspring. [52]

In a different study, exposure to Wi-Fi EMR at 900, 1800, and 2450 MHz, induced progressive reduction in sex steroid hormones (reduction in serum estrogen, progesterone, plasma TAS, vitamin C), and imbalance in oxidative/antioxidative stress parameters in pregnant rats. [53]

Mobile phone waves were also reported to affect the ovaries and increase follicular atresia and cause changes in sex hormone concentration leading to a reduction in fertility rates in female rats. [54]

More data on EMF estrogen disruption is presented in Chapter 6.5.

1.2. Biochemistry of the soul

Depression, anxiety, eating disorders or similar disorders have sometimes carelessly been included in 'diseases of modern civilization' (Diseases of affluence, prosperity diseases), implying that the high standard of living led to the mental suffering.

Elderly people sometimes comment about disoriented young people who are suffering from mental and behavioral issues for no apparent reason: *"They are doing too well. They have everything, so they don't know what to do with their lives!..."*

Nobody is doing too well. Nobody is so happy, confident and healthy that it makes them bored and then they get depressed, anxious and aggressive.

Happy people with a purpose and a fulfilled life are people at their best. Nobody suffers from mental illness *because* they were spoiled, even though you can be spoiled and unhappy. *Affluent neglect* (children being wealthy and neglected at the same time) does obviously exist. When scientists claim that too much happiness makes you unhappy [55], they conflate up happiness with cheerfulness and an outgoing bubbly personality, the latter two can make people susceptible to abuse.

Humans are very complex beings. What one person 'is', how they feal, what they think, it is all a combination of thousands of genes, in virtually infinite numbers of epigenetic activations, life circumstances, innumerable experiences and so on.
There are no sure treatments to cure depression, anxiety and despair; otherwise, everybody could be well. But there are known mechanisms to cause hormonal disruptions and many of these can be prevented and in rare ideal cases, the symptoms can be reversed, without psychological therapy or counseling, without telling the sufferer how they have to 'turn their life around'.
We know what can brake people, but we seldom know how to fix them. A chemical or physical damage to any of the components of the *hypothalamic-pituitary-testicular (HPT) axis* can change a person completely, his or her personality dampened or depressed. And no empathy, analysis or good advice of what that person should do, can cure the condition. Those who have suffered from severe depression know that all good advice on how to 'be more positive' is futile.
Mainstream psychiatry still treats mental illness as a chemical imbalance in the body. While they are mostly wrong in their approaches to 'cure' this imbalance by adding synthetic chemicals such as hormone suppressants or artificial hormone releasing compounds – which may alleviate symptoms for some time - they have a point that in some cases, the illness can have a (mainly or entirely) biochemical cause.
The gonad hormone mechanism is closely connected to the serotonin regulation; and serotonin dysfunction is linked to depression; thus selective serotonin reuptake inhibitors are used as antidepressants (available since 1987). Drugs such as MDMA (or ecstasy) temporarily release serotonin into the brain.
However, administration of synthetic hormones and hormone releasing substances do not involve the full natural activation mechanism and the effects are temporary and then mostly turn counterproductive.

The main reason why we should care about healthy gonad hormones, is happiness and well-being.
If for instance, someone's *hypothalamus* is working insufficiently due to chemical are mechanical damage, the entire gonad-

hormone- serotonin- system can malfunction and dominate and suppress that person's personality and wellbeing.

In women, "Estrogen acts everywhere in the body, including the parts of the brain that control emotion. Some of estrogen's effects include: Increasing serotonin and the number of serotonin receptors in the brain, modifying the production and the effects of endorphins, the "feel-good" chemicals in the brain." [56]

Estrogen has the 'ability to modulate serotonergic function' [57] and it can improve serotonin-linked diseases by stimulating the serotonin system." [58]

"A decrease in serotonin activity in the brain is linked to feelings of depression. Testosterone may play a role in serotonin reuptake in the brain, improving its activity and your overall mood. " [59]

In short: healthy testosterone in men as well as healthy estrogen in women are strongly connected to positive life outlooks, happiness and wellbeing.

Below, we'll see how endocrine disrupting heavy metals can play a role in all of this, for instance, in young adults with low levels of lead exposure, higher blood lead levels are associated with increased odds of **major depression and panic disorders**, and other psychological alterations. [60] Lead suppresses testosterone in men." Exposure to lead even at levels generally considered safe could result in adverse mental health outcomes." [61]

And lead removal from the body has been used in many cases to completely resolve such symptoms. Read about lead poisoning and testosterone on p. 132.

Thought experiment human nature

The human character or human nature cannot be intrinsically changed by education, indoctrination or social developments. While individuals can undergo changes in their personalities and life outlooks, a population does not change their ideologies or behavior just because they wont to. The only known processes that change the essence of human nature in a sustainable way are:

1. natural selection - also in a social context- (by the death or the reproductive disadvantage of those who can cope with or adapt to environmental conditions less well). Social and political changes exert existential pressure on individuals, so that those who were better adapted have more children and these have a higher survival rate.

2. genocide and persecution, when a state or any authority kills off an ideologically or behaviorally distinct segment of the population that they don't want.

3. chemical or electromagnetic influences on a short-term or epigenetic level (what I call Hormonageddon in the case of the past few decades).
4. possible environmental stress that physically changes brain function and hormonal parameters on a genetic or epigenetic level.

No philosophical or ideological movement has changed a population's character on a meaningful and sustainable level over generations. People can be broken and forced to obey, but their children will not have changed biologically. A populations behavior can be altered temporarily, for instance wealth and social security makes people more docile and cooperative, but only until the wealth is gone. Even though personality traits (the Big Five) are only 40-60 percent genetic, they largely define a people's mentality and culture.

As an example of sustainable adaptation: Humans have become more peaceful in the course of the past 900 years and crime, especially violent crime, decreased drastically (see 14.1.).
This was brought about by harsh punishment of violent and even nonviolent crime (somewhat ironically). Even though genetics is only a part in the expression of violence in a person's life history, this radical approach gradually reduced genes associated with a higher risk of violence, a de- facto eugenic process. In the 20th century, with more indulgence and lenient sentences, crime did continue to decline further, but in direct proportion to the increase in living standards and the welfare state, which removed much of the material incentives to commit property related violent crime.
So, the decline in violent crime between the 1800s until the early 2000s in the West, was not due to actual changes in the genetic predisposition of the people. Which means, crime and antisocial behavior must be expected to relapse to the higher levels of the earlier 20th century and beyond once the economy is in fool collapse. This effect could be dampened by the chemically induced decline in gonad hormones in the past 60 years that left an epigenetically lower testosterone level in men. As men today have only half as much testosterone as their grandfathers, they are technically have castrated. But low male testosterone only reduces physical aggression of low-self-control individuals and does not prevent totalitarian regimes, quite to the contrary: it increases the tendencies of passive aggression, (the affected will be more content when the state commits the violence for them).

Humans and groups of humans can be broken and forced to submit to a state., but since there is no genetic adaptation withing one generation, the people will not be intrinsically adapted to conform to – for instance a more collectivist social structure – and thus a society will not function as the population has no motivation to produce and be active for their society. In China, totalitarian collectivism works much better than elsewhere, because the population has evolved with it over centuries and gravitates towards it.

- Koreans used to be very similar across the peninsula before the Korean War. It is sometimes argued that North Korea demonstrates how indoctrination works to change a population.

How can literally starving North Koreans seriously cry at the grave of their dictator, when his heir will put their entire family in a concentration camp if they don't cry enough?

It would seem they must all just pretend, much like the protagonists in Orwell's1984. But testimonies from refugees indicate that most of the funeral attendees were seriously grieving in excess over the death of their dictator. And some refugees want to return to the north. Meanwhile South Korea is an industrial hub and compared with the region, relatively democratic and liberal, respecting individual freedoms.

So, when it is argued that North Korea demonstrates how indoctrination works to change a population, it must be kept mind that the regime has been killing a double-digit percentage of the population, it eliminated most liberal or libertarian minded, all individualist, entrepreneurs, and free thinkers in the past 70 years. So they have changed the publics mentality by eugenics.

This left a population genetically inclined to be more submissive, egalitarian and collectivist, who is more likely to except poverty and suffering so that 'all animals are equal, but some animals are more equal than others', with the leader being almost the only overweight man in the country.

Which means by today, if north-and south Koreans would exchange babies and adopt them across the border, later as adults, they would have on average a smaller chance of integrating into this other society. It can be assumed that babies of South Korean parents raised by North Koreans in North Korea are likely to end up in a concentration camp as enemies of the state in their adult life.

Physical health and stamina
Today in a western country, even people who live healthily and work physically, are much weaker and less energetic than our

ancestors of 300 years ago who were malnourished, overworked and under enormous physical strains. Our distant ancestors were starving and freezing, worked in the fields for 14 hours a day and watched half of their children die. Although we don't have an objective measure of happiness for those generations, we know they didn't kill themselves in droves and they didn't give up. To be spoiled by the comforts of modern life alone does not cause maladaptedness to hard work. To the contrary we should be fitter and more vigorous and motivated now. If the average person would have to work under the brutal conditions of the pre-1800s, most people would just grumble and starve or commit suicide. Even as recent as the 1970s in Europe, it was normal to see unskilled laborers digging ditches by hand all day, right up to their pension at 65. Today only machinists and supervisors work on construction sites at age 65, that's not just because we are spoiled, but grueling hard labor can simply not be realistically expected.

The nuclear family

To have children used to be a universal human desire until the 1950s in the West. And it still is in much of the developing world. Whenever people were asked what is the meaning of life, almost everyone ever used to say, to be a good person and provide a good life to their children. "My children should have a better life than me." [62] Even in 2014 with below -replacement birth rates in the West and half the other countries, family is still valued as the most important aspect in life. [63] To most people, it didn't even occur to opt out.

Never has any state managed to dismantle the nuclear family. Marx and even Plato strongly promoted this, and totalitarian, socialist regimes have tried without much success. People today in the West are the first generation to increasingly abandon not only the extended family as well as the nuclear family, but the wish of having children altogether. Not only is infertility rampant, but they are the first generation to be content with their ethnic group going literally extinct. This novel trend is strongly coincident in time and place with estrogen disruption in western women. See an extended discussion on abolishing the family on page 103.

Chapter 2
Overall decline in male testosterone over time

Low testosterone can directly affect fertility by causing decreased sperm production and indirectly affect fertility by reducing a man's sex drive and causing erectile dysfunction.

However, men with low testosterone levels, called hypogonadism in medical terms and commonly known as low T, can still have enough of the hormone for sperm production." [64]

Michigan University declared *"Low total testosterone in men is widespread, and it is linked to chronic disease. "* [65]

As far as fertility/ sperm production is concerned, we must assume that things may be further advanced than is known. Statistics based on data from infertility clinics may produce a skewed picture. Men and women who don't plan of having a baby are usually not interested in their fertility status and are less likely to participate in volunteer fertility studies, either. The effect is much accelerated after the vaccination efforts since 2021. Since the people who still planned to have children postponed this in the pandemic, nobody has any idea yet of how many will turn out to be infertile since the vaccine. Even female millennials, the oldest of which are 40, say they want to have children later (see p. 106).

2.1. Rates of Overall decline in testosterone over time

"Several studies from the US and Nordic countries have shown a significant decline in serum testosterone among men from the 1970s to the early 2000s. " [66]

For reference, let's keep in mind that between 1973 and 2011, sperm concentration and total sperm count declined by **50–60%** in western countries. [67] As mentioned above, at the current trajectory, male fertility will be at practically 0 by 2045. [68]

And that is only the one aspect of the crisis that people are talking about (and only few people are talking about it). But all other parameters of reproductive health and biologically influenced behavior are spiraling downward at about the same rate (these are largely ignored).

Travon et al estimated an average population-level decline in serum testosterone levels in American men (age-matched trend 1987-2002) of −**1.3% per year**. [69]

Even in Finland, where men are 'comparatively less affected by testicular cancer and other reproductive health problems', a significant secular trend in testosterone (total and free) levels was observed with lower levels in more recently born age-matched men. Serum testosterone level decreased in men aged 60–69 years from 21.9nmol/l (men born 1913–1922) to 13.8nmol/l (men born 1942–1951).

That's a decrease of 37 % in 29 years or 1.27% per year.

This means 65-year-old Finish men in 2012 had 37% less serum testosterone than 65-year-old Finnish men in 1983.

Men born more recently have also been shown to have a higher risk of testicular cancer compared with men born in previous decades. [70]

The decline (or Hormonageddon) began already somewhere in the 1950s-1960s. A man born in 1970 had about 20 percent less testosterone at age 35 than a man of his father's generation at the same age.

In Denmark, men born after the 1930s-40s have lower testosterone levels in the blood than their fathers and grandfathers had in the same age. **A 30 to 40- year-old man today has a level corresponding to that of a 70-year-old then.** [71]

A 2020 study investigated total testosterone (TT) levels for US men from 1999 to 2016.

Mean total testosterone in young men decreased from 605.39 ng/dL in 2000 to 451.22 ng/dL in 2016. **A decline of 25 % in 16 years, or 1.6 % per year in the US.** [72] TT is also lowered with progressively higher body mass index.

Soum Lokeshwar, MD, MBA, incoming urology resident at Yale School of Medicine, New Haven, Connecticut, says

"Testosterone deficiency has a prevalence of 10%-40% among adult males, and 20% among Adolescent and Young Adult men aged 15- 39 years." The authors hypothesized that serum total testosterone levels will further decline in AYA men. [73]

In all of this, we can keep in mind the standard for normal testosterone levels has been corrected, obfuscating the steepness of the slope of the trend.

Dr. Laurie Blanscet commented: *"normal" Testosterone levels for men are determined by testing the blood of a randomly picked group of men—men who are now having lower Testosterone levels than they should. The result is that Testosterone levels that are actually low have been labeled as "normal". This results in men suffering needlessly from low Testosterone but being told that they are normal and nothing is wrong with them. You need optimal Testosterone levels, not "normal".* [74]

The decline in male testosterone over the last few decades is documented less seamlessly for non-western countries, but we know, fortunately, developing countries are behind in the process of Hormonageddon. As an indirect indicator we can add the fact that women in poor countries with low health index prefer men with manlier faces than women in wealthy countries. "Researchers can predict how masculine a woman likes her men based on her nation's World Health Organization statistics for mortality rates, life expectancy and the impact of communicable disease. In countries where poor health is particularly a threat to survival, women leaned toward "manlier" men. That is, they prefer their males to have shorter, broader faces and stronger eyebrows, cheekbones and jaw lines", all indicators of higher testosterone (in utero and present). [75]

Men and women with lower sex specific hormones tend to preferer more androgenous partners; e.g. men with a large 2D:4D finger ratio (a marker of lower androgen exposure in utero and lower T) prefer less feminine women.

Fertility and testosterone

Meanwhile, all parameters of reproductive health are declining at approximately the same rate: sperm count, sperm quality, serum testosterone, male fertility, female estradiol levels, female fertility, genital malformation, including micro penis, cancer of the reproductive organs…

All have been worsening about 1% per year for the last four decades and in the last decade accelerating to around 2% per year.

The best recorded metrics over the past 50 years are sperm- count and quality, which also give us a reliable estimate on where testosterone counts used to be before the 1970s.

Also in studies on other mammalian animals, the two are shown to be strongly corelated. *"Testosterone concentrations showed a clear correlation (r = 0.73) with sperm quality of mink males"* [76]

2.2. Decline in sperm counts

A systematic analysis of the Global Burden of Disease Study in 2017 was conducted including 195 countries and territories.
The results showed that the total fertility rate in all the countries globally declined by **49 % between 1950 and 2017.** [77]
A comprehensive meta-regression analysis reported a significant decline in sperm counts (as measured by sperm concentration (SC) and total sperm count (TSC) between 1973 and 2011, driven by a **50–60%** decline among men unselected by fertility from North America, Europe, Australia and New Zealand.
Between 1973 and 2011, mean Total Sperm Count declined on average by 1.6% per year, an overall decline of 59.3%. [78]

This species- threatening decline in fertility is best summarized in S. Swan's *"Count Down"* 2020. What hadn't been mentioned there is that sperm counts dropped so fast the World Health organization hat to lower the definition of "Normal" sperm numbers within 10 years. In 2010, the WHO said "Over 15 million sperm per milliliter is considered normal." [79] Older definitions state 20 million. " [80] By the old definition, possibly half the male population would already be declared sub-fertile today.
In 2000, earlier findings of a sperm decline from 1934-1996 were reexamined and confirmed the declines in sperm density in the United States (approximately 1.5%/year) and Europe/Australia (approximately 3%/year) were somewhat greater than the average decline reported by Carlsen et al 1992 (approximately 1%/ year). *"However, we found no decline in sperm density in non-Western countries, for which data were very limited. "* [81] But since then, most non-Western countries have been catching up fast.

Overview of declining sperm morphology values over years

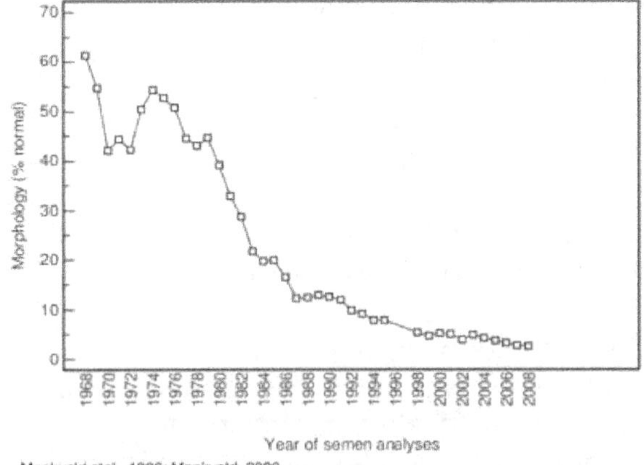

Fig. 1 Overall declining sperm morphology values over years between 1969 and 2008. Menkveld, Roelof. (2010). Clinical significance of the low normal sperm morphology value as proposed in the fifth edition of the WHO Laboratory Manual for the Examination and Processing of Human Semen. Asian journal of andrology. 12. 47-58. 10.1038/aja.2009.14. https://www.researchgate.net/publication/41174359_Clinical_significance_of_the_low_normal_sperm_morphology_value_as_proposed_in_the_fifth_edition_of_the_WHO_Laboratory_Manual_for_the_Examination_and_Processing_of_Human_Semen/citation/download

Invitro fertilization is no solution against spermageddon.

So, if male fertility is going down the drain, but female fertility is only weakened, and not gone completely, why not just make all babies in a test tube?

Well, this "Plan B" will only kick the can down the road for some time because of increased birth defects, including of the reproductive system. Something is happening in the natural process of conception, that is not understood and cannot be bypassed in a test-tube without an increase in birth defects. We don't have to go into speculations on the exact mechanisms, whether some form of "sperm war" is going on (see below). But the outcome is undisputed and will lead to even more infertility after more invitro fertilization. Along the same lines, older men (45+) have not only lower fertility, but a higher risk of fathering children with birth defects. [82] This further demonstrates that conception is not just a sperm cell delivering half the genome like in a two-piece puzzle.

"Babies born after fertility treatment run an increased risk of genetic disorders." [83]

"Overall, the total body of data points to the conclusion that ICSI conceived children are at a higher absolute risk of the following conditions: 1) multiple gestation and its associated sequelae, 2) congenital defects (in particular genitourinary defects), and 3) epigenetic syndromes (such as Beckwith Wiedemann). " [84]
The risk of the latter is increased 4 times in people born after IVF. [85]

Single birth IVF babies have double the risk of heart defects as do naturally conceived babies. **Heart defects are increase four-fold in IVF twins**. [86]
A 2007 study found "birth defects were significantly increased for infants born after IVF, compared with naturally conceived infants (9.0 percent vs. 6.6 percent), even after controlling for maternal factors. Specifically, IVF infants had greater rates of malformations of the eye (0.3 percent vs. 0.2 percent), heart (5.0 percent vs. 3.0 percent) and genitourinary system (1.5 percent vs. 1.0 percent).
"Overall, IVF infants' odds of having birth defects were 1.25 times greater than those of naturally conceived infants with similar maternal characteristics." [87]
Further, IVF babies with birth defects show an increased cancer risk. [88]
The concept of sperm competition after insemination is controversial. Evidence is lacking that natural selection continues in the womb as in a "Sperm War" where the sperm cells are supposed to be 'swimming a race' and the fittest of 250 million gets to fertilize the egg.
However, *"an average human ejaculate contains some 250 million sperm. But a key question remains unanswered: 'Why so many?' In fact, studies show that pregnancy rates tend to decline once a man's ejaculate contains less than 100 million sperm."* [89]
A study by Barbara Luke and her team suggests that epigenetic modifications – changes to the chemical structure of DNA that do not change the sequence of the genes themselves – might occur when an embryo is grown in the lab, contributing to birth defects and cancer risk in children conceived via IVF. [90]
Lu et al 2013 say "the mechanism(s) leading to these changes have not been elucidated. " [91]

Fiction
What we are witnessing resembles the first part of the plot of the dystopian novel *Handmaid's Tale* (1985): which is this: due to environmental pollution and radiation, almost all women are infertile.

But in the novel, a totalitarian regime takes over, changes the nation into a military dictatorship and forces selected women to reproduce.

In contrast to today's reality: due to environmental pollution and radiation, more and more people are becoming infertile, but almost everyone is giggling into their extinction, while demanding more lockdowns and less freedom.

The self-proclaimed 'climate activists' of Extinction Rebellion and feminists alike wear costumes adapted from the Handmaid's Tale, they act like a medieval end-of-the-world cult - much like the Flagellants during and after the climate collapse at the time of the Black Death in the mid 14th century, as documented in my free E-book: Black Death and Abrupt Earth Changes in the 14th century. [92] Apparently, the climate activists are unknowingly up to something when they wear costumes from the *Handmaid's Tale*, their message is: CO2 will kill all of us because you have too many children. In reality, the next Grand Solar Minimum will do a bit of what the man-made- climate change lobby predicts, and by that time, the remaining population will be largely infertile, and it's going to be a minority who will almost literally have to 'replenish' or 'fill' the Earth, as ridiculous as it may sound.

And for the feminist protesters in western countries, they were protesting against Mike Pence from Argentina to the US, the UK and Ireland, their costume was dubbed "one of the most powerful current feminist symbols of protest". [93] Apparently, they are protesting the fact that women in the West are more privileged than anyone anywhere at any time in history. Oh no wait, they thought Pence was going to force them to have children.

2.3. Testosterone decline isn't a necessary part of aging

"From the 1970s onwards, several authors reported an age-associated decline of serum testosterone levels beginning in the fourth or fifth decades of life. Other studies found that the decline in testosterone with age might be more related to comorbidities that develop in many aging men. " [94]

The older someone is, the longer they have been affected by the cumulative effects of endocrine disruptors. Today's over 70-year-olds (post-war generation, boomers) were not affected much at birth, but since then have had a long total time to have their endocrine system weakened by everyday influences. While Boomers today are largely accepting of today's increasingly authoritarian and "politically correct" doctrines, physiologically they are still more "like people used to be": Higher sexual dimorphism, male Boomers have broader faces, smaller 2D:4D finger length ratios, broader shoulders, etc., with a larger difference between sexes than in younger generations who were affected by endocrine disrupters in the womb. You can observe this in everyday life, especially when you meet grandparents with their adult grandchildren.

To date, the American Urology Association (AUA) identifies low blood testosterone (Low-T) as less than 300 nanograms per deciliter (ng/dL). [95]

In a study of men over 40 years of age who self-report very good or excellent health, serum T, DHT and E_2 displayed no decrease associated with age. It was concluded the age-related decline in blood T accompanying non-specific symptoms in older men may be due to accumulating age-related co-morbidities rather than a symptomatic androgen deficiency state. [96]

"A decline in testosterone levels as men grow older is likely the result -- not the cause -- of deteriorating general health, say Australian scientists, whose new study finds that **age, in itself, has no effect on testosterone levels in healthy older men.**" [97] "Declining testosterone levels are not an inevitable part of the aging process, as many people think," said study co-author Gary Wittert, MD, professor of medicine at the University of Adelaide, Australia. *"Testosterone changes are largely explained by smoking behavior and changes in health status, particularly obesity and depression."* Interestingly, unmarried men in the study had greater testosterone reductions than did married men. Wittert attributed this finding to past research showing that married men tend to be healthier and happier than unmarried men. [98]

Chapter 3
Testosterone alone does not cause aggression

The common simplified association that has long been made, is this: men have more testosterone than women, men are more aggressive than women - and aggressive men have more testosterone than non-aggressive ones – ergo: testosterone causes aggression…

Even for female criminals, 'testosterone is related to criminal violence and aggressive dominance in prison among women, similarly as has been reported among men. [99]

But things are much more complex than this. Rather, research shows testosterone does not induce aggression.

A study at the University of Zurich and Royal Holloway London refutes the preconception that testosterone causes aggressive, egocentric, and risky behavior.

"Early research had shown the castration of male rodents evidently led to a reduction in combativeness among the animals. This led to the growing prejudice over decades that testosterone causes aggressive, risky, and egocentric behavior."

It was proven the same effect does not occur in humans, where the hormone increases the sensitivity for status, instead. Here, "prosocial behavior is what secures status, and not aggression."

"Moreover, the study shows that the popular wisdom that the hormone causes aggression is apparently deeply entrenched: during the experiments, those test subjects who believed they had received the testosterone compound and not the placebo, stood out with their conspicuously unfair offers." [100]

The main findings of the Zurich study even manifested in testosterone administration to women:

*"The sublingual administration of a single dose of testosterone in women causes a substantial **increase in fair bargaining behavior,** thereby reducing bargaining conflicts and increasing the efficiency of social interactions. However, subjects who believed that they received testosterone - regardless of whether they actually received it or not -behaved much more unfairly than those who believed that they were treated with placebo."* [101]

Further, castration of rapists does not work to prevent reoffending.

"Therapists who treat rapists and child molesters are united in the view that castration is useless and probably counterproductive in preventing future sexual assaults."

"There's a high degree of folklore about what castration does and doesn't do," said John Money, emeritus professor of medical psychology and pediatrics at Johns Hopkins School of Medicine.

Rape crisis workers say that violence, not sex, is the real problem, which castration fails to address. *"This misfocuses the issue and feeds into the myths about rape,"* said Denise Snyder, executive director of the D.C. *Rape Crisis Center. "Sexual assault is a crime of violence and aggression . . . not the product of an uncontrollable sex drive."* [102]

K. Simpson (2020) explains androgen and estrogen receptors are also found along neurotransmitter pathways. As such, testosterone is able to modulate levels of various neurotransmitters that show evidence of mediating effects on aggressive behavior. However, there is a critical time period early in life, usually within the first few days after birth, during which testosterone exposure is essential to elicit aggression in adulthood.

"Testosterone is only one of a myriad of factors that influence aggression and the effects of previous experience and environmental stimuli have at times been found to correlate more strongly." [103]

Likewise, testosterone administration does not affect men's aggressive mood. T increases *energetic* mood but not aggressiveness or ultimatum game rejections. While testosterone affected subjective ratings of feeling energetic and interested, the evidence produced in clinical trials by Carlo Cueva et al 2017 strongly suggested that testosterone had no effect on ultimatum game rejections or on aggressive mood. [104] Further, endogenous testosterone modulates prefrontal–amygdala connectivity during social emotional behavior. [105]

"Therapeutic increases of androgen levels in deficient males or females do not increase aggression." [106]

Why are some men more aggressive when they are drunk? Well, not only long-term heavy drinking (more than 15 drinks a week for men) decreases testosterone, but already a few drinks can shut down testosterone levels within 30 minutes. [107] So, drunk men who are aggressive and antisocial are not "testosterone driven" but the opposite.

While testosterone has long been considered an aggression hormone, psychology professor Joey Cheng says it's more accurate to consider it a competition hormone that responds to and has an effect on competing for a reputation based on talent and making positive contributions to a group. [108]

In non-human primates closely related to humans like chimpanzees, "alpha males" - who have higher testosterone levels than the other animals of the group - gain their respect and popularity by being empathetic and consoling distressed members of the pack, by acting as mediators in conflicts and often taking the side of the 'underdog', while lower ranking animals always side with their close relatives and mates, according to primatologist Frans de Waal. [109] De Waal is who partly coined the term alpha male (for dominant aggressive humans). In primates, the alpha males are not oppressors but rather kind leaders. Human despots and war mongering politicians are not biological alpha males.

Indeed, often dominance is expressed non-aggressively. Allan Mazur et al, found: "*T not only affects behavior but also responds to it. The act of competing for dominant status affects male T levels in two ways. First, T rises in the face of a challenge, as if it were an anticipatory response to impending competition. Second, after the competition, T rises in winners and declines in losers. Thus, there is a reciprocity between T and dominance behavior, each affecting the other.* " [110]
Similar patterns are observed even in animals: Autumnal territorial aggression is independent of plasma testosterone in mockingbirds. "Current observations contribute to a growing body of work in temperate passerines indicating that the role of androgens in mediating aggressive challenge may be restricted to the breeding season." [111]
Young men who voted Republican or Libertarian in the 2008 presidential election suffered an immediate drop in testosterone when the election results were announced, according to a study by researchers at Duke University and the University of Michigan. [112]

Chapter 4
Symptoms of testosterone deficiency

4.1. List of symptoms in men as reported in the literature

Compare these symptoms in affected individuals to broader societal trends of recent years and decades:
- Increased frequency of anxiety
- Mood swings, depression, [113] low self-perception and perceived quality of life
- reduced quality of life and sexual life in young hypogonadotropic hypogonadism [114]
- fatigue, lethargy
- decreased virility
- memory loss,
- irritability, crankiness, [115] anger
- lack of sex drive
- lack of focus.
- decrease in body hair and skin alterations,
- "Listlessness, hopelessness and suicidal thoughts"
- obesity, enlarged breasts, a decrease in lean body mass with associated decreases in muscle volume and strength and decreased bone mineral density resulting in osteoporosis

Depression and mood swings

Men with borderline testosterone levels have higher rates of depression and depressive symptoms than the general population.

"Over half of men referred for borderline testosterone levels have depression. Men seeking management for borderline testosterone have a very high rate of depression, depressive symptoms, obesity and physical inactivity." [116]

"Low testosterone levels are frequently encountered in obese men who do not otherwise have a recognizable hypothalamic-pituitary-testicular (HPT) axis pathology. Moderate obesity predominantly decreases total testosterone." [117]

For men with below average testosterone, more testosterone means less depression, as expected. But for those with above average testosterone, more testosterone can result in more depression.

"For those with above average testosterone, the relationship disappears when controls for antisocial and risk behaviors and the absence of protective factors such as marriage and steady employment are in the equation. " [118]

Michael Zitzmann further outlines testosterone deficiency influences a wide array of clinical pictures such as various traits of anxiety, from unfocussed fear to phobic anxiousness and open panic syndromes.

*"The steroid modulates pro-active and re-active dimensions of aggression, which has to be seen within the context of gaining or maintaining status. This may also include other strategies impacting the social position: **heroic or parochial altruism and non-aggressive paths of assertiveness, such as posture and social vigilance**. "*

"Testosterone is believed to support maintenance of psychological features representing positive and negative affects within a balance, which is perceived as 'good mood' and an enjoyable quality of life. " [119]

The cells in the male brain are equipped with testosterone receptors. When a man has lower-than-normal testosterone levels, these receptors are, quite literally, left "high and dry." [120]

Research by Tsujimura (2013) further supports the notion that men with low T are more likely to face **depression, irritability, or a lack of focus.** [121] In a 2010 study, American researchers found that 40% of obese male participants had low testosterone. For obese men with diabetes, this number was 50%. [122]

Powerful and assertive people have a more upright and prominent posture, higher testosterone and lower cortisol levels. [123] It turns out in experiments by social psychologist Amy Cuddy, that vice versa, when participants of a trial were consciously assuming a power-emanating posture for 2 minutes, it reflected in their hormone levels. Before as well as after the experiment, their testosterone and cortisol levels were measured and they were given the opportunity to gamble.

The results showed that 86% of the participants with high-power poses chose to gamble and only 60% of participants with low-power poses chose to do so.

The high-power participants showed a 20% increase in testosterone levels whereas the low-power participants showed a 10% decrease. Cortisol levels dropped with 25% in high-power people and increased with 15% in low-power people. [124]

Cognition

Both testosterone levels and cognitive functions - particularly memory - decline with age. [125]

Testosterone has a strong modulatory influence on language-specific gray and white matter structures as well as functional connectivity. [126]

Different reports suggest that testosterone may be important in protecting neurons from Aβ, the peptide suspected of killing neurons in Alzheimer's disease. [127]

Low testosterone levels have not only been observed in patients with Alzheimer's disease (AD) but also with mild cognitive impairment (MCI).

Chemical castration studies in men with prostate cancer suggest low endogenous levels of testosterone may be related to reduced cognitive ability. [128]

Opioid use, some congenital conditions (medical conditions people are born with), loss of or harm to the testicles, diabetes, and obesity can also be reasons for the symptoms associated with testosterone deficiency. [129]

"Additional reported symptoms of late-onset hypogonadism (diminished testicular function) are easily recognized and include diminished sexual desire and erectile quality, particularly in nocturnal erections, changes in mood with concomitant decreases in intellectual activity and spatial orientation, fatigue, depression and anger, a decrease in lean body mass with associated decreases in muscle volume and strength, a decrease in body hair and skin alterations, and decreased bone mineral density resulting in osteoporosis. " [130]

Healthy older men with moderate increases in serum T and/or its metabolites demonstrated significant improvements in verbal and spatial memory. [131]

Falter et al found prenatal testosterone, but not current testosterone plays a substantial role for determining cognitive performance. Sixty-nine subjects were assessed with cognitive tasks of mental rotation, targeting, figure-disembedding and perceptual discrimination.

As we'll see below (p. 96), second-to-fourth finger length ratio (2D:4D) is a putative index of prenatal testosterone exposure.

In one study, the person's sex was found to be the exclusive predictor for the ability of mental rotation, while 2D:4D ratio was found to be the sole predictor of targeting abilities and figure-disembedding performance.

The researchers concluded: "*These findings suggest a substantial role for **prenatal** testosterone but **not current testosterone** in determining cognitive performance.*" [132]

Another study on the relationship between serum total testosterone level and fluid intelligence revealed there was no significant difference between IQs of men and women, but an inverse curvelinear relationship between IQ and T in women and men.

It was concluded that T may be related to IQ, even in subjects exhibiting no sex difference in IQ tests; too low or too high T levels may be disadvantageous for fluid intelligence, especially in women. [133]

4.2. The vicious spiral of disruption of testosterone/ estrogen

The vicious cycle can turn into a downward spiral that can propagate itself, for individuals and society.

Disruption of sex hormones → Depression and lack of motivation → acceptance of depression→ Unwillingness to address root problem → oversensitivity → mental illness → unhealthy life style → more depression and insecurity → aversion against normal people → passive aggression → aversion against children → oikophobia (hatred of the homeland) → misanthropy (hatred of humans) → societies accept and even cherish the extinction of their gene line. → low fertility, low sexual energy → sexual frustration → embracement of low fertility

Low testosterone in men can cause men not wanting to hear that their state of being is in parts a product of their low testosterone.

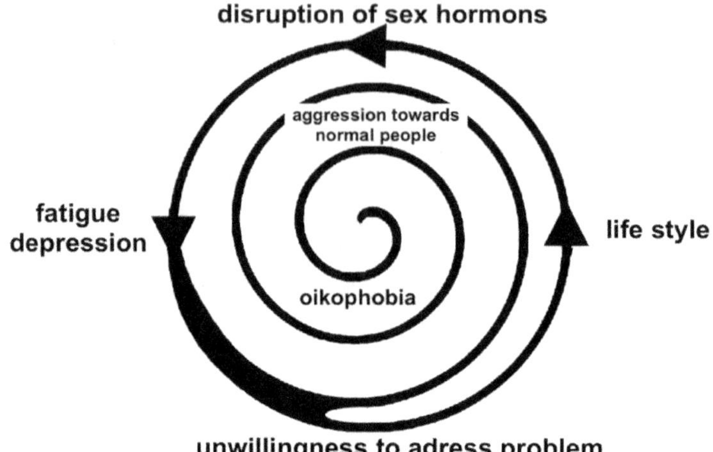

Fig. 2 the vicious spiral of sex hormone disruption

Testosterone replacement therapy (TRT) can accelerate the spiral.

Below we will look at the risks of common treatment for low testosterone which will further demonstrate this vicious spiral (Chapter 13). Testosterone replacement therapy is appropriate in many cases to help alleviate suffering, but as it turns out in practical use, testosterone replacement therapy often ends up doing more of the same. It promises to increase virility and libido, it can reduce depression and hair loss. Leading experts in the field say testosterone replacement therapy is a decision for life and most men will never get away from constant testosterone applications. It also causes an increased risk of heart attack and infertility by shutting down sperm production.

"The most common negative effect of TRT is testicular shrinkage and impotency" (this is then presumably corrected with Viagra).

In spite of such warnings, testosterone prescriptions show no signs of decline.

"In fact, TRT has increased tenfold in the last decade, and is growing steadily at 10 percent per month!" [134]

In short: it turns out that men (including some that don't even have low T levels) will do everything to feel better, feel manlier, to become more sexually active and more successful in business and have more muscles. But what many men end up with is to take serious health risks to become sexually more active, vain and infertile substance- dependents.

The only sustainable solutions against low gonadal hormone levels are: boosting natural T production, reducing additional endocrine disrupting agents in your personal life and in the long run, for the sake of your descendants, imposing legislation that will regulate and prevent exposure to ED agents to future generations. For details, see Chapter 16.

We have already seen that similar risks as for men and TRT apply for women and estrogen treatment:

"Estrogen treatment can improve or at least maintain current levels of cognitive functioning in postmenopausal women." However, research has also shown that the negative emotional effects of psychosocial stress are magnified in normal postmenopausal women after estrogen treatment. [135]

Also, some women are administered testosterone to increase their libido. [136]

Serotonin

As we saw at the beginning, the gonad hormone regulation is closely connected to the serotonin distribution and thus important for well-being and happiness. And here too, hormonal deficits can in some cases be countered with artificial hormone administration for a short-term relief, but external hormones do not involve the very complex natural activation mechanism, and are therefore no sustainable replacement for healthy natural hormone levels. And they mostly cause a homeostatic effect - a further shut down of the natural hormone production and thus quickly turn counterproductive.

About 90% of serotonin is found in the cells lining your gastrointestinal tract. It's released into your blood circulation and absorbed by platelets. Only about 10% is produced in your brain. Serotonin is made from the essential amino acid tryptophan. [137]

Selective serotonin reuptake inhibitors are used as antidepressants (available since 1987).

'They increase the amount of serotonin available in the brain.' 12.7% of the U.S. population over age 12 and 19.1% of older adults (over age 60) are currently on antidepressant medication, according to an analysis from the National Center for Health Statistics. [138] Users are most likely to be women, older adults and non-Hispanic whites.

Other drugs release serotonin.

"By releasing large amounts of serotonin, MDMA or ecstasy, causes the brain to become significantly depleted of this important neurotransmitter, contributing to the negative psychological after-effects that people may experience for several days after taking MDMA." [139] "Abnormal regulation of the brain neurotransmitters, as well as the increased oxidative stress causes damage to the brain neurons after the MDMA exposure." [140]

Other Drugs that stimulate serotonin receptors include buspirone; dihydroergotamine; lithium; lysergic acid diethylamide (LSD); meperidine; metoclopramide; and triptans (e.g, sumatriptan). [141]

Lithium drugs are commonly used in the management of bipolar disease. "long-term lithium treatment is relatively frequently associated with different endocrine complications." [142] "It has been suggested that adding trace Lithium to drinking water could be a safe and effective way to reduce suicide." [143]

Similarly, artificial administration of oxytocin "known as the bonding hormone" has been proposed for mass administration to the public to make them more accepting of immigrants and more compliant with covid mandates.

Naturally released oxytocin is commonly associated with cuddly love and bonding between group members, but it can make people more racist and xenophobic, especially when given artificially and on a mass scale (See also p. 112).

By the way, oxytocin and testosterone are also directly linked.

"It seems counterintuitive that oxytocin and testosterone would rise in tandem in a male individual." [144] In indigenous hunter- gatherers, successful hunters experienced a surge in testosterone that lasted from the moment they made a kill until their return home – a "winner effect. hunters returning home also have increased oxytocin levels, especially if they were gone for a long time, and if their testosterone was high.

TRT as treatment for depression

"Depression, anxiety, decreased quality of life and symptoms of sexual dysfunction are the most common psychopathological conditions in young hypogonadal men."

After 6 months of TRT, a team of Umit Aydoganet et al 2012 observed improvements in the above parameters, suggesting that low endogenous levels of testosterone might be related to the increased incidence of psychological symptoms. [145]

A meta-analysis of the data from seven studies showed a significant positive effect of TT therapy on depressed patients. The researchers concluded "*TT may have an antidepressant effect in depressed patients, especially those with hypogonadism or HIV/AIDS and elderly subpopulations.*" [146]
"Some people living with HIV may have low levels of certain hormones—most commonly, testosterone, thyroid hormones and DHEA (a hormone that leads to the production of androgens and estrogens, male and female sex hormones)." [147]

Chapter 5
Causes

As for the known causes of endocrine disruption in recent decades, we can distinguish between chemical and electromagnetic sources. For practical reasons, we call Endocrine Disrupters Endocrine Disrupting Agents and separate them into
1.) classic Endocrine Disrupting Chemicals (EDCs)
and we introduce and new term of
2.) Endocrine Disrupting Non- Ionizing Radiation (EDNR).
To my knowledge this is the first research project to systematically build a case for the strong contribution of electromagnetic sources to the current hormonal crisis.
Further below, we will also investigate the effects of natural variations in solar radio flux and its connection to solar and geomagnetic activity.

5.1. Endocrine Disrupting Chemicals (EDCs)

As stated above, the chemical part of the problem of fertility has been analyzed in depth for instance by S. Swan 2021; little could be added from my part: here we focus on EDC effects on testosterone and estrogen, the following is a summary of the current state of insight and some new scientific findings on the effects of EDCs not just on general fertility but specifically on testosterone function in men via pesticides, plastics, industrial- and household goods.
As a general rule, we can say chemicals that decrease fertility and sperm count also reduce testosterone in men and estrogen in women, at roughly the same rate.
As we have seen at the beginning, the world's largest reinsurance company Swiss Re categorized EDCs as one of the highest risk categories in a 4 to 10-year projection beginning 2013. They ranked it among the top 7 global risks for reassurance companies to pay out a lot of money by liability claims in the coming years. In 2020, Christopher D. Kassotis pointed out that
"Endocrine-disrupting chemicals (EDCs) substantially cost society as a result of increases in disease and disability but—unlike other toxicant classes such as carcinogens—have yet to be codified into regulations as a hazard category." [148]

According to a survey of the Danish Environmental Protection Agency;
"Endocrine disruptors have for years been suspected to be a contributory cause of reproductive adverse effects, especially in boys and men." [149]

The multigenerational death spiral

Endocrine Disrupting Chemicals can cause a progressive decrease in sperm counts over multiple generations- - a phenomenon that environmental scientist Pete Myers referred to as a "**male fertility death spiral.**" [150] Frederick vom Saal, Curators' Distinguished Professor Emeritus of Biological Sciences at the University of Missouri used the same strong language: "We are in a death spiral of infertility in men." [151]
Even when EDCs are removed from the environment, this death spiral can continue: In 2007, a relation was established between employment in agriculture of Spanish women during pregnancy and serum levels of organochlorine endocrine disruptor pesticides, including DDT and isomers (despite their being banned in Spain since 1977). [152]
"More than a dozen papers have now been published on "transgenerational epigenetic inheritance," where exposure in a great-grandmother causes adverse effects in great-grandsons." [153]
Washington State University's Distinguished Professor of Molecular Biosciences, Patricia Hunt says: "*Things get progressively worse as subsequent generations are exposed. These large changes in human sperm count and concentration reveal that we are already well down the road."* [154]
In male mice as well, germline and reproductive tract effects intensify with successive generations of estrogenic exposure.
"Transgenerational effects in mammals–presumably resulting from epigenetic changes to the germline–have been reported in numerous studies." [155] Not only pesticides but various other environmental pollutants, including organochlorine pesticides, polychlorinated biphenyls, bisphenol A, phthalates, dioxins and furans have estrogenic and anti-androgenic activity and are thus considered as endocrine-disrupting chemicals (EDCs). [156] The mechanism by which Endocrine disrupting chemicals are known to work is they are structurally similar to steroids or amine hormones and have the potential to mimic endocrine endpoints at the receptor level. *"However, more recently, epigenetic-induced alteration in gene expression has*

emerged as an alternative way in which environmental compounds may exert endocrine effects." [157]

Finally, in 2021, the EU proposes to add two new hazard classes to the EU CLP regulation to cover endocrine disruptors. In mid-October 2020, the EU released its Chemical Sustainability Strategy as a roadmap for how the EU wishes the chemical industry to move forward in the foreseeable future. [158]

Unfortunately, as history has shown, whenever one EDC is banned, 3 others are introduced at the same time.

5.2. Genital malformation is associated with EDC exposure

The Danish Environmental Protection Agency reported in 2012 that **9% of Danish boys are now born with cryptorchidism (testicles undescended to the scrotum)**. Cryptorchidism is associated with an increased risk of low semen quality and testicular cancer. [159]

The increase in genital malformation, including micropenis, is staggering: *"In 2000, in the United States, the incidence of micropenis was reported as 1.5 in 10 000 male children born between 1997 and 2000."* That was a prevalence of 0.015%. [160] In 2010; F. Paris referred to the condition as a fairly common occurrence, without giving a specific number. [161]

In 2018, the Cleveland Clinic reported that "Micropenis is affecting an estimated 0.6 percent of males worldwide. " [162]

Compare the two numbers. Given the measurement standards are consistent, even when comparing the US with the world, that would mean a **40-fold increase in these 18 years.**

An increasing trend of genital anomalies was reported in Scotland by Ahmed et al 2004, examining genital anomalies in single births (excluding multiple births). Prevalence in hypospadias and other genital anomalies increased over an 8-year period of time from 4.0 per 1,000 births (1988) to 5.9 per 1,000 births (1996). [163] **An increase of 33% in 8 years, or 4% per year.**

Genital malformation and EDC exposure in diverse places of the world

Spain

A population-based case–control study was carried out on pregnant women and male children living in ten health districts of

Andalusia classified as areas of high and low environmental exposure to pesticides according to agronomic criteria. Data were collected from computerized hospital records between 1998 and 2005. Prevalence rates and risk of miscarriage, low birth weight, hypospadias, cryptorchidism and micropenis were significantly greater in areas with higher use of pesticides in relation to those with lower use. [164]

Brazil:

In Northeastern Brazil, 2710 male newborns were examined for genital malformations. It was found that 2.07% had genital malformation, including 0.85% cryptorchidism, 0.55% had hypospadias and 0.66% micropenis. All cases exhibited normal or subnormal testosterone production. More than 92% of these newborns presented foetal contamination by EDCs, as their mothers reported daily domestic use of pesticides (i.e., DDT) and other EDCs.

"Most of these undervirilized male newborns presented additional EDC contamination, as 80.36% of the mothers and 58.63% of the fathers reported paid or unpaid work that entailed the use of pesticides and other EDCs before/during pregnancy for the mothers and around the time of fertilization for the fathers. " [165]

From the progression of recent decades, we must assume that the prevalence of micropenis has already reached around 1 percent of the male population by 2021(see below).

France:

Prenatal environmental risk factors were identified for genital malformations. Over a 16-month period, 1442 full-term newborn males were examined for the same genital malformations as in Brazil (above). Reported were **2.70% genital malformation**, including 1.25% cryptorchidism; 0.97% hypospadias; 0.35% micropenis; 0.14% of 46, XY disorders of sexual differentiation (DSD). There was a significant relationship between newborn cryptorchidism, hypospadias or micropenis and parental occupational exposure to pesticides. [166]

Egypt:

Similarly, a study was conducted to determine normal penile length and prevalence of male genital anomalies in full-term neonates and whether they were influenced by prenatal parental exposure to endocrine-disrupting chemicals. The results showed the prevalence of genital anomalies was **1.8 %** (of which 83.33 % were hypospadias). There was **a 6 times higher rate** of anomalies in those exposed to endocrine disruptors (EDCs; 7.4 %) than in the non-exposed (1.2 %). Mean penile length showed a linear relationship

with free testosterone and was lower in neonates exposed to EDCs. [167]

5.3. Pesticides

What we just saw in the above data is often overlooked in the context of environmental toxins i.e., the fact that farmers are much more exposed to pesticides than the general population - who eat the produce - and even the urban population. So, the notion that farmers and agricultural workers are always in 'nature' in the fresh air, away from city pollution and this should be a healthy lifestyle, is not true today, it only applies to some extent to organic farmers. Agricultural workers and gardeners are more often and more severely affected by EDC pesticides like atrazine than urban populations, and actually have higher rates of Genital Malformation in male offspring. [168] For instance, lowered total testosterone levels are associated to pesticides in the blood of Thai farmers. [169]
Carmen Freire et al found an association between serum levels of organochlorine pesticides and sex hormones in adults living in a heavily contaminated agricultural area in Brazil. They concluded pesticides may have triggered *anti-androgenic effects in men and estrogenic effects in women* in these regions. [170] An elevation in serum PCB (chlorinated pesticides) levels is associated with a lower concentration of serum testosterone in Native American men (Mohawk adults 18–95 years of age who resided at Akwesasne). [171]

And pesticide use in Sri Lanka is associated with suicide rates. A restriction on the import and sales of WHO Class I toxicity pesticides in 1995 and endosulfan in 1998, coincided with reductions in suicide in both men and women of all ages. [172]
The same pesticides are also associated with cancer and a host of other diseases. In Spain, 81% of cases of breast cancer reported in the female population were observed in areas of high pesticide (EDC) contamination. [173]

Glyphosate

Prepubertal exposure to commercial formulation of the herbicide glyphosate alters testosterone levels and testicular morphology. Glyphosate is an herbicide widely used to kill weeds both in agricultural and non-agricultural landscapes. It causes an in vitro reduction in testosterone and estradiol synthesis, as a potent endocrine disruptor in vivo. A study on prepubertal Wistar rats showed that the herbicide significantly changed the progression of puberty and reduced the **testosterone** production. [174]

Roundup, a major herbicide used worldwide, is a glyphosate-based pesticide with adjuvants. *"At lower nontoxic concentrations of Roundup and glyphosate (1ppm), the main endocrine disruption effect is a* **testosterone decrease by 35%."** [175]

Atrazine

Atrazine is one of the world's most widely used pesticides, it was invented in 1958 in the Geigy laboratories, Basel Switzerland. The Headquarters of producer Syngenta are still in Basel, the pesticide is banned in this country and the EU. [176]

In 2006, the EPA stated, *"the risks associated with the pesticide residues pose a reasonable certainty of no harm".*

In 2007, the EPA said: "*The primary target of atrazine in humans and animals is the endocrine (hormonal) system. Studies thus far suggest that atrazine is an endocrine disruptor; an agent that has been shown to alter the natural hormonal system in animals."*

"Implications of possible endocrine disruption for children's health are related to effects during pregnancy and during sexual development, though few studies are available." [177]

But in fact, many studies are available, indeed.

For instance, the Berkley University reported: Pesticide atrazine can turn male frogs into females.

Atrazine wreaks havoc with the sex lives of adult male frogs, emasculating three-quarters of them and turning one in 10 into females, according to a new study by University of California, Berkeley, biologists.

"The 75 percent that are chemically castrated are essentially "dead" because of their inability to reproduce in the wild", reports UC Berkeley's Tyrone B. Hayes, professor of integrative biology.

"These male frogs are **missing testosterone** *and all the things that testosterone controls, including sperm. So, their fertility is as low as 10 percent in some cases, and that is only if we isolate those animals and pair them with females,"* he said. *"In an environment where they are competing with unexposed animals, they have zero chance of reproducing."* [178]

Dr. Hayes conducted different trials in which ten percent of exposed genetic male frogs developed into functional females that copulated with unexposed males and produced viable eggs. *"Atrazine-exposed males suffered from* **depressed testosterone***, decreased* *breeding gland size, demasculinized/feminized laryngeal development, suppressed mating behavior, reduced spermatogenesis, and decreased fertility."* [179]

Also in male rats, atrazine causes inhibition of testosterone production following peripubertal exposure. [180]

A study by Rey et al found that neonatal caiman exposed in ovum to Atrazine altered the histoarchitecture of the testis and organization of the seminiferous tubules. [181]

In order to justify the health risks of atrazine, a great economic benefit is presumed. But in reality, some cost–benefit studies have assumed that atrazine boosts corn yields by only 6%; an extensive review found a 3%–4% average yield increase; other research suggests only a 1%, or perhaps 0 %, yield effect. Italy and Germany both banned atrazine in 1991, with no decrease in corn yields or harvested area. [182] So, nobody can really explain why such a dangerous sterilizing chemical is still being used proficiently in the US and the third world.

Its use was banned in the European Union in 2004, when the EU found groundwater levels exceeding the limits set by regulators, and Syngenta could not show that this could be prevented nor that these levels were safe. [183]

"As of 2001, atrazine was the most commonly detected pesticide contaminating drinking water in the U.S."

"The European Union (EU) allows the export of certain pesticides even though it bans their use on its own fields. It is allowing agrochemical companies to flood low- and middle-income countries (LMICs) and also the USA with substances deemed too dangerous for European agriculture." [184]

By 2022, Switzerland plans to finally ban the export of five dangerous pesticides, including atrazine and paraquat. [185] The latter has been banned in Switzerland since 1989 but is still widely used in other countries, it's also endocrine disrupting, of course. [186]

DDT

The pesticide DDT was seen as a breakthrough miracle intervention in the prevention of malaria by killing off mosquitoes and Tsetse flies for half a century. But as it turned out in the 1970s, DDT has many health risks, it is not only implicated in having contributed to the polio epidemic [187], but it reduces testosterone in serum and testis, as well. [188]

Also, officially *"more polio cases are now caused by the vaccine than by the wild virus."* [189]

As DDT is an endocrine disruptor,[190] studies document decreases in semen quality among men with high exposures (generally from indoor residual spraying). [191]

There is also a strong link between pesticides (DDT), Alzheimer disease and decreased testosterone in these patients.

"Reported elevated levels of DDE (similar to DDT) in patients with Alzheimer disease raises the strong possibility that the missing link is the **antitestosterone** *effect of many pesticides causing increased β-amyloid production."* [192]

"Various studies have consistently demonstrated a higher risk for prostate cancer in agricultural populations than in the general population." [193]

Results of a 2005 Lancet review on the health risks of DDT revealed white male workers showed increased risk of liver cancer and biliary tract cancer, but not white women or black men. [194]

Also in Italy, pesticides (in particular DDT) were associated with a statistically significant higher rate of prostate cancer among farmers (exposed to organochloride pesticides) in a multi-site case-control study carried out in five rural areas between 1990–92. *"Higher prevalence of cryptorchidism and hypospadias was found in areas with extensive farming and pesticide use and in sons of women working as gardeners."* [195]

DDT in streams, rivers and thus fish was also what almost brought the bald eagle - the US national symbol since 1782 - to extinction in the post-World War II era. [196] This upset not only Americans. It is telling that a population heavily affected by endocrine disrupting pesticides is more concerned about a bird than about their own children. It took decades after the US ban of DDT in 1972 and the bald eagle has started to recover. The bird is now making a comeback, human confidence and virility is not.

Phthalates are endocrine disrupting chemicals used in plastics, mostly as plasticizers where they are not molecularly bound to the main material, they can then leach out into food, toys, household goods, water and soil. As far as infertility is concerned, Dr. S. Swan has delivered the most comprehensive coverage on the detrimental effects, in particular, on sperm count/ quality.

Here, we again focus on the effects on testosterone, estrogen and the behavioral and social ramifications of these substances.

In general, occupational exposure load to phthalate esters is often higher than environmental exposure. [197]

Decreased serum free testosterone was observed in workers exposed to high levels of phthalates. Pan et al, 2006, examined male workers at a Chinese factory producing different unfoamed phthalates (DBP) and (DEHP). The exposed workers had substantially elevated concentrations of phthalates. Free **testosterone** (fT) was significantly lower in exposed workers. FT was negatively correlated to phthalate concentrations. [198]

It was also shown that "Prenatal phthalate exposure **causes Phthalate Syndrome** in males." [199]

The *phthalate syndrome* or "testicular dysgenesis syndrome" is a real thing, and it's the only syndrome named after a specific synthetic chemical. Other chemically, environmentally caused syndromes are more generalized, such as *Multiple Chemical Sensitivity Syndrome* or *Toxic shock Syndrome*, for instance.

The symptoms of PhS are: the anogenital distance is shorter and the penis is smaller than expected for a boy of his size, testicles are less completely descended.

Phthalate esters also inhibit fetal testicular testosterone production in rats. Kembra Howdeshell et al determined that exposure to certain phthalates during sexual differentiation causes reproductive tract malformations in male rats. In the trials, individual phthalates and the mixtures thereof also induced fetal mortality, due to pregnancy loss.

"These data demonstrate that individual phthalates with a similar mechanism of action can elicit cumulative, dose additive effects on fetal testosterone production and pregnancy when administered as a mixture." [200] Similarly, S. Park et al found the plasticizer diethylhexyl phthalate induces malformations by decreasing fetal testosterone synthesis during sexual differentiation in the male rat. [201]

Phthalates cause estrogenic activity in females. 6 different types of Phthalates were tested, using a 72 h zebrafish embryo toxicity test. Four types were demonstrated to have estrogenic endocrine disrupting activity on intact organisms and two proved to be developmental toxins. [202] The phthalate called DEHP is a known reproductive toxicant and a carcinogen in rodent animal models. It prevents ovulation in adult female rats. [203]

BPA is another chemical in everyday plastics. Significant positive associations between prenatal BPA and symptoms of depression and anxiety were observed among boys 10-12 years of age. [204]

A combination of stress and perinatal BPA exposure may increase sensitivity to stress in adults. [205]

Ultraviolet (UV) filters, sunscreen

Ultraviolet (UV) filters are used widely in **cosmetics, sunscreens, plastics, adhesives and other industrial products to protect**

human skin or products against direct exposure to deleterious UV radiation.
"Exposure to UV filters induce various endocrine disrupting effects, as revealed by an increasing number of toxicological studies performed in recent years." ED- UV filters include benzophenones, camphor derivatives and cinnamate derivatives. [206]

Heavy metals

Cadmium (Cd), mercury (Hg), arsenic (As), lead (PB), and d large concentrations of manganese (Mn), and zinc (Zn) are endocrine-disrupting chemicals (EDCs). [207]
Mercury has been shown to decrease luteinizing hormone. [208] Lead and other heavy metals have been shown to decrease testosterone as well (see also the fall of the Roman Empire, page 132). Further, different heavy metals can have estrogen-mimicking effects on the body and are associated with delayed maturation markers in adolescents (the metals also included Tl and Cupper). [209]

Leaded gasoline
From the 1930s to the 1990s (and still in developing countries, due to the increased accessibility of cars, the main exposure for the public concentrated between the 1960s and the 1990s.
For most of the mid-twentieth century, lead gasoline was considered normal. But lead is a poison, and burning it has had dire consequences.
From 1924 onward, the lead additive solved a problem: it enabled engines to use higher compression ratios, which made cars more powerful and it decreased knocking sounds of the engine.
Researchers are still puzzled why the petrol companies push tetraethyl lead instead of the much less toxic of ethyl alcohol, which had much the same effect on the engines.
"Research has shown that lead exposure in children is linked to "a whole raft of complications later in life, among them lower IQ, hyperactivity, behavioral problems and learning disabilities." A significant body of research links lead exposure in children to violent crime. [210]

Arsenic
Arsenic is found in drinking water, it is a potent endocrine disruptor at low, environmentally relevant levels, it alters steroid signaling at the level of receptor-mediated gene regulation for all five steroid

receptors. "Arsenic contamination continues to be a serious, ongoing public environmental health problem affecting hundreds of millions of people." [211]

Smoking

Don't smoke while pregnant and during breast feeding should be known to every future mother, or at least someone must tell her. It turns out future fathers should quit before conception, too. Exposure to maternal smoking is associated with reduced semen quality and reduced testis size in adulthood. [212]

If the mother smoked during pregnancy, later, a young man's sperm count is reduced by 40 %, if the father smoked at the time of conception, the son's sperm count is also reduced by 40%. Both is irreversible. If the young man smokes himself, his sperm count is reduced by 15%, but that is reversible. [213]

"The incidence of bilateral cryptorchidism is increased and the fertility potential is reduced in sons born to mothers who have smoked during pregnancy. " [214]

Differently, for testosterone in daughters, when women smoke during pregnancy, their daughters have higher testosterone and higher risk of becoming smokers themselves. *"Self-reported smoking in pregnancy has a direct effect. Smoking among daughters during adolescence was determined by maternal prenatal testosterone and self-reported maternal smoking during pregnancy and postnatally."* [215]

"In utero exposure to constituents of cigarette smoke has been associated with earlier age of menarche (first menstruation) and - to a lesser extent - changes in the testosterone profile of the young women." [216] A 2019 study found that women who smoked marijuana when they underwent infertility treatment with ART had more than double the miscarriage rate of those who didn't. [217]

Speaking of smoking, the main reason why nicotine is extremely addictive is also directly connected to testosterone: in men luteinizing hormone (LH) spikes for 42 minutes after a cigarette (similarly as with cocaine) and then drops to below baseline levels. Serum testosterone increases slightly after nicotine intake and then drops off steeply after 16 minutes to remain below baseline indefinitely or until the next dose of nicotine, leading to depression, feeling of unease or fatigue. [218] Male active chain smokers can have increased testosterone levels just after intake for a few minutes, at least for the first few months, until the addiction takes on a life of its own (when the same recreational drug is used both as an upper and as a downer, for stimulation and relaxation, and then all the additional toxins contained in tobacco smoke can destroy the endocrine system). With additional years of smoking, testosterone levels drop gradually and sustainably. Lead, mercury and dozens of other neurotoxins contained in tobacco are well established endocrine disrupters. "Cigarette smoking is associated with higher blood lead levels." [219]

After quitting, it can take months to years to reach normal testosterone regulation.

It may be that back in the days when smoking was encouraged by movie stars and mainstream culture, tobacco was less laden with the known additional neurotoxins. So, pure tobacco could make men appear more 'manly' and mor confident, immediately while smoking, because of testosterone effects, not just because smoking was thought to look "cool". And they were perceived as such by women of the last millennium, enough so that women tolerated the smell and the coughing.

In early adolescence, male and female smokers had higher T levels than non-smokers. A longitudinal study by Zmuda et al (1997) found that across time, T declined faster in male smokers than non-smokers. [220]

Pharmaceutical drugs

Vaccines (Update of 6.2.2022):

A vaccine to deliberately sterilize women and chemically castrate men.

In 1992; two vaccines were set into Phase I/Phase II clinical trials in patients of prostate carcinoma at the National Institute of Immunology (NII) in New Delhi, India.

The application of this vaccine effectively chemically castrates the male prostate cancer patient and prevents pregnancy in women.

As of May 1991, some of the women participants had experienced 179 pregnancy-free cycles.

After the leading pharma corporations and governments have admitted many unintended side effects in the current global vaccine - and ingredients are secret - it remains to be seen what other endocrine disrupting and sterilizing compounds are in the new vaccine in addition to the known ones (nanoparticles, see below). [221]

In the trials of 1991, the two tested vaccines were: the human **chorionic gonadotropin (hCG) vaccine and the gonadotropin releasing hormone (GnRH)** vaccine.

Gonadotropin-releasing hormone (GnRH) is a releasing hormone responsible for the release of follicle-stimulating hormone (FSH) and luteinizing hormone (LH) from the anterior pituitary.

It constitutes the initial step in the hypothalamic–pituitary–gonadal axis.

In a follow-up paper in 2013, G.P. Talwar reported

"The first-ever efficacy trials on a birth control vaccine established high efficacy (one pregnancy in 1224 cycles). [222]

A 2019 study on Heberprovac, a GnRH based vaccine, showed significant reductions in serum levels of testosterone and PSA after four immunizations. Castrate levels of testosterone were observed in all patients at the end of the immunization schedule, which remained at the lowest level for at least 20 months. [223]

Jerri Caldeira, 2015 utilized two different approaches attempting to produce virus-like particles (VLPs) to induce antibodies that neutralize hCG."

"Immunization of mice with some virus-like particles (VLPs) yielded antisera that bound the hormone and neutralized hCG biological activity." [224]

With these sterilizing vaccines in trial, it may be assumed that they are only given under full consent and after detailed information of the recipients in these developing countries, to make sure they really understand the goal is they cannot have children for a certain time or never again.

But in fact, after countless UN vaccination scandals, we don't know. Globalist philanthropists like Ted Turner or Bill Gates on the one hand insist they want to reduce the world population and on the other, they vow they want to vaccinate the entire world population. Thus, it must be assumed that these sterilizing vaccines have been contained in other vaccines or administered under false labels, for the greater good....

There are numerous reports of entire town populations being infertile after UN vaccination visits. [225] It was found that UN administered tetanus vaccines may contain sterilizing substances.

Kenya's Catholic Doctors Association leaders say they have proof that the doses given to Kenyan women by the UN since March 2014 are 'laced' with a fertility inhibiting hormone. [226] The Association sent samples from around Kenya to laboratories in South Africa. "They tested positive for the hCG antigen." [227]
And now a byproduct of a Covid 19 vaccine ingredient is also linked to reduced testosterone, a study shows. [228]

And here is the most important update to this book of June 2022:
As it turns out the Covld vaccine is accelerating the progress of Hormonageddon at a staggering pace.
Infertility after the vaccine, especially in women, is widespread, or rather, women are the ones to have noticed the loss of periods and loss of pregnancies. And as many women in their late 30s postponed pregnancy because of the pandemic, and most men have no intention of having children, vaccinated men in general haven't even noticed their possible sudden infertility. Since the pandemic, we know from animal studies that nano particles of the type that are officially used in the mRNA vaccines, *"are accumulating in the liver and the spleen and in the gonads, that means in the ovaries and the testicles, which leads to inflammation and possible infertility."*
And of course, important here is what causes infertility via the gonads, also decreases testosterone in men and estrogen in women. Which agrees very well with the manifestation of a society who just sits there for two years obediently waiting for the government to give them their life back, as the process of *Hormonageddon* has just been put in overdrive by the covid vaccinees. Thus, when the UN and other well-meaning organizations speak of population control by contraceptives and vaccines, this means both population numbers can be controlled and populations' behaviors can be controlled or populations are induced to control themselves more easily via gonad hormonal disruption.
For more than two years now, experts have tried to deny that the FDA-approved Pfizer vaccine might impact fertility in both men and women. In June 2022, a medical study confirmed, the mRNA COVID vaccine by Pfizer, caused men to experience a drop in fertility of more than 20%. [229]
And now official data is available to prove birth rates have indeed dropped massively in the United Kingdom, Germany, Sweden, Netherlands, Switzerland, Hungary and Taiwan in the first months of 2022 of up to 15 %. This is unprecedented in peace times or non- famine times, normally birth rates fluctuate only in the 1 %

range from year to year. The decline did not begin in the first two years of the pandemic, mind you, but only a year after the vaccination campaigns. So, this large decline in birth rates was not a result of family planning of those who postponed pregnancy because of the pandemic. Naturally all governments and institutions deny a link to the vaccine. [230]

Here are a few excerpts from the Nanoparticle article, read the full text here. [231]

The Nanoparticle Pandemic COVID: how the global bio-tech and Insurance Industry predicted a Nanotech Disaster

Eight years before the COVID vaccine, the World's largest Re-Insurance company predicted "unforeseen consequences of nano-technology" as one of the highest insurance risks in a 4 to 10- year timeframe.

Almost all global political and economic leaders are dead set to vaccinate the entire world population with COVID vaccines which are still experimental as of mid 2022.
The nanoparticles which are being marketed as essential ingredients of the COVID vaccines are lipid nanoparticles, further, ferritin nano- vaccines will be released shortly. [232] The lipid nanoparticles are used as a medium to deliver the mRNA into the cells.
Independent researchers also announced to have detected graphene and graphene oxide nanoparticles in the currently administered doses, graphene oxide is also an official compound of many types of masks, mandatory in many countries.
At the same time, 2021 saw an exorbitant increase in heart inflammation [233] as reported by the CDC- VEARS [234] data base as vaccine side effects (up to 240 times more myocarditis in 2021 than in any other year; from an average of 100 cases reported per year to 24,211 cases in 2021).
The problem has become prominent enough that even science magazine reported:
"Suspicions grow that nanoparticles in Pfizer's COVID -19 vaccine trigger rare allergic reactions." [235]
In Feb 2022 the CDC confirms an increased risk of heart inflammation after COVID Vaccines. [236]
As we've seen at the beginning of this book, for a decade, the global insurance industry had been preoccupied with the long-term consequences of nanoparticles.

As a side note, the report also listed [for risks with a 1-3 year time frame], "The topics "prolonged power blackout", "run-away inflation and surging bond yields" and "big data" were assessed as being of highest concern as they could have a high impact on the entire insurance industry and might occur within a short period of time."
"the SONAR report pointed out (in 2013).
"Healthcare costs are becoming unsustainable, due largely to a chronic disease epidemic fuelled by unhealthy lifestyles and ageing populations. Increasingly, early death is less of an economic concern than decades spent alive and sick. "

Already in 2007, the German insurance company ADAC changed their policies for accident insurance to exclude mass vaccine damage: *"Insurance does not pay compensation in cases of vaccination injuries as a consequence of mandatory mass vaccination."* [237]
cas.org describes the application of nanotechnology in COVID -19 vaccines:
"Lipid nanoparticles are a vital component of the Pfizer/BioNTech and Moderna mRNA COVID-19 vaccines, playing a key role in protecting and transporting the mRNA effectively to the right place in cells." [238]
Dr. Wodarg, a former leading epidemiologist for the German Government, warned:
"If it [the vaccine] does not go into the vein, then it is distributed throughout the body via the lymph system and the tissue fluids, and here also, we know from animal studies that these nano particles are accumulating in the liver and the spleen and in the gonads, that means in the ovaries and the testicles, which leads to inflammation and possible infertility." [239]
"In a recent bioRxiv preprint research paper, Botond Z. Igyártó and colleagues from Thomas Jefferson University demonstrated the inflammatory nature of the lipid nanoparticles (LNPs) in the Pfizer/BioNTech and Moderna vaccines."
In a study the connection to the hypothalamus (at the initial stages of the gonad hormone axis) was elucidated:
"LNPs might also diffuse from the periphery and reach any organs in the body, including CNS (hypothalamus) where they could directly induce side effects; " [240]
On Dez. 21. 2021, The US Army declared they "Created a single COVID-19 vaccine using a spike ferritin nanoparticle vaccine, against all COVID & SARS variants (even future ones)." [241]

Further, there are several institutions, chemists and physicians who also published evidence of the presence of graphene oxide and reduced graphene oxide (all nanoparticles) in the vaccines.

In 2020, a Chinese study proposed that graphene oxide (GO) should be used in vaccines, citing it does not break down in the body over time as a drawback. [242]

A Chinese patent for a covid vaccination that uses graphene oxide also exists: "Nano coronavirus recombinant vaccine taking graphene oxide as a carrier, A61K39/12 Viral antigens. "The new corona vaccine contains graphene oxide, carnosine, CpG and new corona virus RBD." [243]

"By tracking the top 10 graphene applications through the years, one can see how 'medicine' rises to become the most popular application of graphene in 2020, ranked by the number of posts written. Beginning with 2015, where medicine was 4th; 2016, 3rd; 2018, 3rd; 2019, 2nd; and finally, 2020,1st on the list. Covid-19 is cited as the obvious reason graphene's use in medicine was the most popular discussion on the Graphene-info website." [244]

"According to preliminary results of a study done by the University of Almería in Spain, graphene has been found in the Covid-19 vaccines. By examining the contents of a Pfizer / BioNTech vial researchers discovered, there is mRNA, but graphene oxide makes up between 98% and 99% of its contents: 'this is not a vaccine but a dose of pure graphene oxide into the vein.'." [245]

There is an urgent need to replicate this analysis. Graphene-family nanomaterials (GFNs), including graphene oxide and reduced graphene oxide, are toxic. [246]

Symptoms of graphene oxide poisoning include: bilateral pneumonias; thrombogenicity; blood clots; post inflammatory syndrome or systemic / multi-organ inflammations; alteration of the immune system; and, ultimately collapse of the immune system and a cytokine storm. [...] When inhaled, graphene causes inflammation of the mucous membranes and possible loss of taste and smell. Sounds familiar?" [247]

Dr. Robert Young also reported that scanning & transmission electron microscopy reveals graphene oxide in CoV-19 vaccines:

"The observations under optical microscopy revealed and abundance of transparent 2D laminar objects that show great similarity with images from the literature (Xu et al, 2019), and with images obtained from rGO standard (SIGMA) (Figures 1, 2 and 3).

All these laminar objects were widespread in the aqueous fraction of the blood (Figure 1) or vaccine samples (Figures 2 and 3) and no component described by the registered patent can be associated with these sheets. [248]

The Effects of Nanomaterials as Endocrine Disruptors
I. Iavicoli et al found that: "Current data support the notion that different types of nanoparticles are capable of altering the normal and physiological activity of the endocrine system." [249]

Nanoparticles for sterilization of animals
In 2020, a patent was filed for "A method for non-surgical sterilization of mammals using an antibody-guided nanoparticle carrying cytotoxin to kill gonadal cells exhibiting anti-Mullerian hormone II receptors." [250]

Researchers at Tufts University have devised a novel, fast, and non-surgical means to induce apoptosis in animal gonads for sterilization. Lipid-like carriers are used for targeted intracellular delivery of proteins and antibodies that induce cell apoptosis. The procedure is done through single intravenous (IV) injection that does not require anesthesia.

in 2018, Wang et al explained:

Numerous types of NPs are not only able to pass certain biological barriers and exert toxic effects on crucial organs (after inhalation, ingestion, or injection), such as the brain, liver, and kidney, but NPs can also pass through the **blood–testis barrier**, placental barrier, and epithelial barrier, which protect reproductive tissues, and then accumulate in reproductive organs. NP accumulation damages organs (testis, epididymis, ovary, and uterus) by destroying Sertoli cells, Leydig cells, and germ cells, causing reproductive organ dysfunction that adversely affects sperm quality, quantity, morphology, and motility or reduces the number of mature oocytes and disrupts primary and secondary follicular development. In addition, NPs can disrupt the levels of secreted hormones, causing changes in sexual behavior. "

"Several studies have demonstrated that various NPs can pass through the blood–testis barrier (BTB) and exert their toxic actions on spermatogenesis. Regarding deposition and translocation, the ability of NPs to cross both the blood–brain barrier and the BTB is highly important. " [251]

It had been known for years that the "blood–brain barrier can be permeated by graphene nanomaterials." [252]

Further studies on the effects of graphene oxide on gonads conducted by Dziewięcka M. et al 2017 revealed: Short-term in vivo exposure to graphene oxide can cause damage to the gut and testis of A. domesticus.

"Upon analysing histological specimens, we found numerous degenerative changes in the cells of the gut and testis of Acheta domesticus as early as ten days after applying GO." [253]

Nanoparticles (29.5 +/- 6.3 nm in diameter) can damage human fibroblast cells across an intact cellular barrier **"without having to cross the barrier."** The outcome, which includes DNA damage without significant cell death, is different from that observed in cells subjected to direct exposure to nanoparticles. [254]

Other types of nanoparticles, such as titanium dioxide nanoparticles, reduce pituitary-testicular axis hormones and decrease reproductive potential of male sex. [255]

Exposure to silver nanoparticles decreases the weight of the reproductive organs, sexual behavior, oxidative defense parameters, sperm count and their motility in male mice. In addition, serum testosterone, apoptotic germ cells and testicular histology are also disrupted. [256]

Before the pandemic, a CDC study of 2016 reported that 1/6 children in the US now is diagnosed with Developmental Disabilities. [257] German researcher Hans Tolzin pointed out that US boys are affected significantly more often by suspected vacclne side effects in connection with autism than girls. *"We also find this effect in the number of reports of serious vacclnation side effects in the databases of the responsible authorities - for instance in the German Paul Ehrlich Institute (PEI) - where boys are also much more often affected than girls."*

"At this time, there are no responses from officials on this striking inequality. Some studies indicate that the male hormone testosterone and the female hormone estrogen react differently to environmental and medical toxins. " [translation mine]. [258]

Differently this time around, women have more severe side effects from the COVLD vacclne than men. 79 percent of side effects reported came from women, although only 61 percent of the vaccines were given to women. [259]

Pain medication

A 2017 Scientific Report article found that ibuprofen (a widely used over-the-counter mild analgesics) reduces steroidogenic enzymes, testosterone synthesis, and Leydig cell function in 8-to-9-week-gestation-age testicular tissue. [260]

In 2018, a study published in the journal Proceedings of the National Academy of Sciences of the United States of America showed Ibuprofen alters human testicular physiology to produce a state of compensated hypogonadism. [261] *"Interested patients, such as men attempting to father children, may use acetaminophen as an alternative for mild pain."*

Here is a list of prescription pharmaceutical drugs that can reduce T in men as a side effect, ideally, they are replaced or avoided all together:

Ibuprofen, Ketoconazole (Extina, Nizoral, Ketoderm); Cimetidine (Tagamet); Spironolactone (Aldactone); Certain antidepressants; Opioids like morphine, codeine, hydrocodone (Vicodin), and oxycodone (OxyContin, Percocet). [262]

Fluoride disrupts testosterone in males

"High fluoride will influence sperm count and quality and damage testis, epididymis and prostate structure so as to influence male reproductive ability." [263]

In a study conducted on 31 male adults (20-55 years old) in a high fluoride area, the serum level of testosterone (T) was significantly decreased (P<0.01) as compared to the control group. "This indicates that high fluoride exposure may affect the reproductive endocrine function of the male human body." [264]

In a different study on subjects age 25-35, semen volume, liquefaction time, viability, motility and semen viscosity were found to be significantly (p<0.05) reduced in all groups of fluorotic patients as compared with the controls. [265]

In Chinese male farmers aged 18-55 years, markedly lower T levels were observed in male farmers from the higher fluoride exposure group than in those from the lower fluoride exposure group. Furthermore, younger farmers, 18-29 and 30-39 years old, may be the most likely to have lower T levels when exposed to fluoride (P < 0.05). "These results supported that excess fluoride exposure decreased serum T levels of male farmers with age-specificity." [266]

"Soy Boys"

Some natural foods, such as soy, have endocrine disrupting properties as well, they are endocrine disrupting substances, but technically not EDCs.

Many young men are becoming vegetarian or vegan these days - as is promoted heavily by politicians, the media and the technocrat establishment – and they then resort to soy as protein substitution. This led to the derogative term of the "Soy Boy".

And it doesn't help that virtually all the soy is of heavy pesticide GMO production and extensively processed.

However, cause and effect may be partly mix up here. The rapid increase in veganism and soy consumption might be partly *caused* by low testosterone, rather than vice versa. Hypogonadism - and subsequently low testosterone - can lead to depression, oversensitivity and irritability which may have contributed to the exorbitant increase in veganism in recent years.

When I turned vegetarian 30 years ago, most people, and especially other young men, were laughing at the idea. The past couple years that I've been eating meat again and coincidently repaired my health, the same people are suddenly lecturing me on the evils of meat eating, as they see it in every TV show, political movement and youth culture pushed by celebrities. What's more, even people who eat meat themselves demand more government control to reduce meat consumption (for the climate, for justice).

More decisive for the testosterone levels of a young man than his own current soy consumption is his soy intake in childhood - which is determined by the parents - on the one hand, and the soy intake of the mother during pregnancy, on the other. I'm opposed to derogative and insulting terms for well-meaning, empathetic people, especially if these terms are not leading to problem solutions, but since the term '*Soy Boys*' is being used, technically, the phenomenon may be more accurately be called "sons-of-soy-mothers".

"Endocrine disruption by dietary phyto-oestrogens has an impact on dimorphic sexual systems and behaviours. Because soya is a hormonally active diet, soya can be endocrine disrupting, particularly when exposure occurs during development."

"Consumption by infants and small children is of particular concern because their hormone-sensitive organs, including the brain and reproductive system, are still undergoing sexual differentiation and maturation. Thus, their susceptibility to the endocrine-disrupting activities of soya phyto-oestrogens may be especially high. " [267]

"Early-life soy exposure was associated with less female-typical play behavior in girls at 42 months of age. Soy exposure was not significantly associated with play behavior in boys at the same age." [268]

The "*Grass Eaters*" of Japan

"A particularly interesting example of low nationwide male fecundity is the emergence of "grass eaters" (soshokukei danshi) in the wake of the continuing 20-year-long Japanese economic impotency. These are men who are uninterested in sex or reproduction. They supposedly lack adequate testosterone." [269]

On Wikipedia, we read in connection to *Grass Eaters*: "Many women refuse men who do not have steady jobs (such as freeters and NEETs). Other women feel that self-proclaimed sōshoku-kei danshi (herbivore men) are weak and not masculine, while some men apparently are not attracted to "independent" women. In a 2011 poll of Japanese boys aged between 16 and 19, 36% described themselves as indifferent or averse towards having sex; the figure for girls in the same age group was at 59%." [270]

If you grew up in the last century, you might find it hard to imagine an 18-year-old boy in your generation who was 'indifferent or averse towards having sex'.

On the women's side, developments in sports may serve as a further indicator of estrogen decline, and the loss of natural motherly feelings and the biological urge for self-preservation.

The ban on women's boxing was lifted in England in 1996 and the sport became Olympic in 2012, Mixed Martial arts followed. Female athletes compete in running competitions in the 6th month of pregnancy. Not after decades of studies that proved there are no long-term health consequences for the child. No, just after empowered women and selected experts said there are no studies to prove that pregnant sprinting is harmful and because women can do what they want. Evolutionary biology makes it clear, that throughout human existence, babies of pregnant women who had to run for their life or ran just for fun, were eliminated from the gene pool. Thus, everyone is the descendent of a woman who did everything to prevent sprinting in pregnancy. And thus, everyone was hardwired to protect pregnant women from physical stress, until a few years ago.

Vegetarianism is a well-intended experiment, which may or may not succeed. It will take decades of studies of isolated groups to see how many can live and function at their best without meat, without the food their ancestors have evolved to survive on for millennia. We cannot just willingly alter our physical body and metabolism to adapt to a new diet.

To make the transition to a fully vegetarian society, where enough people can still do physical hard work, will require an enormous selection process, wherein everyone who cannot be healthy without meat or dairy will die, become infertile or is prevented from having children by poverty or state power. Here as well, human groups don't just change because they want to or because society or the state told them to. This is true for physiology and psychology. Humans evolve only by the above- mentioned processes such as natural selection.

Chapter 6
Electromagnetic fields and testosterone/ estrogen

6.1. Endocrine Disrupting Non- Ionizing Radiation (EDNR).

Non- Ionizing radiation in the radio- and microwave frequency range is almost everywhere. The main sources are smart phones, Wi-Fi, modems, computers, tablets, microwave ovens, walkie talkies and cellphone towers and even baby phones. For the sake of simplicity, we hitherto refer to them as wireless radiation.

Long before any cellphones or radios operating in microwave frequencies were available to the public, it was known that microwave radiation decreases testosterone and inhibits testicular function.

*"The 1971/ 72 U.S. Office of Naval Medical Research study reported the following changes induced by microwave and radio waves related to testis or sperm: **Decreased testosterone** leading to lowered testis size; histological changes in testicular epithelial structure; gross testicular histological changes; decreased spermatogenesis."* [271]

Because rapidly dividing germ cells go through meiosis and mitosis, they are more sensitive to EMF in contrast to other slower-growing cell types.

Long-term exposure to EMF decreases sperm motility and fertilization. [272]

Here a little anecdote: in the late 1990s, a funny colleague showed off his latest cellphone gadget, which was an earphone with a microphone, as is standard today. At the time, the increased risk of brain tumor from mobile phone users was rather speculative, but more people were still concerned than today, now, few people even care anymore. He was joking how with the cable speaker on his ear and the phone in his pocket, he won't get a brain tumor like the rest of us, but on the other hand, he might get testicular cancer instead. Little did he know, he was unwittingly foreseeing a public health disaster.

Ethics of testing

The following is how safety standards for wireless radiation are determined. To date, all a mobile phone or another microwave emitting device requires in order to pass regulations is this: the radiation doesn't raise the temperature of a human body too much (usually tested on a water filled dummy head). [273] The rationale behind this is the consensus says that non-ionizing radiation up to a certain energy (or watt per surface area) – is safe for humans.

Some have made the comparison that authorities in Fukushima might as well declare the reactor as safe for humans, as long as that human doesn't heat up too much. The comparison is lacking, for nuclear radiation is ionizing radiation, but there is a point to it. It was back in the 80s when I last heard an old lady making the news for drying her little dog in a microwave, the dog was boiled inside and obviously died.

Now, only if you're crazy, you would put your baby in a microwave oven, even at a very low power output, even if a federal regulator bureaucrat ensured you the energy output was so little that your baby only warms up a little bit. But with wireless technology, this is exactly what we are doing.

To request that men expose their reproductive organs to mobile phone radiation as an experimental condition in order to analyze changes in testosterone levels is not an approved approach by the WHO or other health regulation organizations. [274] So, trust the WHO when they say there are no health risks.

Experiments on testosterone levels and mobile phone exposure are typically conducted on animals including rats and rabbits.

But human studies do exist and show a similar, consistent picture, i.e., mobile radiation disrupts sex hormone regulation, and reduces testosterone in men and estrogen in women.

Here are summaries of studies of recent years. We are beginning with EMF-MF exposure at 50 Hertz (Hz). This is the frequency of the generic power grid, and we've been living with this in increasing doses for a hundred years. The 50 Hz peak is visible in brain wave measurements, EEG, as a very distinct peak. EMF effects on human brain activity and the endocrine system are amplitude dependent.

Then we move to animal and human studies of wireless, mobile phone, Wi-Fi and other radio/ microwave radiation. These are distinguished by EMF emissions at a complex combination of frequencies, including ELFs (Extremely Low Frequencies) even below 10 Hertz. Frequencies below 50 Hz are not considered at all in regulations by governments.

The following is a short selection of about 50 peer-reviewed studies that confirm more or less the same effects, so it might be a bit repetitive. But the basic content of the literature is crucial for the understanding of the premise of this book. If you want to skip the details, the short of it is this:

Wireless/ EMFs are disrupting not only fertility, but also testosterone and estrogen production/ function in humans and animals.
Thus, we introduce a new term: **Endocrine Disrupting Non- Ionizing Radiation (EDNR).**

Mobile phone and Wi-fi technology are listed as RF- EMF (radio frequencies) in the literature, which is a bit misleading since they actually operate in the microwave and millimeter frequency spectrum.
Radio waves range from 1 Hz to 300 MHz, microwaves range from 300 MHz to 300 GHz. ELFs, Extremely Low Frequencies, range between 3 to 30 Hz. Magnetic field (MF) is non-ionizing radiation.
In wireless communication, the term radio-frequency (RF) encompasses both microwaves and radio waves.
But wireless providers use frequencies from 700MHz to 3000 MHz and high-band 5G uses frequencies of 25–39 GHz or 39,000MHz.
Thus, when we talk of wireless radiation we are almost exclusively talking about microwaves and millimeter waves. Millimeter waves used to be called high frequency microwaves.
Microwave ovens operate at a frequency of 2.45 GHz or 2,450 MHz, even though they use much higher amplitudes, its much the same as wireless/mobile radiation. Being dosed in radio frequency electromagnetic fields just sounds more reassuring than getting your brains microwaved 24/7. The same is true for body scanners at the airport etc. undergoing a millimeter-wave clothing penetration examination sounds more welcoming than "getting microwaved" at the airport.
The frequency of a microwave oven is close to that of the solar radio flux to Earth, which is strongly corelated with solar flares.
"The 2,800 MHz, or 10.7 cm, responds to the same conditions that produce changes in the visible and X-ray wavelengths." [275] (See Chapter 12).
As pointed out above, most of the research on the endocrine disrupting effects of wireless /mobile radiation is conducted in Middle Eastern countries, where growing infertility and disruption of family structures are still recognized as a problem for the future, while in

the West, these trends are generally embraced. If things continue at the current trajectory, humanity is going to owe a lot to the institutions in these countries.

6.2. EMF general frequencies (not mobile radiation specific)

EMF 50 Hz, animal studies

- When adult male rats were exposed to a 50 Hz sinusoidal magnetic field at approximately 25 µT (rms), testosterone levels were significantly decreased after 6 and 12 weeks of the exposure period. " [276]

- Exposure of mice to EMF (50Hz) induced a significant reduction in sperm count, viability and progressive motility. EMF exposure caused abnormalities in sperm and a significant decrease in testosterone levels. [277]
- In adult mice that were exposed to EMF (50 Hz at 3 milliTesla) during the developmental period, there were several intercellular spaces and spermatogenic cells with condensed nuclei. [278]

- 50 Hz EMF caused testosterone disruption in the 2nd generation of rats. In a 2014 study by Gharamaleki et al, pregnant rats were exposed to 3mT EMF, 50 Hz for 21 days. The male pups were kept until maturity, then their Total Antioxydant Capacity (TAC), MDA and testosterone levels were analyzed. TAC was significantly increased in pregnant rats.
In the male offspring in adulthood, TAC and the testosterone level was significantly decreased. Spermatogenic cells were disrupted. [279]

- EMFs were shown to include changes in serum levels of testosterone in rats. EMF exposure may cause profound changes in the vesicle seminal tissues. Therefore, exposure to EMF may result in pathological changes that lead to sub fertility and infertility. [280]

- Long-term exposure to low frequency EMF significantly decreased the diameter of the seminiferous tubules and increased the number of seminiferous tubules per unit area of testes in male rats.

In addition, low frequency EMF (1 microTesla, 50 Hz) significantly reduced sperm motility and testosterone levels. [281]

- Adult female rats were exposed to a 50 Hz sinusoidal magnetic field at approximately 25 microTesla for 18 weeks. A significant reduction in absolute and relative ovarian weights in exposed rats was observed. The reduction in the levels of gonadotropins (FSH and LH) was significant after six weeks of exposure. The level of progesterone and estrogen was significantly decreased after 12 weeks of exposure. The level of estrogen was still significantly reduced at 12 weeks **after removing the field.** [282]

- EMF (50 Hz) exposure causes profound changes in the genital organs of male rats. [283]

- Exposure of mice to EMF (50 Hz) induced a significant reduction in sperm count, viability and progressive motility in comparison with control group. EMF caused abnormalities in sperm and a significant **decrease in testosterone** level. Date palm pollen (Phoenix dactylifera) had a protective effect [284] (See also p. 145).
- Electromagnetic field (EMF) exposure at 50 Hz for 42 consecutive days caused a significant decrease of Serum Testosterone in Rats. [285]

EMF 50 Hz human studies

- In a human study on testicular tissue, it was found that the number of cells in the spermatogenesis cycle was reduced significantly after exposure of 50 Hz. [286]

- Male workers of an electric power plant with high EMF exposure and with walkie-talkies usage had statistically significantly lower levels of plasma testosterone and lower testosterone/estradiol (T/E2) ratio than colleagues with lower exposure. [287]

6.3. Wireless/ EMF and testosterone

Children absorb more microwave radiation (MWR) than adults, and the *"fetus is in even greater danger than children from exposure to MWR."* MWR is a Class 2B (possible) carcinogen.
The legal exposure limits have remained unchanged for decades.

Cellphone manuals warnings and the 20 cm rule for tablets/laptops violate the "normal operating position" regulation. [288]
- M. Pall, 2016 found "Microwave frequency electromagnetic fields (EMFs) produce widespread **neuropsychiatric effects including depression**."
26 studies show EMF associations with neuropsychiatric effects; 5 criteria show causality. "Microwave Electromagnetic Fields cause at least 13 different neuropsychiatric effects including depression in humans." [289]
- Another representative analysis of 23 scientific studies on the effects of Wi-Fi radiation on animals as well as on humans confirmed degenerative changes in testes, reduced testosterone levels, increased apoptotic cells, and DNA damage. The authors concluded exposure to 2.45 GHz RF-EMR emitted by a Wi-Fi transmitters is hazardous on the male reproductive system. [290]

Wireless EMF / testosterone, animal studies

- Mice were exposed to RF-EMR from a mobile phone (Samsung Note 9) for 14 days. Serum levels of male sex hormones (follicle-stimulating hormone and **testosterone**) decreased significantly.
The study shows that chronic exposure to RF-EMR from a cell phone causes impaired testicular function accompanied by a decrease in the value of sexual hormones. Sperm count was also decreased. [291]

- Three-week old male mice were exposed to mobile phone (1800 MHz) radiation for 3 hours per day for 120 days in different operative modes.
*"Decreased seminiferous tubule diameter, sperm count, and viability along with increased germ cells apoptosis and a **decreased serum testosterone level**, was observed in the testes of all the mobile phone exposed mice."* The researchers concluded that long-term mobile phone radiation exposure induced oxidative stress leading to apoptosis of testicular cells and thus impairment of testicular function. [292]

- After being irradiated for 24 h at 1950 MHz, 3 W/kg radiation, cell proliferation in mice obviously decreased. Secretion capacity of testosterone was reduced. [293]

- EMFs created by mobile phones caused morphologic and histological changes by affecting germinal epithelium tissue of rats negatively.
The cortisol levels in the EMF-exposed groups were significantly higher. [294]

- Mobile cell radiation exposure in male rats induced a significant decrease in serum FSH (follicle stimulating hormone), LH (luteinizing hormone), decreases in testosterone levels, epididymal sperm count and sperm quality. However, administration of vitamin D resulted in a significant recovery of all the above- mentioned parameters in the mobile radiation exposed rats' group. The authors confirm the harmful effect of mobile phone radiations on testicular function in male albino rats. In addition, they confirmed the protective effect of Vitamin D on the testicular functions via restoring steroidogenesis and spermatogenesis in exposed rats. [295] (See also: remedies, p. 141).

- Adult male rats were exposed to 30 minutes per day, 5 days a week for 4 weeks to 900 MHz EMF. The diameter of the seminiferous tubules and the mean height of the germinal epithelium were significantly decreased in the EMF group. There was a significant decrease in serum total testosterone levels. It was concluded that testicular morphologic alterations may be due to hormonal changes. [296]

- Exposure to mobile phone radiation for 60 minutes per day for the total period of 3 months significantly decrease the serum testosterone level in Wistar Albino rats compared to their matched control. "Long-term exposure to mobile phone radiation leads to a reduction in serum testosterone levels. " [297] Animals exposed for 60 min per day **had half the serum testosterone** levels of the unexposed (in ng /ml). This can be likened to radiological semi-castration.

- Rats exposed to 900 MHz EMF had decreased wet weight of testes and serum testosterone levels. [298]

- Rabbits were exposed to a period of simulated mobile phone radiation (950 MHz; 3 and 6 W) for 2 hours per day for 2 weeks. The results showed a decrease in the concentration of testosterone in both the 3 and 6 W groups. *"However, cortisol concentration as a marker of adrenal gland function was not affected."* [299]

- Experiments showed that male Wistar rats, who had been exposed to microwave radiation (2.45 GHz for 2 hours/day for 60 days), had significant **decreases in testosterone** and melatonin. *"This finding emphasizes that reactive oxygen species (a potential inducer of cancer) are the primary cause of DNA damage. "*
However, pulsed electromagnetic field exposure (100 Hz, 2 hours/day for 60 days) relieved the effect of microwave exposure by inducing Faraday currents. [300]

- Exposure to 10 GHz fields decrease testosterone and caused shrinkage of the lumen of the seminiferous tubules and DNA strand breaks in rats. The **testosterone** level was found significantly decreased with the shrinkage of testicular size. [301]

- 900 MHz RF-EMF **decreased testosterone**. Rats were exposed to 900 MHz RF-EMF for 1, 2, or 4 h/day over a period of 30 days. A significant decrease in serum testosterone levels in the LTE group was found compared to short and moderate time exposed (MTE) groups after 30 days RF-EMF exposure. [302]

- 1800MHz RF-EMF decreased testosterone in rats.
Radiofrequency fields (RF) at 1800 MHz are known to affect melatonin (MEL) and testosterone in male rats. In this trial, RF exposure was 2 h/day for 32 days. The circadian rhythms of T and melatonin were disturbed after exposure to RF, with the effect being more pronounced on MEL than on testosterone. [303]

- Exposure to 1,800 MHz RF had adverse effects on testosterone synthesis, antioxidant levels, and clock gene expression in primary Leydig cells of mice. Pretreatment with CeO2NPs (Cerium oxide nanoparticles) prevented the adverse effects on testosterone synthesis induced by RF exposure by regulating their antioxidant capacity and clock gene expression in vitro. [304]

- Microwave oven leakage decreased testosterone in rats.
Test groups of rats were exposed to 2450 MHZ produced by a microwave oven. Leakage of the microwave oven resulted in decreased testosterone production by testes in mature rats which may be due to the direct effect of microwave on Leydig cells or its indirect effect on pituitary and hypothalamus. [305]

- Germ Cell apoptosis in testes (cell death) in rats was induced by ELF-MF. *"Testosterone levels in rats significantly decreased after 6 and 12 weeks of ELF-MF exposure."* It was concluded that "deprivation of gonadotropin or testosterone induces germ cell apoptosis." [306]

- Male mice were exposed to 1800 MHz RF at 208 microW/cm2 power (wireless frequencies) for 32 days with 2 hours per day. "Microwave radiation induced reduced level in testicular sperm head count and serum testosterone, while the level of serum estradiol increased. [307]

- Male rabbits were exposed to MPs (800 MHz) in a standby position for 8 h daily for 12 weeks. Exposed rabbits showed altered sexual behavior, lack of ejaculation, increase biting/grasping during copulation. The researchers concluded that the pulsed radiofrequency emitted by a conventional MP, which was kept on a standby position, could affect the sexual behavior in the rabbit. [308]
- 1800 MHz radiofrequency fields for 2 h per day for 32 days inhibits testosterone production in mice via CaMKI /RORα pathway. [309]

Wireless EMF/ testosterone, human studies

- Long term exposure to base stations and mobile phones affects human hormone profiles. A study over a 6-year monitoring period with human volunteers revealed that high radio frequency radiation effects emitted either from mobile phones or from base stations (wi-fi routers) on the pituitary–adrenal axis represented in a **reduction** of adrenocorticotropic hormone (ACTH), cortisol, thyroid hormones, prolactin in young females, and a **reduction in the testosterone level in both genders**. [310]

6.4. Mobile phone EMFs and additional hormone disruption

Playing hormone roulette

- Operators of satellite stations exposed to low level radiofrequency electromagnetic radiation showed heightened excretion of stress hormones in operators during 24-hour shifts. The satellite stations are used for TV communications and space research. [311]

- After Wistar rats were exposed to mobile RF for 6 hours daily, for 4–8 weeks at RF900 MHz, enhanced plasma adrenocorticotropic hormone (ACTH) and cortisol levels were found.

It was concluded that *"cell phone RF exposure induced significant hormonal and structural changes in adrenal gland and brain tissues. Therefore, the public should be aware and limit their exposure as much as possible."* [312]

- Mobile phone radiation increases Thyroid Stimulating Hormone (TSH) in Humans. A higher than normal TSH level, low mean T4 and normal T3 concentrations in mobile users (students) were observed. *"It seems that minor degrees of thyroid dysfunction with a compensatory rise in TSH may occur following excessive use of mobile phones."* [313]

- Short, medium, and long-term exposure to extremely low frequency electromagnetic field (ELF-EMF) (1 and 5 Hz radiation) on behavioral, hormonal, and metabolic changes in male Wistar rats were studied.

Plasma adrenocorticotropic hormone (ACTH) concentration increased in both frequencies, whereas noradrenaline concentration showed an overall reduction. [314]

- Wi-fi increased the extent of lipid peroxidation in the kidney and testis of rats. Wi-Fi- and mobile phone-induced EMR exposure to rats for 4-6 weeks caused oxidative damage by increasing the extent of lipid peroxidation and the iron level, while decreasing total antioxidant status, copper, and GSH values. *"Wi-Fi- and mobile phone-induced EMR may cause precocious puberty and oxidative kidney and testis injury in growing rats."* [315]

6.5. Wireless EMF and sperm cells, fertility

Wireless EMF and sperm cells, fertility - human studies

- K. Kesari et al, 2018 noted that cell phones, laptops, Wi-Fi and microwave ovens are the most common sources of non-ionizing radiation.

"From currently available studies it is clear that radiofrequency electromagnetic fields (RF-EMF) have deleterious effects on sperm

parameters (like sperm count, morphology, motility), they affect the endocrine system and produce genotoxicity, genomic instability and oxidative stress. " [316]

- Martin Pall 2018 cautions: "Wi-Fi is an important threat to human health". Established Wi-Fi effects include: apoptosis, Neuropsychological DNA impact; hormone change and Ca2+ overload.
"Each of these effects are also caused by exposures to other microwave frequency EMFs, with each such effect being documented in from 10 to 16 reviews. Both the lowered male fertility and lowered female fertility are associated with and presumably caused by the oxidative stress in the male and female reproductive organs. Spontaneous abortion is often caused by chromosomal mutations, so the germ line mutations may have a causal role. Lowered libido may be caused by lowered estrogen, progesterone and testosterone levels." [317]

- Sid- Salman (2019) found that a Wi-Fi router increased antibiotic resistance and motility of E Coli and increased metabolic activity and biofilm production in Staphylococcus Aureus and Staphylococcus Epidermis. *"The [Wi-Fi] exposed cells, as compared to the unexposed control, showed an increased metabolic activity and biofilm formation ability in Escherichia coli 0157H7, Staphylococcus aureus and Staphylococcus epidermis."* [318]
This should be carefully considered in a current virus crisis that also involves bacterial infections, when people are forced to wear masks in which bacteria and fungi can proliferate.

- "Many laptops show magnetic field readings higher than 200 milligauss (600 times more than the 0.3 milligauss level that is considered safe). " [319]

- In 2012, Avendaño et al showed that the use of laptop computers connected to internet through Wi-Fi decreases human sperm motility and increases sperm DNA fragmentation. [320]

- When human spermatozoa were exposed to mobile phones RF-EMR they have decreased motility, morphometric abnormalities, and increased oxidative stress. Further, men using mobile phones have decreased sperm concentration, decreased motility (particularly rapid progressive motility), normal morphology, and decreased viability. *"These abnormalities seem to be directly related to the duration of mobile phone use."* [321]

- In an observational study at the Cleveland Clinic, Ohio, men undergoing infertility evaluation were analyzed for their active cell phone use. The laboratory values of mean sperm count, motility, viability, and normal morphology decreased in cell phone users as the duration of daily exposure to cell phones increased. [322]

Wireless/ EMF and sperm cells, fertility - animal studies

- Wistar rats were exposed to 60 Hz / 1 milliTesla EMF three times per day for 30 min, between the 13th day of gestation and the 21st postnatal day. Histomorphometric analysis showed that exposure to EMF can promote a delay in testicular development. [323]

- Rats exposed to Wi-Fi (2.45 GHz) for 1-hour and 7-hours showed a decrease in sperm parameters in a time dependent pattern. [324]

- In a similar study by Bruno Tenorio, et al 2012, Wistar rats were exposed to EMF (60 Hz, 1 milliTesla) from day 13 of gestation to postnatal day 21 or 90, in three daily applications of 30 min. Testicular degeneration was shown in a subset of animals exposed to EMF. It was confirmed that exposure to 60 Hz EMF can disturb spermatogenesis and may produce subfertility or infertility. [325]

- EMFs caused cell death in testicular germ cells in mice. [326]

- An experimental group of rats were exposed to a magnetic field (0.8 mT) for 5 weeks, 3 hr per day. Experimental groups had more sperm malformation. Testosterone levels were also found to be altered (p<.05). Decreased spermatogenesis in testis' seminiferous tubules were observed. [327]

- 950-MHz cell phone microwave exposure of rats led to decreased total sperm motility, diminished percentage of normal sperm morphology, reduced percentage of sperm viability (which is expected to increase the possibility of male factor infertility with varying degrees over time). [328]

- Wi-Fi router radiation causes changes in lung tissues.
When rats were exposed to Wi-Fi router radiation for 6 and 24 h, at 25 cm distance, they showed marked histological and immune-histochemical changes in the lung tissues. The research team of R. Ibrahim et al concluded: "The exposure to such devices can cause

bad effects on the lung tissue which increases with prolonged exposure time." [329]

Wireless EMFs disrupt fertility in female animals:
- EMFs disturb estrous cycles in female mice.
Female mice post weaning were exposed to 20 kHz sawtooth electric and magnetic fields (EMF) with 6.25 microTesla peak intensity for 6 weeks. The EMF exposed groups had less estrous cycles than the sham control group. Furthermore, in the EMF-exposed group, the duration of proestrous and metestrous stages of the estrous cycle was significantly increased. [330]

- Female mice were exposed to a Wi-Fi radio frequency of 2.5 GHz. The exposure group was placed 24 cm closer to the radiation source.
"No oocytes count was determined in the exposure group. In other words, the group underwent anovulation. " [331]

-In female mice, 2.45 GHz microwave irradiation-induced oxidative stress affects pregnancy or implantation [attachment of the fertilized egg or blastocyst to the wall of the uterus at the start of pregnancy]. Implantation sites were affected significantly. A low level of MW irradiation-induced oxidative stress not only suppresses implantation, but it may also lead to deformity of the embryo in case pregnancy continues. [332]

Chapter 7
Wireless/ EMF exposure: additional cerebral and cognitive effects (not restricted to endocrine disruptors)

7.1. Mobile phones emit ELF-MFs in the frequency of Alpha brain waves and the first mode Schumann resonance.

Here is a crucial novelty of this new millennium, which humans did not have to deal with in previous centuries:

Mobile phones emit ELF at 8.3 Hz, in the frequency of the Alpha brain waves and the first mode Schumann resonance (ELFs, Extremely Low Frequencies, range between 3 to 30 Hz,).

There is a very limited coverage in the literature about this specific frequency in mobile devices. Research focuses on the high frequencies (Microwaves) 2.4 GHz, 10 GHz, the 5G network and other frequencies as listed above. As far as the intensity of the magnetic field in the most widely used cellphone transmission system (GMS until 2020) is concerned, we have only limited information on the intensity of the combined emission cocktail, and we don't know the individual intensity of this 8.3 Hz ELF that is used today. An ETHZ study (Zurich Institute of Technology) of 2005 measured 217 Hz and 8.3 Hz fields between 8 microTesla and 75 microTesla emitted from mobile phones at 5 mm distance. [333]

Other measurements revealed intensities of up to 94 MicroTesla. [334] One of the problems with this is that brainwave entrainment occurs from at least 100 NanoTesla upwards, and very possibly below that (100 nT= 0.1 MicroTesla)." [335] *"Brain-wave entrainment can be demonstrated electroencephalographically when subjects are in the vicinity of oscillations in the frequency range of approximately 3–20 Hz at intensities below 100 nT (nanotesla)."* [336]

The fields emitted by the cellphones were almost 100 times stronger.

So, this 8.3 Hz frequency is contained in the mobile phone emission cocktail. For reference, this happens at a magnetic flux about the strength of the Earth magnetic field and hundreds of times stronger than the magnetic field of the Earth's Schuman Resonance.

The combined field intensity of the different frequencies of a cell-phone is ten to several tens of MicroTesla.

Thus, virtually everyone is carrying a powerful little "Schumann Resonance Generator" in their pockets, dosing them in 8.3 Hz, likely stimulating the alpha brainwaves to different degrees and possibly impeding the full activation of the beta and low gamma brainwave potential as in intense cognitive operations and consciousness.

No one can tell at this point whether this 8.3 Hz part of the spectrum is the main endocrine disrupting effect of mobile phone radiation.

The iPhone 7 contained an official warning not to hold it closer than 5 mm to the body, it must not be held in direct contact to the ear or carried in pants pockets because of radiation danger. The vast majority of mobile phone users do just this. For other phones, the official distance is at least 1.5 cm (about 0.6 inches). [337]

But even if used correctly, radiofrequency radiation exposure from the iPhone 7 was measured 'over the legal safety limit and more than double what Apple reported to federal regulators from its own testing.' [338]

A 2011 study by D. Henshaw corroborated:

*"Mobile phones typically have three types of EMF emissions associated with them: in the GSM system: a 900 MHz radio frequency, a 217 Hz pulsing signal and an extremely **low frequency magnetic field (ELF MF) associated with the battery.** The ELF component has so far been ignored in all epidemiological studies of mobile phone exposure and cancer. During phone use, this ELF component exposes the whole brain to MFs ranging **from a few to tens of micro-tesla,** above the intensity of power frequency ELF-MFs that have been repeatedly associated with increased risk of brain tumours in adults."* [339]

75µT (Microtesla, some mobile phones emit over 90 µT) is just below the confirmed intensity needed for brain wave entrainment in short term experiments.

For permanent, long-term exposure, brain wave entrainment at 75µT and far below is very probable, it has been observed with very low power settings down to one half of a milliwatt. [340]

Artificial electromagnetic frequencies applied to the skull can also change behavior therapeutically, but Transcranial Magnetic Stimulation at ELFs of 1-10 Hz to the head disrupts people's ability to make **moral judgements.** For this, the stimulation needs to be directed at the TPJ region, which is located above and behind the right ear, not just nearby, and at frequencies of 1-10 Hz. Unfortunately, we saw that mobile phone use at the right ear not only has different health risks including hormonal disturbances, but - as far-fetched as it may sound - it may literally interfere with people's ability to make moral judgements. *"By disrupting brain activity in a particular region, neuroscientists can sway people's views of moral situations."* [341]

That's well within the carrier frequency of 8.3 Hertz emitted by cellphones and smartphones at an amplitude high enough to be bioactive.

"When we judge an action as morally right or wrong, we rely on our capacity to infer the actor's mental states (e.g., beliefs, intentions)." In additional experiments by L. Young et al, transcranial magnetic stimulation to the right temporoparietal junction RTPJ led participants to rely less on the actor's mental states. Thus, interfering with activity in the RTPJ disrupts the capacity to use mental states in moral judgment, especially in the case of attempted harms." [342]

The right ear is where most people hold their phone or where the earphones - which serve as antennas via the cables up to the speakers - are placed. Beyond this, we don't know the exact frequency modulation cocktail of wireless routers and mobile towers, of which 5G frequencies might be just the latest of the unknown unknowns (another reason to use speaker mode or non-radiation airtube headphones (see Remedies, Chapter 16).

The legal limit for electro- magnetic field exposure above 50 Hz in Switzerland and most European countries, for example, is 100 microtesla, but for ELFs below 50 Hz, no limits are defined. For comparison, the natural Earth's magnetic field is 25 to 65 microteslas. [343]

10 Hz frequencies in WLAN (WIFI) affect humans

Dr. Rütger Wever (Max Planck Institute for Behavioral Physiology, Seewiesen and Erling-Andechs) examined the effect of the 10 Hz frequency in the range of the alpha waves of 8 to 13 Hz, (5 to 100 microvolts) on the human circadian rhythm.

He concluded: *"With the proof of an effect of 10 Hz fields on the circadian periodicity of humans, also the question of a possible effect of these fields on humans is broadly answered. For this question as well, the frequency of approx. 10 Hz is interesting: the particularly stable αWave component of the electroencephalogram has a frequency of 10 Hz, further, the entire body surface of warm-*

blooded species mechanically vibrates in a frequency of about 10 Hz."
"The Schumann waves make life on our planet possible, they influence our health profoundly." We could not live without Schumann resonances. The 10 Hz pulsation of the Wi-Fi is pulsed electromagnetic radiation, not a sinus wave and it disturbs all life processes, it is profoundly harmful to human health, because with it - analogous to the pain memory - a WLAN pulsation- stress memory with permanent long-term exposure can develop. This means that even if Wi-Fi is turned off, the effect of stress is still present!" [Translation mine]. [344]

Declining eye sight in children from screen devices.

Kristof Vandekerckhove, board member of the Swiss Society for Ophthalmology stated: "There are already clear indications that due to the lockdown and other COVID -19 measures, myopia [near-sightedness] worldwide has accelerated." [345]

The experts' single explanation that parents want to believe: children are looking at screens close up for longer periods of time then children did years ago.

It is true that children are looking more at screens than they used to look at books 20 years ago. However, children have spent hours in school reading and writing close up and then watched TV and played video games for decades, so something new is going on with eyesight.

What is new is the tablets and screens emit microwave EMFs, these are known to cause damage to eyesight in themselves.

Research found teenagers with the most frequent life-long smartphone use had three times the incidence of eye-related problems in comparison with teenagers whose life-long use was much more restricted. [346]

"The American Academy of Ophthalmology is concerned that too much screen time is now affecting children's vision, including myopia [near sightedness] and dry eye symptoms. Retinal phototoxicity from blue light is now established as a risk. Sleep and human circadian sleep disruption by blue light is considered essentially proven by health authorities. Increased screen time is now identified as a risk factor for dry eye syndrome and computer vision syndrome. Research has revealed damage to skin from radiation from digital screens as well." [347]

Dr. O. P. Gandhi's work showed that the eyes of a ten-year-old absorb five times more cell phone radiation than adult eyes, while

five-year-old eyes absorb 12 times more. These absorption numbers were calculated already in 1996. [348]
The Specific Absorption Rate (SAR) for a 10-year-old is up to 153% higher than the SAR for the Specific Anthropomorphic Mannequin (SAM) model. When electrical properties are considered, a child's head's absorption can be over two times greater, and absorption of the skull's bone marrow can be ten times greater than adults. Therefore, a new certification process is needed that incorporates different modes. [349]

Already in 1988, long before cellphones and Wi-Fi, researchers with the University of Chicago determined microwave and ionizing radiation can induce cataracts. "Microwaves most commonly cause anterior and/or posterior subcapsular lenticular opacities in experimental animals and in human subjects." [350] In 2014, scientists reported oxidative stress in the eyes of rats that were exposed for only one hour per day to 2.45 GHz Wi-Fi radiation. Oxidative stress and thus ROS, are believed to be a principal cause of noncongenital cataract. [351]
During sleep, melatonin stimulates testosterone production, and also acts as an aromatase inhibitor to prevent the conversion of testosterone to estrogen. [352] Exposure to microwave radiation from cellphones, WIFI, and other wireless devices also reduces melatonin levels, as does blue light from screens used after sunset. "Blue light is a circadian signal that tells your brain that it is daytime, and that melatonin is not needed. Exposure to artificial blue light before bed stops melatonin production at the very time when it is needed. " [353]

Chapter 8
Blurring gender lines

In Psychology Today, 2019 an article by Robert Hedaya, MD - a clinical professor of psychiatry at the Georgetown University School of Medicine - read:

"It is nothing short of astounding that after hundreds of thousands of years of human history, the fundamental facts of human gender are becoming blurry. "

"There are many likely causes of this, but one that I haven't seen discussed is the influence of endocrine disrupting chemicals, EDC." [354]

To study the biological and possible epigenetic influences on personal orientation is a very sensitive field.

In this book, the intention is not to question the identity or the perception of self of any human being and much less so to judge any form of identity or lifestyle choices.

Quite to the contrary, I hope that some biological facts from the literature can increase understanding and mindfulness in this topic. And it should further be understood that if scientific facts indicate any role of prenatal hormone exposure in the development of gender or sexual orientation, this must not be addressed lightly or carelessly.

Imagine someone suggested to you that the things you truly feel and believe, who you identify as, whom you are attracted to, whom you love or get along with, your personality – imagine someone told you all these things were affected by artificial chemical interventions in utero and in childhood. Who would want to know? This would be especially harsh for people who were marginalized and rejected by their family for their identity or orientation.

And on an individual level, it doesn't matter what contributed to what. But for humanity as a whole, it will be a matter of survival rather soon.

In the words of Dr. Hedaya:

"There will be less blame and judgment, less guilt and shame, more respect and compassion [in the dialogue around gender identity disorders]. Recognition of the likely link between EDC's and gender dysphoria might also motivate a change in some of our laws, which are too permissive of these chemicals' presence in our lives." [355]

8.1. Intersex Variation

In the context of gender reassignment and transgender people, conservatives sometimes site data that claim ambiguous genitalia or intersex variation are very rare conditions and therefore this would need no public discussion. But the prevalence has increase exponentially in recent years, it is a physiologically as well as psychologically very real experience for many young people today.

A description of Intersex Variation:
"Intersex variation (IV) is a morphological and physiological anomaly where an individual is born with "congenital conditions in which development of chromosomal, gonadal, or anatomical sex is atypical". [356]
Today, Victoria Health Services say "Intersex variations are natural biological variations and occur in up to 1.7 per cent of all births." [357]
A much lower percentage of only 0.05 % was given in the late 1980s: An early study by Lilford and Dear (1987), suggested that one in 2,000 newborns had some form of external genital ambiguity. [358]

First, here is an explanation of the biological mechanisms of fetal genital differentiation and its toxicological dysregulation by A.L. Rich:
Differentiation in male or female external genitalia in the fetus begins during the **seventh week** of gestation. Masculinization is initiated by testicular androgens (derived from the Greek term "andro" meaning male) in the fetus, defining the androgynous external genitalia into a recognizable form or *sex* **between 8 and 12 weeks** of gestation.
Abnormal hormone production, or action, can disrupt this process, resulting in incomplete masculinization. In the absence of the hormonal influence of dihydrotestosterone, a fetus will essentially develop into a female. External genitalia differentiation is therefore **strongly hormonally dependent**." [359]
Or in other words, a fetus carrying the Y chromosome becomes a phenotypic male if the **testes** produce sufficient amounts of androgens at the right time during gestation; if endocrine-disrupting chemicals interfere with this process, the fetus will essentially develop into a female (the default gender, biologically speaking) or develop ambiguous genitalia (that is, have elements of both male and female reproductive organs). [360]

"Evidence supports the premise that at critical stages in fetal development exposure to exogenous chemicals known as endocrine-disrupting chemicals (EDCs) can disrupt reproductive organ differentiation and development in utero, leading to an IV condition." [361]
This can also affect later development of secondary sex characteristics.
"Animal studies on fish and reptile embryos exhibited IV and sex reversal when exposed to EDCs. Occupational studies verified higher prevalence of offspring with IV in chemically exposed workers (male and female)."
Intersex individuals may have concurrent physical disorders requiring lifelong medical intervention and experience gender dysphoria. " [362]

The human rights organization Heinrich Böll Stiftung advised in 2013:
"Since intersex is heavily stigmatized in South Africa, it is difficult for intersex individuals to come out, organize and speak up on their own behalf." In an apparently racist remark, they claim that:
"This applies especially – but not exclusively – to the black part of the population in rural areas, because everything that is included in LGBTI is generally considered to be a disease imported by the West that «by nature» does not exist among black individuals." [363]
Does the Heinrich Böll foundation imply that black Africans are transphobic?
K.G. Behrens (2020) reported:
"Intersex infanticide or attempted infanticide has been reported from Uganda, Kenya and China. It is likely that the most vulnerable intersex infants are those born in rural communities, where births take place in private homes and out of sight of authorities." [364]

8.2. Gender identity

"Gender assignment in infants born with a difference in sexual development (DSD) remains one of the many difficult decisions faced by the multi-disciplinary treatment team as some of these children develop gender identity disorder (GID) when they become adults." [365]

A study by Elisabeth Sievert and colleagues concluded that "claims that gender affirmation through transitioning socially [e.g. changes in name, pronoun, and clothing] is beneficial for children with Gender Dysphoria (GD), could not be supported from the present results. Instead, the study highlights the importance of individual social support provided by peers and family, independent of exploring additional possibilities of gender transition during counseling." [366]

Louis Gooren 2006, points out that prenatal androgenization does not decisively predispose to a male gender identity development. [367]

As researchers at the University of North Texas noted, EDCs like phthalates can interfere with the complex biochemical pathways of the brain, *"which could affect the way a person associates with his/her physiological sex or personifies his/her gender behaviorally."* [368] Also recall that exposure to already "very low doses of endocrine disrupting chemicals during fetal life permanently alters brain development and behavior in animals and humans." [369]

Artificial testosterone and estrogen actually alter adult human brain structures. "*Magnetic resonance brain images demonstrated: Anti-androgen Cestrogen treatment **decreased brain volumes** of adult male-to-female subjects towards female proportions, while androgen treatment in female-to-male subjects **increased** total brain and hypothalamus volumes towards male proportions.*"

The authors suggest that "throughout life, gonadal hormones remain essential for maintaining aspects of sex-specific differences in the human brain. [370] Prenatal exposure to endocrine-disrupting chemicals can also influence the way boys play. Boys who were exposed in the womb to higher levels of a potent phthalate (DEHP), which can lower fetal testosterone levels, scored significantly lower on the "masculine scale" - in other words, they were more likely to play with dolls and less likely to play with trucks and guns. [371] Similarly, a 2014 study from the Netherlands used the same play-behavior questionnaire and found that exposure to dioxins and PCBs was associated with more feminine behavior in boys, whereas in girls, exposure to these chemicals was associated with less feminine play behavior. [372]

It was suggested by Gerhard Winneke et al, 2014 that the way EDCs modify behavioral sexual dimorphism in children, is by interacting with the hypothalamic-pituitary-gonadal axis. [373]

Sex hormones in prenatal life also play a role in the development of sexual orientation. For example, girls born with congenital adrenal hyperplasia (CAH) - which results in naturally increased levels of male sex hormones - show relatively high rates of same-sex attractions as adults. [374]

Whatever influences gender differentiation and maturation of the brain during pregnancy is likely to influence sexual orientation. This leads us to a rather depressing notion involving intolerance. The low heritability of homosexuality is still subject of much speculation. Throughout the centuries, homosexuals were often imprisoned or executed and rarely had any children. There is no clear pattern as of the psychological profile or political orientation of parents of homosexuals.

[375] *"The best-established facts in relation to homosexuality point to developmental-psychological, not genetic or physiological, causation."* [376]

In the 1970s at the eve of the emancipation of gays in San Francisco, there arose the concept of the 'Farm Boy', it was obvious that a strikingly large proportion of young gay men arriving in the city were from the rural Midwest from conservative families, rather than from liberal families of coastal cities, even though exact statistics are difficult to come by. The Book "Farm Boy ' by Will Fellows undermines the cliche that Homosexuality is a purely urban experience, far removed from rural and small-town life.

Imagine the tragic hypothetical discussion:

The young son of a conservative Christian farmer family comes out as gay and is disowned and cast out by the disappointed parents, who ask themselves what they did wrong. 'You are no son of mine!' Should the son than suggest that the parents handling and spraying tons of atrazine all over the farm and during the mother's gestation in the 8th to 12th week could have anything to do with the son's feelings and orientation, the situation could only get more absurdly tragic. "Now you are blaming us?!"

But it is now clear that such a connection must be taken into the equation in many cases. Recall that children of agricultural workers have increased rates of genital malformation due to endocrine active pesticides exposure of the parents.

Homosexual men have significantly higher (less male sex typical) 2D:4D digit ratios than heterosexual men; and these results tend to be consistent across ethnic groups. [377]

A study from Eric Vilain's lab at the University of California (UC), Los Angeles finds that epigenetic effects, chemical modifications of the human genome that alter gene activity without changing the DNA sequence, may have a major influence on sexual orientation. **"Homosexuality may be caused by chemical modifications to DNA"**
[378]

"PET and MRI studies performed in 2008 have shown that the two halves of the brain are more symmetrical in homosexual men and heterosexual women than in heterosexual men and homosexual

women. These studies have also revealed that connections in the amygdalas of gay men resemble those of straight women; in gay women, connections in the amygdala resemble those of straight men. The amygdala has many receptors for sex hormones and is associated with the processing of emotions. " [379]
The approval for homosexual marriage in the American Population has increased in 15 years from (between 2004 and 2019) from 31% to 61%. [380] Never before has any public opinion on a matter of social structures and reproduction changed that rapidly.

8.3. Digit ratio (2D:4D)

In males, the 2D:4D digit ratio is generally small (negative number = the ring finger is longer than the index finger). Contrarily, in females, the ratio is generally large (positive number = the index is longer than the ring finger). The difference is large enough since thousands of years that archeologists can tell with reasonable certainty in cave paintings – where hands were used like stencils to spray on pigments and thus leave a silluette of the hand –whether the hand belonged to a man or a woman.

A low 2D:4D is an Indicator of high prenatal testosterone (i.e., masculinization) in males or females.

Van Dongen et al report there is a wealth of studies supporting a link between 2D:4D ratio and prenatal exposure to testosterone and oestrogen. *"Furthermore, 2D:4D ratios appear to relate to several aspects of human sexual behaviour, which suggests that these characteristics are determined in early embryological stages and are not largely affected by factors later in life."* [381]

A low second to fourth digit ratio (2D:4D) has been related not only to high testosterone levels but also to markers of high status.

Kobe et al had predicted that a low 2D:4D would be associated with high levels of egoism and altruism and low levels of common cooperativeness (i.e., contributing exactly one's fair share). However, they found the exact opposite: *"Participants with a low 2D:4D (more masculinized) were more likely to act cooperatively and less likely to act altruistically and egoistically."* [382]

In 2003, research found that the 2D:4D ratio is related to sexual orientation in men, but not in women; meaning heterosexual men had significantly lower (more male typical) 2D:4D ratios than gay men; and these results tended to be consistent across ethnic groups. [383]

In a 2008 study, women with gender identity disorder (GID) were found to have a significantly more masculinized digit ratio. *"This finding was consistent with the prediction that a variance in prenatal hormone exposure contributes to a departure from a sex-typical gender identity in women."* But no evidence of an altered 2D:4D ratio in men with gender identity disorder was found. [384]

Female Olympic athletes from Sweden were shown to have a significantly lower 2D:4D digit ratio than non-athletes. [385]

These differences and their general associations with personality traits are obvious enough that many must have been ware of them long before systematic studies were published.

Could this be why more people believe in palm reading than in other types of fortune telling? Differences in 2D:4D between sexes and individuals allow making general assumptions about someone's personality traits and even guesses about their childhood. This is something that you can observed within your social cycles.

Not only BPA (bisphenol A), but other BPs, which are promoted as safer alternatives to BPA, can have the same effect in prenatal exposure. In children at ages 4 and 6, it was shown that prenatal exposure to BPA alternatives of the mother was associated with offspring's higher 2D:4D digit ratio (more feminized). [386]

Kirchengast et al 2020 showed age at menopause correlates significantly (and positively) with the digit ratio. A more feminine digit ratio is associated with a higher age at menopause, while a low digit ratio, interpreted as a hint of a higher androgen exposure during prenatal phase, was associated with a lower age at menopause. [387]

A Chinese study showed an association between high 2D:4D ratio and coronary artery disease (CAD) in both hands in men (males with less testosterone in utero had more CAD). There were no significant differences in mean 2D:4D between women with CAD and controls. [388]

In a sample of male patients of an infertility clinic, **there were negative associations between 2D:4D and testicular function.**

Adult levels of testosterone may be related to aspects of 2D:4D in samples which contain men with compromised testicular function, but not in men from normative samples. The researchers concluded that *"Associations between 2D:4D and fertility-associated traits probably arise from early organisational effects of testosterone rather than from activational effects of current testosterone."* [389]

Chapter 9
Accidental social engineering?

How were people in the past riled up so easily into following totalitarian leaders into wars and genocides, one might wonder? In times when people were still subjected only to naturally induced hormonal effects?

Well, one important differentiation should be made: propaganda applied by totalitarian leaders traditionally aimed to rile up the masses against "the others", against other nations or minority groups within the nation.

Only since WWII, and particularly since around 2000, propaganda in the West is mostly directed against the self and against average people. Western countries and only western countries have to de-industrialize for climate change, have to pay reparations for the atrocities committed by their ancestors centuries ago, have to accept millions of refugees without a plan or an economy to accommodate them, have to apologize for "toxic masculinity", whatever that means.

The "War on Terror" and the Iraq War (2003) was so far the last incident where westerners (in this case Americans) were incited to invade "the others", the Patriot Act is today used mostly against domestic terrorists and US political dissidents. Later (and also illegal) NATO wars were waged under a low profile and were barely televised.

Neither Hitler, Stalin, Mao or emperor Nero would ever have managed to drive the people against their own interests and make them apologize for even existing, as we are witnessing it today.

Biochemical and Electromagnetic consolidation of propaganda?

Is TV propaganda? Sounds like a wild conspiracy theory? It could just be a silly accident. I will suggest that the way modern day TV, internet and cinema film propaganda can work more efficiently is this: Since EDCs have been disrupting gonadal hormones biochemically, newspapers, radio, cinema and TV became more effective tools for politicians to convince the people of what is good for them. And since the last two decades, the actual content of the ideologically charged programs is not even that important anymore. Today, TV sets are connected to the Wi-fi routers (in most western countries the two practically must be installed in the same room, which is mostly the living room, or the router is connected to the smart TV by another strong wireless signal). The computers, phones, tablets, routers connected to the TV, etc. emit microwave EMFs that can disrupt hormones, especially testosterone and estrogen, as we saw above. Further we saw that extremely low frequencies (ELF) also emitted in the wireless spectrum, can enhance alpha brain wave amplitude (which are associated with a semiconscious state of brain wave activation, it is the frequency range in the brain wave spectrum that is enhanced in a half-conscious state or while a person is falling asleep, as visualized in an electroencephalogram, EEG.

I propose that the endocrine imbalance - in particular low testosterone in men - is what makes people more susceptible to current ideologies in the first place.

Ideologies de jour include Increasingly totalitarian collectivist ideas targeting the interests of their own people, at that. Depression, inner confusion, hypersensitivity, lethargy, extreme self-criticism and oikophobia to the point of outright auto- racism. In this way, the propaganda can easily take hold.

I propose that without these endocrine disrupting chemical and radiological influences to human biology, few people would still watch TV or believe anything a politician or a (social) media mogul has to say.

And I will further propose that it is the same hormonal disruptions, that further push people to react to the before said defensively, to jump up and say these ideologies are not totalitarian at all, and those who think so, should be censored and punished.

As it happens, since the beginning of the lockdowns, when everyone is sitting at home, a few people have wondered what happened to their friends and families, and how they can just sit there while they are losing everything they ever had. Lethargic and frightened, while they watch on TV how politicians keep breaking their own lockdown orders.

Did the chemically assisted reduction in testosterone help reduce wars and interpersonal violence in the post-war era?

This would mean that chemical social engineering (deliberate or accidental) would have had a positive aspect for a period of time. To be precise, if it was accidental, then it's technically not engineering.

We have seen that testosterone alone does not cause aggression. However, for outwards expression of collective violence, such as wars genocides and persecutions, a certain minimal testosterone threshold seems to be required. So, what we have been seeing in the last 5 decades in terms of low ethnocentrism, low future-orientedness, and lack of engagement in the general population, it all seems nice and heartwarming - not only to those who's hormones have been compromised already - but it all is leading straight towards a very likely massive population reduction event. A certain population decline would have been unavoidable in a Grand Solar Minimum and would have come along in the next decade(s) anyways, due to climate disruption and crop failure. But for the time being, this chemical and electromagnetic tempering with human behavior (accidental or deliberate) apparently made the world a more peaceful place with much lower reactive aggression.

Are people - especially men - "nicer" now than decades ago?
"Dr. Charles Ryan has a clinic in San Francisco at which he regularly relieves men of their testosterone. This "chemical castration", as it is sometimes known, is not a punishment, but a common treatment for prostate cancer. Testosterone doesn't cause the disease (currently the third most deadly cancer in the UK), but it fuels it, so oncologists use drugs to reduce the amount produced by the testicles."

"We do see increases in the empathy scores in many patients on the treatment". In his new book, *The Virility Paradox*, he argues that "the fact that reducing testosterone in these ageing men may lead to increased empathy, more emotional engagement in relationships and a softening of aggression could be something of a silver lining". [390]

In some men with underlying aggression issues, chemical castration may bring alleviation, but in the above conclusion it has to be kept in mind that patients with a serious and potentially fatal illness and already compromised hormones may have an altogether different outlook on assessing their own wellbeing. And again, low male testosterone leads to lower self-confidence and more self-doubt.

9.2. A global conspiracy?

Not necessarily. Kind of. Can thousands of doctors, experts and politicians prevent a public shut down of the discussion of the causes of infertility and "Hormonageddon"?

Did they allow these chemicals to pass knowingly or are they just as clueless and careless as the rest of us? Are they all in some secret society with funny hats and secret handshakes to cover up the causes and the effects of hormonal havoc, especially testosterone collapse?

Consider this example, in the 1920s, it became known that asbestos can cause lung cancer. It took over 70 years of private research, activism, lobbing, and political pressure to ban it in industrial countries. The big corporations, producers and corrupt politicians of course were interested in covering up the health issues. But it was not only those in power who could afford to protect themselves from asbestos exposure, but also small bureaucrats, doctors and other people who lived in asbestos contaminated buildings themselves. Some retired doctors who had helped to cover up the health risks, were still vowing that asbestos is completely safe in the early 2000s. Beginning in the 1990s, it was banned in European and then in all industrial countries.

Some of the low-level enablers even thought it would be better for society as a whole if we tolerate some health risks in exchange for the huge benefits of asbestos to the industry and the associated increase in living standards of the masses, for 'the greater good'. Of course, they couldn't tell this to the masses, who are short sighted, with a 'que sera, sera' - mentality. Asbestos insulation for buildings was cheap, highly effective, resistant to weathering and fireproof, rapidly reducing disease and preventing millions of early deaths by exposure to cold or heat, mold and poverty. Asbestos was one of the prerequisites for the post -war economic progress.

So, from a purely rationalist point of view, lying about the health risks did indeed save more lives for a certain time than it destroyed. Most of us know people, friends and families who are capable of going along with this without flinching.

The low-level enablers did not have to be part of the big boys' club the convince themselves it would be better to have a few victims of lung diseases in exchange for a massive uplift in general health and wealth.

What applies to asbestos, is true for dozens of technological advances with short term benefits for humanity as a whole, that were - after much lobbying and corruption - proven to be harmful to health and ultimately were banned: lead paint, leaded gasoline, thalidomide causing deformed limbs in babies, X-rays directly into the doctor's face, arsenic in newspapers, spraying DDT into children's faces, radioactive bottled water, mercury as treatment for syphilis, radioactive watch dials…and so on.

Here is a short history of the rise and fall of asbestos by Michelle Whitmer:

"Court documents provide irrefutable proof the asbestos industry leveraged its power and influence to keep workers and the public in the dark about the hazards of asbestos. Dozens of companies are implicated in the decades-long cover-up."

"As early as the late 19th century, scattered reports on the health risks of asbestos emerged in Canada, Europe and the U.S. By the 1920s, leading medical journals had published articles linking asbestos to asbestosis, a new and sometimes fatal lung condition where inhaled asbestos scars the lungs and makes breathing difficult."

"The disease was a serious problem for asbestos workers, who often toiled in thick clouds of asbestos dust each day. Even in the 1920s, doctors believed asbestosis could be prevented by limiting exposure to asbestos. It would take several decades, however, before asbestos was properly regulated in the U.S. and workers learned their jobs could lead to cancer and other serious health complications years down the line."

"Between 1940 and 1980, the business expanded into a multibillion-dollar industry that employed more than 200,000 people." [391]

9.3. Abolishing the nuclear family

Not only the role of the extended family, but of the nuclear family is being dissolved from within. Today's western societies are the first to have given up on this most archaic social instinct of having children and of investing much of their resources and energy to raise them. And non-Western nations are catching up fast, even more traditionalist societies, for instance in the Middle East.

The nuclear family has always been the backbone of any society in history, even totalitarian collectivist states have not been able to break it. This includes biological influenced gender roles. It would be every totalitarian collectivist state's dream to dismantle the family completely, and to force women to hand over their anonymous babies, to be raised by state run nursing homes from infancy on. The abolishment of the family was proposed by Marx and Engels. [392] Already Plato believed that the interests of the state are best preserved if children are raised and educated by the society as a whole, rather than by their biological parents. So he proposed a simple (if startlingly unfamiliar) scheme for the breeding, nurturing, and training of children in the guardian class. [393]

But even though communist leaders have largely managed to break up strong affiliations to the extended family, they have never seriously tried to implement the end of the nuclear family. The modern-day inclination to destroy the family is unprecedented and it strongly coincides with the biological endocrinal disruption in the population.

In most communist/ socialist societies, 10 percent of the population were murdered at the start and then more later on. It is always the more individualist, libertarian, and conservative and more family-oriented citizens that are executed first. But even in North Korea, with all the social engineering, executions and reeducation camps over three generations, where already small children are forced to learn that the state is above everything and interpersonal relations must take a subordinate role, where people are induced to rat out their grandma for "thought crime"; even there, the human instinct for the nuclear family could not be broken. If dissidents escape over the border, the state kills the entire family left behind, this threat works to keep almost anyone at bay.

Similarly, China has a 70-year-old communist agenda that endorses gender equality even though the party just "banned feminism" altogether and they just banned "effeminate men" from TV. [394] And loyalty to the state is held as the highest merit, but here too, the nuclear family always remained undisrupted.

And that is not only because the state needs a steady supply of new citizens. Even during the one-child- policy, the nuclear family was not challenged.

In 1923 the Soviet Regime promoted the new Soviet woman: "single, confident, and committed to a life of edifying political-agitational work."

"Worker first, mother second, wife never again! " Author Alexandra Kollontai, former director of the Women's Department of the

Communist Party (Zhenotdel), used fiction to promote new social relations under Socialism."

"Like the institution of the state under complete Communism, the family would "wither away not because it is being forcibly destroyed by the state, but because the family ceases to be a necessity."

So, the ideal family is a single working mom household with the children raised in nurseries.

"Trotsky argued: women would have to be relieved of housekeeping and childcare duties, and freed from the bonds of marriage. New Socialist institutions such as canteens, laundries, and nurseries would permit Soviet women to practice domestic independence—and, crucially, to enter the workforce." [395]

Not only did communism as envisioned by Marx never happen, but the socialist and inaccurately self-declared communist states never really tried to dissolve the nuclear family completely, as in a socialist dystopia, where mothers hand over their babies to be raised in state run nurseries.

According to Marx, communism is when the socialist state, a temporary entity, has withered away to leave the citizen self-governing. The only thing that was fulfilled under 'communism' indeed however, was Vladimir Lenin's demand: *"He who does not work shall not eat", as* a necessary principle under socialism.

(Vladimir Lenin: The State and Revolution, 1917)

At the end of the book, we revisit the decline and Fall of the Roman Empire, where similar trends as today were rampant in the upper classes, the citizens. Plummeting birth rates, abortion, contraception, obsession with pleasure and status, sex orgies. But the middle classes were much less affected than the upper classes (citizens), whereas the peasants in the provinces showed no disruption of the nuclear family. Thus, the "Romans" are still around, today's Italians are largely genetic descendants of imperial Romans. [396]

Chapter 10
Theories and proposals for population control

"Perhaps by means of injections and drugs and chemicals the population could be induced to bear whatever its scientific masters may decide to be for its good. "

Lord Bertrand Russell, the scientific outlook 1931.

As we have seen, whatever decreases fertility is ultimately also reducing testosterone. Disrupting testosterone secretion is actually the pathway by which certain EDCs disturb fertility. The two go hand in hand, when the talk is of population control (population numbers) by pharmaceutical intervention and chemical sterilization, then this ultimately includes 'weakening the human character' and reducing virility by disrupting gonadal hormones.

Many prominent intellectuals, politicians and industrialists have called for efforts to bring about population reduction in order to prevent food collapse, over-aging or climate change. among those are of course eugenic methods to selectively kill off the "unfit." Eugenicists have not gone away after the 70s, even Obama's top science advisor has called for sterilization and forced adoption of babies of single mothers (see below). In general, globalist power brokers like Ted Turner restrict themselves to propose that the population "should" decline by 50-90%, without specifying the means by which this should come about. Only because they want to do exactly what has been happening to fertility and gonadal hormones, does not prove they have deliberately let it happen or even made it happen. But, if I had to guess…
Others such as Malthus have warned that population numbers will collapse inevitably without deliberate intervention, from scarcity of food and land. The latter can hardly be disputed. One thing is clear, if solar- and geomagnetic activity continue to decline – and there is no indication to a stop – then the world population will be reduced to some extent inevitably in the next decades(s). Fertility is declining at an accelerating rate, so the overpopulation problem will solve itself sooner than the people would like (at the latest from 2045 onwards). But as I've proposed, it is the parallel decline in gonadal hormones, which is a prerequisite for people to react with indifference to or even cheer on their genetic extinction. The human race

is not going extinct any time soon, but many gene lines, families and peoples are.

The population in the world doubled since 1960 - increasing the effects of other problems such as natural climate change, crop failure and food shortages that come with declining solar activity.

Populations in poverty have on average higher birth rates. In Europe and Northeast- and northern Asia, birth rates were very high until the early Modern Age and the Industrial Revolution, with a high mortality rate, leading to high fluctuation, but stable population numbers.

When Thomas Malthus anonymously published his sensational work "An Essay on the Principle of Population" in 1798, he wrote: *'Populations tend to always grow faster than the production of food, part of society seemed to be condemned to misery, hunger or epidemics: these are the scourges that slow down population growth and that, in Malthus' opinion, are the principal obstacles to the progress of society.'* [397]

Contrary to his prediction, the *'Malthusian Trap'* did not snap shut in the 20th century, rather, the Agricultural Revolution was able to keep up the food production, and the British are still around today.

Ever since, dozens of well-connected people have proposed methods for population reduction.

In his 1968 book *"The Population Bomb"*, Stanford University Professor Paul Ehrlich himself reached fame for predicting: *"Dire famine' by 1975."* The newspapers wrote: Experts chart worst failures in 'eco-polcalyptic' predictions." [398]

Ehrlich said the famine is due to overpopulation; *"birth control may have to be accomplished by making it involuntary and by putting sterilizing agents into staple foods and drinking water."*

Surely, he didn't mean they should just do it, and he later added they shouldn't, but this happens to be exactly what turned out to go on since: sterilizing or fertility-reducing chemicals have been introduced in pesticides, pharmaceuticals, packaging materials, flame retardants and so on, ending up **in food, soil and drinking water** in accumulative quantities, with a coinciding bottomless drop in fertility and testosterone levels and unprecedented rates of defects in reproductive health.

Nobody is saying secret government operatives are driving tanker trucks to water treatment facilities and dump sterilizing chemicals into reservoirs in the middle of the night. But the chemicals with these side effects are there. Mr. Ehrlich advised in 1967 that:

"The United States is already too big, that birth control may have to be accomplished by making it involuntary and by putting sterilizing agents into staple foods and drinking water, and that the Roman Catholic Church should be pressured into going along."

"The US would have to lead international efforts due to its prominence in the world. In order to avoid charges of hypocrisy or racism it would have to take the lead in population reduction efforts." [399]

The proposal of adding sterilants to drinking water brought a charge from one newspaper critic that Ehrlich was 'worse than Hitler.' [400] But Ehrlich was just thinking out loud, for he later added:

"It might be possible to develop such population control tools, although the task would not be simple.... Technical problems aside, I suspect you'll agree with me that society would probably dissolve before sterilants were added to the water supply by the government. Just consider the fluoridation controversy. Some other way will have to be found." [401]

Well, "sterilants" were NOT "added to the water supply by the government." Sterilizing properties are just a side effect of useful chemicals that were coincidentally released, mostly by private enterprises in the form of pesticides, plastics and hundreds of industrial and household products, that ended up in the groundwater, drinking water and soil. Governments just happened to let this pass.

Another globalist 'philanthropist', Julian Huxley, was a United Nations advisor, co-founder of UNESCO and the brother of author Aldous Huxley. Julian was not only concerned with the population numbers, but he was an adamant eugenicist:

"The lowest strata are reproducing too fast. Therefore... they must not have too easy access to relief or hospital treatment lest the removal of the last check on natural selection should make it too easy for children to be produced or to survive; long unemployment should be a ground for sterilisation."   Julian Huxley (1944). "Man in the Modern World" [402]

Professor Paul Weindling 2012 explains:

"[Julian] Huxley redefined eugenics as "a form of applied human genetics.[...] Huxley pointed out that what the immunologist Peter "Medawar called "genetic engineering" was really a new form of negative eugenics. Eugenics remained at the core of Huxley's humanism." [403]

Julian's brother Aldous Huxley is sometimes credited with having sent out the most vivid warning of humanity's future in the dystopian novel **Brave New World**, published already in the 1930s.

Did he just make well informed guesses, or did he get some insider information from his family into ongoing research?

The novel did anticipate invitro fertilization, the dismantling of the nuclear family and of monogamous relationships, all children raised in state nurseries, everyone on Soma or anti- depressant drugs, general sex addiction, sex pills, medical rejuvenation procedures, multi-senses theater (the feelies), human shallowness, general narcissism and 'idiocracy', the despise for old and 'unfit' people, sexualization of everything, separation of intellectual classes.

The only thing that hasn't come true, and probably won't, is the complete lab baby grown without a womb.

But what has been happening extensively in the past 50 years, is chemical interference in the fertilization and gestation process, leading to epigenetic changes in the born human, dulling character, virility and intelligence. Today, men born with (chemically induced) hypogonadism and low testosterone are literally more docile, mellow and superficial. All of this probably came to pass purely accidentally as an unintended side effect of the chemical and agricultural progress. In *Brave New World*:

"Lower caste fetuses are created by receiving alcohol transfusions to reduce intelligence and height, thus conditioning them for simple, menial tasks. Connections between alcohol and incubating embryos are made multiple times in the novel. " [404]

The fictional director of the hatchery explains: *"Bokanovskification (splitting eggs into multiples to produce serial twin workers) consists of a series of arrests of development. We check the normal growth and, paradoxically enough, the egg responds by budding."*

Fertilized eggs of the lower cast were treated with eight minutes of hard X-rays, in the 'social predestination room.'

As it turns out, today's real- life invitro fertilization leads not only to birth defects and further infertility in the offspring (see p.35), but coincidently to higher rates of twin birth.

What Huxley insinuated was more or less fetal alcohol syndrome, but systematically induced, with the aim to produce docile and stupid workers.

In real life, fetal alcohol exposure not only results in well-characterized neurobehavioural deficits in offspring, which form the basis for diagnosing fetal alcohol spectrum disorder; but in addition, "in females it delays age at first menarche/puberty onset in alcohol-oexposed offspring. In males, offspring exposed to prenatal alcohol had **altered testosterone levels**, reduced testes and accessory gland weights and reduced sperm concentration and semen volume." [405] "Alcohol exposure during development has been shown to reduce testosterone in males and estrogen in females." [406] This wasn't publicly known in 1932. These are similar effects that would decades later be induced by Endocrine Disrupting Chemicals and radiation. Huxley envisioned X-rays (ionizing radiation) instead of microwaves (non- ionizing) to treat the fetus to produce stupid and docile workers.

Aldous Huxley's death wasn't highly publicized, because he died on the same day as then-President John F. Kennedy, on November 22, 1963.

Lord Bertrand Russell was more outspoken on his ideas of stealth population control:

"Just as the sun worship of the Aztecs demanded the painful death of thousands of human beings annually, so the new scientific religion will demand its holocausts of sacred victims. ..."

"Perhaps by means of injections and drugs and chemicals the population could be induced to bear whatever its scientific masters may decide to be for its good. "

Lord Bertrand Russell, the Scientific Outlook 1931

"I do not pretend that birth control is the only way in which population can be kept from increasing. There are others, which, one must suppose, opponents of birth control would prefer. War, as I remarked a moment ago, has hitherto been disappointing in this respect, but perhaps bacteriological war may prove more effective. If a Black Death could be spread throughout the world once every generation, survivors could procreate freely without making the world too full."

(Lord Bertrand Russell: "Can A Scientific Society Be Stable?' 1949 [407])

What today's modern-day democrats and pro-abortion activists do not mention is that abortion and in parts contraception has always been a means proposed by self-declared "valuable people" to dispose of the "unfit". Margret Sanger, the founder of Planned Parenthood wrote: *"We don't want word to go out that we want to exterminate the Negro Race."* She had also advocated for 'compulsory sterilization and segregation for people with disabilities.' [408]

To deliberately sterilize the population involuntarily by putting sterilants in food and drinking water is genocide by the UN definition; Article II of the United Nations Genocide Convention:

"Genocide means any of the following acts committed with intent to destroy, in whole or in part, a national, ethnical, racial or religious group, as such:
-(c) Deliberately inflicting on the group conditions of life calculated to bring about its physical destruction in whole or in part;
-(d) Imposing measures intended to prevent births within the group.
" [409]

In a similar tone, Obama's top science advisor John Holdren advocated for mass sterilizations, forced abortions and a global police force. Holdren advocated the following proposals in the 1977 book entitled "Ecoscience", [410] which he co-authored with Paul and Anne Ehrlich:
"Indeed, it has been concluded that compulsory population-control laws, even including laws requiring compulsory abortion, could be sustained under the existing Constitution if the population crisis became sufficiently severe to endanger the society."
(Page 837)

"One way to carry out this disapproval might be to insist that all illegitimate babies be put up for adoption—especially those born to minors, who generally are not capable of caring properly for a child alone." (page 786)
A single mother would have to apply for permission to adopt her own children in order to keep them.

Again today, elitist globalists are proposing different methods to reduce the population in order to 'combat climate change', the refugee crisis and injustice, and they're specifically calling on western people to not have children.
Update: in July 2022 the famous Georgia Guide stones were damaged in a bomb attack by unknown perpetrators and then completely demolished within hours for "Safety concerns". The area could have easily been cordoned off until the structural safety was assessed. So the destruction of the monument was apparently planned by the land owners or financers. The 20 feet tall monument erected in 1980 by anonymous commissioners famously said in several languages in its '10 commandments': "Maintain humanity under 500,000,000 in perpetual balance with nature." and " Guide reproduction wisely."

Under-population
Between 1964 and 2018 the global fertility rate fell from 5.06 births per woman to 2.4. [411]

Today, all industrialized countries, not only in the West, have fertility rates below the replacement threshold of 2.1 children per woman (first and foremost among the wealthy classes), *'this is happening in about half of all nations.'* In July 2020, the BBC reported: *"Jaw-dropping' global crash in children being born."* [412] Researchers at the University of Washington's Institute for Health Metrics and Evaluation showed: the global fertility rate nearly halved to 2.4 in 2017 - and their study - published in the Lancet - projects it will fall below 1.7 by 2100. [413] Even in China - after decades of one-child policy to allegedly prevent over population - as of 2018, China's local authorities *'are scrambling to incentivize women to have more children, as the country's birth rate continues to drop'* [414] (I had postulated in *Solar Behavior* that the one-child policy was a stealth eugenic program, that indeed raised the Chinese IQ in one generation).

Only westerners are not concerned at all about their biological extinction, quite to the contrary.

Again, given the ongoing testosterone crisis keeps proceeding unchecked at the same time, the problem of global overpopulation will solve itself faster than people would think. Now, the minority of millennials who were theoretically going to have children are canceling this because of COVID, but they speak of postponing it, [415] which is a bit ironic because the older millennials are now 40 years old - and in case of women - past reproduction age. It is the same age group of women who say they want to have children some day and then start looking for a partner when they are 38. At midlife, between a third and a half of all successful career women in the United States do not have children. [416]

Update Dec 14, 2021: Even Elon Musk chimed in recently saying: *"There are not enough people. Low and rapidly declining birth rates are one of the biggest risks to civilization."* [417] He further pointed out that in Japan, the number of adult diapers used has surpassed the number of baby diapers about 10 years ago.

Recent proposals for chemical behavioral control

In recent years, scientists have again proposed to mass- administer neuro-biological substances to mold the collective mind to their liking.

For instance, some want to distribute the bonding hormone oxytocin to reduce racism and xenophobia by fostering altruism toward refugees. They claim that *'Oxytocin-enforced norm compliance reduces xenophobic outgroup rejection.'* [418]

Also the Rockefeller University proposed doping Western Cultures With oxytocin will cure hatred of refugees. "UNESCO has emphasized the importance of developing neurobiologically informed strategies for reducing xenophobic, hostile, and discriminatory attitudes." [419]

In the long run, collectivist authoritarians who think a broad scale oxytocin distribution would foster a multi-cultural utopia, have it coming for them, because oxytocin enhances in-group preferences as it is in nature most relevant in mother-child bonding, so it would ultimately lead to the opposite outcome, it promotes human ethnocentrism, more xenophobia, not less. [420]

More recently, a medical ethics professor proposed governments add psychoactive drugs to tap water to reduce dissent from lockdowns; to make cor0na defectors comply. [421]

Some theorists argue that moral bioenhancement ought to be compulsory. In an article in *Bioethics*, Parker Crutchfield proposed that "if moral bioenhancement ought to be compulsory, then its administration ought to be covert rather than overt." [422]

Chapter 11
Solar- and geomagnetic activity

11.1. The Glitch

To say it up front, the type of today's self-abandonment, self-criticism to the point of oikophobia and outright auto-racism as in the West did not happen at the end of previous Grand Solar Maxima in historic times and it is not a common symptom of a Grand Solar Minimum, either. Otherwise, humans would not be around. Something new has happened in the past 50 years.

Not only the social and political trends in the context of Solar- and geomagnetic activity, but also the solar radio flux relationship, suggest male testosterone levels are generally higher in solar minima, and especially Grand Solar Minima (the bad-weather periods, which are also the periods of increased peace and rationality). On the other side of the spectrum, deaths from war, genocide, persecution etc. are highly concentrated in Grand Solar Maxima, and interpersonal violence, homicide and so on are highly concentrated in the solar maxima within the 11-year solar cycles. This was empirically demonstrated in detail in my book *Solar History* (2018). In grand solar maximum decades, there are 4.6 times more deaths from war and persecution than in the same time span in grand solar minimum. Or in other words. 78.2% of anthropogenic death were generated in grand solar maximum.

As the most severe outbursts of violence against "the others" were at the peaks of 11- years solar cycles and at Grand Solar Maxima, this was when totalitarian collectivist war mongers had the most success in starting wars and persecutions. Already Alexander Tchijevsky, a hundred years ago, pointed out that many despots and statesmen were puzzled how a certain war or radical intervention was strongly opposed by the public one year, only to be approved of a few years later. As it turned out, the approval to war by the public usually came at the peak of solar maxima.

In the Modern Grand Solar Maximum of roughly the past century, the pattern of violence and solar activity seems to have been interrupted sharply after the 1950s. After two world wars, fascist and communist massacres, solar and geomagnetic activity kept increasing to record levels in the 1960s and remained high only to drop off in the early 2000s. But interpersonal violence, wars and genocides leveled off precipitously after the 1950s. As can be seen in Fig. 3, it is obvious that not all peaks of Grand Solar Maxima are punctuated by wars and persecution, but the second half of the 20th century was special, marking the phase of the highest prolonged solar activity in the past 1500 years, when high social excitability, war and revolutions should have been expected.

In *Solar Behavior* (2020), I had proposed a hypothesis of what could have contributed to this deviation, which I defend unaltered. This hypothesis is based on evolutionary trends relating to solar- and geomagnetic activity, taking latitudinal differences into account.
What I had underestimated, was the gravity of the impact that artificial chemical and electromagnetic influences could have had on hormone balances and thus on human behavior in recent decades. After WWII, the continuing and increasing, unprecedented prolonged Modern Grand Solar Maximum, to a millennium high, should have predicted a further spree of violence and heightened human excitability between the 1950s to 2000, possibly amounting to WWIII.

Limited amounts of Endocrine Disrupting Chemicals had been around in pre-war decades, but the industrial use and production exploded in the late 1950s and 1960s.
The pesticide atrazine was introduced in 1958, and hundreds of Endocrine Disrupting Chemicals such as DDT were used proficiently and increasing to this day, many with accumulative environmental effects and multi- generational defects to the endocrine system.
And since the late 1990s we can add to this an endless increase of sources of **endocrine disrupting non-ionizing radiation**, in mobile/ wireless technology, the full ramifications of which we do not even have a chance to comprehend, yet.
The (accidental or deliberate) chemical alteration of human nature and human interaction, did not only make humans more docile and behave in non-sustainable, non- future oriented ways; but on a more positive note, it can make unstable people less confrontational and less aggressive. This has certainly contributed to passivity, social disintegration, lack of foresight and an unsustainable economy. A population who wants to give everything to the

"others", shut down the industry which our lives depend on; all for climate change, for "justice", for refugees, short-term altruism.

This will almost inevitably cause hundreds of millions to billions of victims in the near future, but for the time being, the world was probably a less violent place for a couple decades than should have been expected at the height of this Grand Modern Maximum at the end of the 20th century. It could be speculated it may have prevented WWIII to take place between the 1950s and 2000.

Did those politicians, industrialists and lobbyists who covered up or downplayed the endocrine disrupting effects of EDCs and lobbied for more of the same (deliberately or by carelessness), do something good for humanity for a limited time span? Do we owe them a drink?

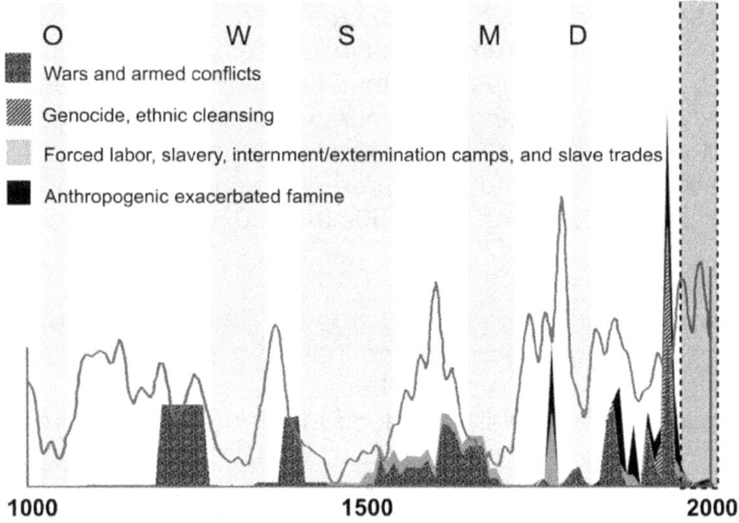

Fig. 3 Anthropogenic (man-made) deaths rates by decade (number of casualties per decade adjusted for world population in comparison to solar activity (14C, radiocarbon). The dark gray bar marks the post war era. Note the very low anthropogenic death rate, the "glitch" in the phase of the highest solar activity roughly 1950-2000, (highest in 1500 years). The 1780-1790 peak in solar activity was more pronounced, but of short duration. No exact data are available for interpersonal violence (violent crime) prior to 1800, therefore this was not included in the statistical analysis. However, historical and archeological examinations suggest that "blank spots" in wars and genocide during solar maximum were marked by increased interpersonal violence. Solar data: Muscheler et al 2007). Chart: Sacha Dobler, Solar History 2018.

My assertion that male testosterone levels are higher in Grand Solar Minimum – the times of peace and a harsher climate - is based not only on circumstantial evidence but also on the Solar Radio Flux connection. In particular, the behavioral patterns indicate higher testosterone in males in periods of peace, rationality and invention. The wars and genocides, erupting primarily in solar maxima, are not typical for high testosterone masculinity, but rather the opposite.

We are going to look at Indicators of higher male testosterone levels in either Grand Solar Minimum or Grand Solar Maximum in Chapter 12.

Chapter 12
Gonad hormones in solar maximum and minimum

Cold winters

The wars and genocides - erupting primarily in solar maxima - are not typical for high testosterone and masculinity and femininity, but rather the opposite.

We don't have reliable direct data on male testosterone level measurements reaching further back than 1975. The indirect evidence of how testosterone and estrogen levels are related to solar- and geomagnetic cycles – or rather whether testosterone is generally higher in solar maximum or minimum - gives a mixed picture, as listed below.

Geomagnetic and atmospheric conditions during Grand Solar Minima are leaning toward conditions in more northerly latitudes and in terms of seasons, to winter conditions. This is explained in detail in *Solar Behavior (2020)*. Here is a short summary:

During a Grand Minimum, the conditions in climate and energetic state of the atmosphere at a particular location shift towards the conditions that would be present in a more northerly altitude.

If we compare a location A at 20° North to location B at 50° North, the more southerly location A has on average less cosmic ray flux [423], a weaker static geo-magnetic field, higher (first mode) Schumann Resonance intensity, higher UV radiation but less UV variability, and more lightening than the northern location B. In Grand Minimum, these parameters are enhanced in location A and the conditions in location B shift to become more similar to those at location A.

Generally speaking, in a beginning Grand Minimum, the conditions at a particular location change as if everyone is moving a bit northward (or away from the Equator). These parameters can all influence human behavior.

Indicators of higher male testosterone levels in grand solar minimum

Solar Radio Flux density (solar microwave radiation on Earth) is higher in solar maximum. To repeat: in today's definition, radio waves range from 1 Hz to 300 MHz, microwaves range from 300 MHz to 300 GHz.

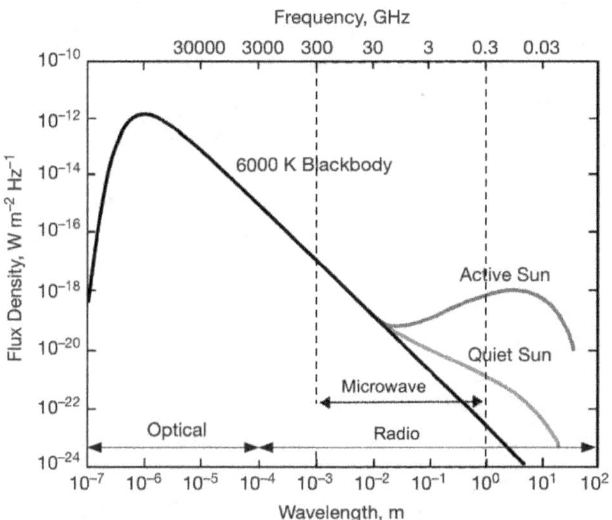

Fig. 4 The solar flux density is equal to that from a blackbody radiator at 6000 K at wavelengths less than about 1.0 cm (a frequency greater than about 30 GHz), but the spectral density becomes much greater at longer wavelengths for both a quiet and disturbed Sun. An active Sun [solar maximum] has much larger flux density than does a quiet Sun [solar minimum] in the frequency range between 100 MHz (3-m wavelength) and 30 GHz (1 cm wavelength). These elevated fluxes come mainly from the contribution of the solar **corona** and the chromosphere, a thin layer just above the visible photosphere. The scales of 'active' and 'quiet' sun here refer to 11-year-solar cycles, they can be extrapolated to much greater fluctuations for grand solar cycles. Graphic: *Ho, Christian et al 2008: Solar Brightness Temperature and Corresponding Antenna Noise Temperature at Microwave Frequencies; IPN Progress Report 42-175; November 15, 2008; https://ipnpr.jpl.nasa.gov/progress_report/42-175/175E.pdf*

Solar activity is measured mostly in 10.7 cm solar radio flux on Earth, which is within the microwave spectrum similar to a microwave oven, but of course in a much lower amplitude.
"The 2,800 MHz, or 10.7 cm, responds to the same conditions that produce changes in the visible and X-ray wavelengths." [424]
In solar maximum, people are exposed to a greater dose of this very weak, but stable microwave flux from the sun. Could this

steady flux be enough to slightly lower testosterone in men and estrogen in women, in a similar way as artificial short term, high amplitude artificial microwaves do? The effect couldn't be large, as the detrimental fall in gonad hormones in the past 70 years is unprecedented and not subject to notable 11-year fluctuations.

The microwave wavelength 2800 MHz daily radio flux correlates highly with the daily sunspot number and the two databases are used interchangeably.

"Unlike many solar indices, the F10.7 radio flux can easily be measured reliably on a day-to-day basis from the Earth's surface, in all types of weather. Reported in "solar flux units", (s.f.u.), the F10.7 can vary from below 50 s.f.u. to above 300 s.f.u., over the course of a solar cycle. " [425]

"The solar microwave flux is nominally an absolute flux, one solar flux unit is defined as [the very small amount of] 10-22 Watt per square meter per Hertz." [426]

Professor Svalgaard elucidates the recently "changing relationship between Sunspot Number and F10.7": Sunspot Number and the 10.7cm solar radio flux are the most widely-used indices of solar activity. Despite their differing nature and origins at different places in the Sun, these two indices are highly-correlated to the point where one can be used as a proxy for the other. *"However, during Solar Activity Cycle 23 we started to see a small but definite change in this relationship*." [427]

Solar cycle 23 lasted between 1996 and 2008, that's when the two measurements began to drift apart.

"The progressive drift is much larger than the 3% correction and is therefore not due to the correction. It seems inescapable that the relation between the sunspot number and the microwave flux has changed significantly in recent years." [428]

To be sure, the fact that the first global response to an infectious disease in history – with government measures thousands of times more severe than during the Spanish Flue – is about a C0R0NAVIRUS, has nothing to do with the solar corona of this beginning solar minimum, nothing at all.

Male testosterone is lower in winter in northern latitudes.

A 2003 study found that the testosterone levels of men in one Norwegian town bottomed out in summer and reached a high in late fall. A study of Danish men found similar seasonal variations (on a slightly different schedule). But studies done in sunny San Diego and snowy Boston failed to replicate the Scandinavian findings. [429]

Space flight has decreased testosterone in astronauts.
Space flight in low orbit or outer space results in increased cosmic ray exposure. on Earth, cosmic ray flux is greater in solar minimum. "Alterations in HPG and HPA axes functioning have been reported following spaceflight. Most evaluations focused on the reduced levels of circulating testosterone in men that appear to rebound after return to Earth." [430]

Ethnic differences in hormones of people living in Zambia.
The concentrations of progesterone, oestradiol, testosterone and cortisol have been measured in blood plasma from groups of men and women living in Zambia, but having European, African or Asian origins. Oestradiol concentration was higher in blood from African men than from men of the other two groups. Asian women showed the lowest luteal phase plasma oestrogen level. African men had **lower mean testosterone** in plasma than the other groups, while African women had higher results. There were no ethnic differences in progesterone concentrations. [431]

Testosterone, latitude and culture.
A new study out of Durham University in the United Kingdom suggests that the childhood environment of males determines their testosterone level, undermining the previous prevailing theories that race or genes govern the amount of the hormone in each individual. *"Bangladeshi men who grew up and lived as adults in the UK had significantly higher levels of testosterone compared with the men who grew up and lived in Bangladesh as adults."* [432] However, what was not considered in the conclusion of this study, is that people growing up in third world countries, even the middle class, which was observed here, have on average higher exposure rates of environmental chemical toxins, including EDCs, in drinking water, food, and consumer goods, then residents of western countries.

Contrarily, there are indicators for higher testosterone levels in Grand Solar Maximum

Most indirect evidence suggesting higher testosterone in solar maximum as well as in Grand Solar Maximum are derived from data that associate higher testosterone with sunlight exposure in vivo as well as in utero.
Sunlight exposure boosts testosterone production in men. Overall, sunlight is more abundant in solar maximum.

Exposure to bright light increases testosterone levels and leads to greater sexual satisfaction in men with low sexual desire. A group of scientists from the University of Siena in Italy have tested sexual and physiological responses to bright light. They found that regular, early-morning, use of a light box -- similar to those used to combat Seasonal Affective Disorder - led both to increased testosterone levels and greater reported levels of sexual satisfaction. [433]

Sunlight and Digit ratio (2D:4D)
More sunlight in gestation coincided with lower 2D:4D digit ratio (greater masculinization) in men and women in Poland. The solstitial-melatonin-testosterone hypothesis posits that melatonin inhibits the production of foetal testosterone and melatonin levels are at their lowest in months when light levels are high. Polish men and women born between 1907 and 1997 were examined. Participants born in late-Autumn and who experienced long days in the 2nd and 3rd prenatal months had a **low 2D:4D digit ratio**. "*The effects were strongest for participants born in the first half of the 20th Century, where photoperiods would be less disrupted by artificial light.*" [434]
The researchers assumed that the differences between subjects born before 1950 and subjects born after 1950 would be due to light pollution at night. What was not addressed in the study is the fact that those born in the second half of the 20th Century, where the effect was less pronounced, are also the generation of the period when EDCs were introduced proficiently, with an overall disruption of androgenization in gestation.

A study by Myerson (1939) showed that even exposure of the genital area to UV light 'greatly stimulated androsterone production in men and increased testosterone production by 200%. [435]
Melatonin is a ubiquitous molecule and exhibits different effects in long-day and short-day breeding animals. Testosterone, the main resource of androgens in the testis, is produced by Leydig cells but regulated mainly by cytokine secreted by Sertoli cells. Melatonin acts as a local modulator of the endocrine activity in Leydig cells. In Sertoli cells, melatonin influences cellular proliferation and energy metabolism and, consequently, can regulate steroidogenesis. This suggests melatonin as a key player in the regulation of steroidogenesis. However, the melatonin-induced regulation of steroid hormones may differ among species, and the literature data indicate that melatonin has important effects on steroidogenesis and male reproduction. [436]

Chapter 13
Treatments and attempted treatments for male testosterone deficiency

13.1. Testosterone Replacement Therapy

So, why don't we just fix this social collapse by putting men on testosterone replacement medication? And women on estrogen? Well, this is no solution and can even accelerate the decline. Let's see why.

Testosterone Replacement Therapy does have a positive impact on depression in patients with late-onset testosterone deficiency.

"TRT reduces depressive symptoms, according to data coming from small-sized, placebo-controlled RCTs of patients with pretreatment clinical mild depression. This impact was not noticed in men with major depressive disorders. In patients without pretreatment depression, TRT leads to a reduction of scores for depressive symptoms." [437]

Additional research showed that "Overall, the quality of life in older hypogonadal men can be positively influenced by testosterone substitution, as has been demonstrated in large placebo-controlled trials. " [438]

A phenomenon in Western countries?

Prescriptions for Testosterone Replacement Therapy more than doubled from 2010 to 2013. This has been partially attributed to drug marketing campaigns urging older men to boost "low T" levels, even if they don't need it. [439]

The figure below shows the distribution of testosterone replacement treatment use in selected countries worldwide in 2011. Note the top countries are all western countries, who are incidentally also leading in social progressivism, oikophobia and negative ethnocentrism.

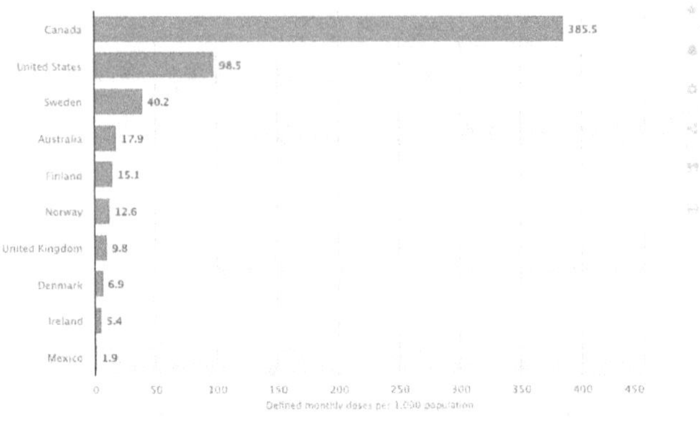

Fig. 5 Testosterone use worldwide by select countries per 1,000 people 2011; Published by Statista Research Department, Aug 13, 2013https://www.statista.com/statistics/302923/testosterone-use-globally-per-1-000-population/

Physicians were interviewed on diagnosing and treating testosterone (T) deficiency in Germany, Spain, the United Kingdom, Brazil and Saudi Arabia. Erectile dysfunction (ED) and lack of libido (2006) but also depression and obesity (2010) were regarded as symptoms of T deficiency. For 70% of physicians, severity of complaints was more significant than the laboratory value of T to prescribe T, more so in Germany (96%) than in Spain and Saudi Arabia. Concerns about prostate disease remained strong and, therefore, 11% of eligible patients did not receive T. [440]

"In the United States, men spend over 3 billion dollars annually on TRT." [441]

13.2. The risks of TRT

Dr. Puneet Masson, Penn Medicine cautions: *"Many times people feel that, 'Oh, I have low testosterone—it affects fertility—I should take a testosterone supplement. That's actually something we do not want them to do. If a man is taking any extra testosterone, it can basically shut off his body's ability to make its own testosterone—and the body's ability to make its own sperm."* The number of men taking testosterone supplements has noticeably increased in the last decade. This growth is even among men who don't need to because their testosterone levels are normal, according to a March 2014 study in the Journal of Endocrinology and Metabolism. Dr. Masson adds: *"There's a lot of misuse of these supplements and treatments," "People take them as a sort of anti-aging treatment when they have normal testosterone. Testosterone replacement therapy should be given to someone who has low testosterone and is symptomatic from it."* [442]

Dr. Thomas O'Connor, a prominent men's health internal medicine physician cautions:

"Testosterone Replacement Therapy has to be considered for life. …. most men don't want to stop - and depending on circumstances they may not be able to." [443]

Testosterone replacement therapy can increase men's risk of stroke and heart attack. [444]

In particular, "Studies showed men over 65 - who were prescribed testosterone - had twice the risk of suffering from a heart attack. Men under 50 with a history of heart problems have a three-fold increased risk of a heart attack during the first 90 days of TRT. " [445]

Further, Obstructive Sleep Apnea Syndrome has been associated with testosterone administration. [446]

 A short background of TRT by Ana Marcella Rivas et al:

"Already from the 1970s onwards, several authors reported an age-associated decline of serum testosterone levels beginning in the fourth or fifth decades of life. Other studies found that the decline in testosterone with age might be more related to comorbidities that develop in many aging men. Aggressive marketing campaigns by pharmaceutical companies have led to warped perceptions. Many men with low testosterone levels have no symptoms, and many men with symptoms who receive treatment and reach goal testosterone levels have no improvement in their symptoms. " [447]

As we have seen, **the actual prevalence of hypogonadism has been estimated to be 39% in men aged 45 years or older in the United States** "(p. 21).

"Erectile dysfunction is associated with low bioactive testosterone levels and visceral adiposity in men with type 2 diabetes." [448]

In addition, Dr. Friedman points out that just as hormone replacement therapy was shown to cause serious health risks to women in the early 2000s, men are now experiencing adverse reactions to TRT, such as an increased risk of stroke and heart attack."

"TRT can also cause an increase in red blood cells, which thickens the blood, leading to blood clots. A study published in the August 2013 issue of Clinical and Applied Thrombosis/Hemostasis found that blood clots may develop as quickly as three weeks after beginning testosterone drugs. [449] Finally, the most common negative effect of TRT is testicular shrinkage and impotency. In spite of such warnings, testosterone prescriptions show no signs of decline. In fact, TRT has increased tenfold in the last decade, and is growing steadily at 10 percent per month!" [450]

In summary: other than in well warranted cases of acute hypogonadism, artificial testosterone (TRT) further shuts down natural testosterone production, causes infertility and impotency, a host of additional health problems and makes most users dependent on a lifetime steady dose of T. Since the testosterone is not regulated. By the natural complex activation cycles, other hormonal and neural imbalances can be propagated. Male and female gonad hormones must be regenerated by natural means to mitigate and reverse the process of Hormonageddon.

Chapter 14
Historic precedents of oikophobia and low ethnocentrism

14.1. natural variations in testosterone over time, solar cycles and the Pacification Process in the Middle Ages, self-domestication

Grand Solar Minima are times of peace. People living in the post war area tend to imagine this means cuddly love and tolerance for everyone, even for repeat violent criminals, no matter what harm they cause to society. In the past millennium, the increased desire to establish peace and security manifested in harsh punishment of violent crime, to such severity that it altered the gene pool in the direction of more impulse control and lowered reactive aggression, which contributed to peacefulness, self-control and enforcement of human rights during the last millennium. The effects last till today and are a defining part of the collective personality of civil societies. However, the process has long started to reverse.

In this 'War on Crime' which began already in the 12th century, lethal interpersonal violence dropped in Europe roughly by a factor of between 10:1 to 50:1 in the period from the fifteenth to the twentieth century. [451] This coincided with a cluster of several grand solar minima, which again coincided with the cold period known as the Little Ice Age (1350- 1850). And the trend was enhanced in each Grand Solar Minimum. All of this was detailed in *Solar Behavior (2020)*.

This phenomenon can be added to the indicators of higher testosterone levels in Grand Solar Minimum, and it is also consistent with the fact that testosterone alone does not cause aggression, but confidence and dominance.

Imagine what the world was like with 50 times more violent crime than today.

Before the 11th century, it was considered honorable and manly to settle disputes from 'man to man', if need be, by violence. From the 12th century onward, violent crime was punished often by death so "the innocent could live in peace".

Over a lifetime, one or two out of every two hundred men would end up being executed. A comparable trend is observed in Japan, which was culturally completely isolated from Europe, in the same timeframe.

On a large scale, this decline in violence since the early Middle Ages had a significant genetic component. The rigorous execution of even non-violent criminals is considered cruel and inhumane by our modern laws and ethical standards; to most of us, hanging a thief on the town square is unthinkable. Plus, the ineffective justice system of the time meant more innocent suspects were unjustly executed than today. Even today, due to errors or corruption, convicts are sometimes found innocent after years of incarceration or even on death row, which makes a strong case against the death penalty.
But despite of all these problems, in a cynical way, it was among other things the merciless implementation of the rule of law in the Middle Ages that led to the low criminality and high empathy of today's society. The exact magnitude of the genetic contribution in this pacification process is still debated, but since it does exist, it had a long-lasting effect (likely for many generations to come).
As a side effect of lowered aggression and heightened altruistic sociability and trust, this also fostered the rise of a 'servile people' - overly trusting in authorities – particularly in western and northern cultures.

Chapter 15
The Fall of the Roman Empire and EDCs

We can see strong parallels between the decline and fall of the Roman Empire and today's decisive period in history.

Late-stage Roman society saw a similar social mood as we are seeing in the West today, low fertility, low family-orientedness and low ethnocentrism, low in-group preference (high levels of oikophobia), narcissism and so on, from the early years of its decline – from around 200 A.D. onward. This was a much more lengthily and tedious process than today. Another striking difference is that the low in-group preference and low birthrates were long confined to the aristocracy and the upper middle class, while the peasants were not or little affected.

Lead poisoning in Roman society has long been argued to have contributed to their decline and fall, usually it was assumed, in the form of general health decline and stupidity. But lead is an endocrine disruptor, it not only causes cognitive and nervous devastation, infertility, low birth rates and low family- orientedness, but just as today, the EDC effects led to people and peoples to not even care about their own genetic extinction.

Did something similar happen to the Romans and Greeks as is happening to us?

By the way, the lead came not primarily from lead pipes in drinking water in ancient Rome, but from cookware, wine cauldrons and to a smaller degree, from fumes of lead factories. [452]

The fall of the empire began in 2nd and 3rd century Rome. Hugh Trevor-Roper describes the decline of Rome as having begun around 200 A.D:

"All the great structures […] the aqueducts, the amphitheaters and the city walls – were raised before the beginning of the third century. After that, there was almost nothing. More and more historians began to discern "a fundamental structural change" at the time, "which the great emperors at the end of that century, and Constantine himself at the beginning of the next, did but stabilize." [453]

In 1920, Professor O. Seeck pointed out a 'problem of the biological order' in the late Roman Empire:

"The cruelty and suspiciousness of the emperors removed and killed all persons who, by their mental qualities, capacity, and energy, raised themselves above the average. Through an artificial, inverted selection, independence and originality were stamped out and a servile people bred." [454]

Overall population started to decline by falling birth-rates 'already from 100 A.D. onwards during the earlier years of the Empire. '[455]

"We see in our own days how the fall of the birth-rate commences in the upper classes and soon spreads down to the lower. This decline seems to be common to a high culture, at least the same phenomenon appeared among the civilized populations of the [British] Empire, the Greeks and the Romans. " [456]

Cultural progress - except in technology – declined; before, it had been 'depending on the upper class'. *"This Roman upper class, beginning about the second or first century B.C., died out with extreme rapidity. Each generation was perhaps a fourth of the previous one, largely through rearing very few children."* [457]

A. H. Jones noted, referring to the 4th century: *"On our evidence the peasantry were in general apathetic and docile; of any spontaneous action on either side [of two peasant armies] there is scarcely any trace."* [458]

As early as in the 18th century – in *'The Decline and Fall of the Roman Empire'* - Edward Gibbon identified five major causes that contributed to the fall of the Roman Empire: ***First, the breakdown of the family. Second, increased taxation. Third, an insatiable craving for pleasure. Fourth, an unsustainable buildup of armaments. Fifth, the decay of religion***. [459]

"The nation of soldiers, magistrates, and legislators, who composed the thirty-five tribes of the Roman people, was dissolved into the common mass of mankind, and confounded with the millions of servile provincials, who had received the name, without adopting the spirit, of Romans." [460]

Thomas Cahill surmised that "Rome fell gradually and Romans for many decades scarcely noticed what was happening." [461]

Kenneth Clark wrote in *Civilizations*:

"Civilizations require a modicum of material prosperity – enough to provide a little leisure. But, far more, it requires confidence – confidence in the society in which one lives, belief in its philosophy, belief in its laws, and confidence in one's own mental powers…

Vigor, energy, vitality: all the great civilizations – or civilizing epochs – have had a weight of energy behind them. People sometimes think that civilization consists in fine sensibilities and good conversation and all that. These can be among the agreeable results of civilization, but they are not what make a civilization, and a society can have these amenities and yet be dead and rigid." [462]

As the decline began with low birth rates - especially among the upper classes - it was then accompanied by promiscuity, abortions, widespread infanticide of unwanted newborns [463], orgies and venereal diseases among the establishment, replacement of Roman soldiers with non-Roman soldiers, non- Roman emperors from the provinces, Emperors obsessed with sexual deviancies, but uninterested in governing, mass immigration; it all seems familiar in regards to current developments in the West. Unwanted children were disposed of on the street. Gibbon: *"In ancient times the parents had a right to expose children whom they did not desire to educate. Where the supply of food is scarce among primitive peoples this may be excused. Among a civilized people, when economic egotism has obliterated the natural feelings of the parents, it is nothing but legalized infanticide."* [464]

Seneca (died 65 AD) warned one of the foundational reasons Rome would fall was the fact that *"they divorce in order to remarry. They marry in order to divorce."* Already Augustus knew that the falling birth rates were not the result of abstinence, but of contraceptives, he enacted laws to create positive and negative incentives, but the upper class could not even be bribed into wanting children. [465]

"Mass population transfers were tried, whether to people recently conquered lands, to replenish newly depopulated ones, or as political policy." [466]

Meisenberg (2007) has observed that when civilizations become advanced the standard of living among the higher classes increased to such an extent that their stress levels drop to a point where they start questioning their religiosity. He claims that this is what happened towards the end of the Roman Civilization, and it likely helped to explain the *'low levels of ethnocentrism observed at this point in Rom's history, when foreigners were effectively permitted to take over the city.'* [467]

Murray (2003) observed *"[…]* *"Taken as whole, the Roman world throughout its history, whether republic or empire, was a near intellectual void when it came to the arts and sciences - "peopled by a race of pygmies" in Gibbon's contemptuous words. Scientific, philosophic, and artistic progress did not come to an end when Rome fell, but, without much exaggeration, when Rome rose."* [468]

Lead poisoning inhibits endocrine function

Already the Greeks exposed themselves to high levels of lead.
Even the Egyptian used it in small quantities:
"Galena (argentiferous lead ore, PbS), was used as eye-paint in Egypt during the prehistoric Baderian period, about 5000 years B.C. the practice of using galena for eye-paint survives to the present day, particularly in India, where it is known as surma." [469]
The Greek philosopher Nikander of Colophon in 250 BC already reported on the colic and anemia resulting from lead poisoning.
Hippocrates related gout to the food and wine, the association between gout and lead poisoning was not recognized during this period (450-380 BC) although he did described colic, or upset stomach, in metal workers. [470]
"The role of manufacturing sugar lead goes all the way back to the Greeks, but the Romans popularized it". [471]
In the first century A.D., Dioscorides, another Greek physician, noticed that exposure to lead could cause paralysis and delirium in addition to intestinal problems and swelling. [472]
During the Roman period, gout was prevalent among the upper classes of Roman society and is believed to be a result of the enormous lead intake." [473] Lead toxicity involves alterations on calcitropic hormones' homeostasis, which increase the risk of skeletal disorders. [474]

"Nriagu estimates the aristocracy of Rome to have consumed two liters of wine a day or almost three bottles (which would seem to make alcoholism more suspect than lead poisoning) and the resulting lead intake to have averaged 180 µg daily. He further estimates the total amount of lead absorbed from all sources to be 250 µg per day and lead concentration in the blood to be 50 µg/dL, at least for the gluttonous and bibulous (as he phrases it) and those with an appetite for adulterated wines and sweetened dainties—who he presumes most Roman emperors to have been." [475]
"Pliny, in his Natural Histories, wrote about the noxious fumes that emanated from lead furnaces, he also wrote that sapa and onion are effective elements towards inducing abortions." [476] (The sweetener *sapa* was prepared from boiling grapes in lead pots). Vitruvius and Celsus were aware of the toxicity of lead and advised against its usage. [477]
Joanna Moore et al argued that lead also contributed to the high infant mortality rates within Roman populations. [478]
Lead enhanced one-fifth of the 450 recipes in the Roman Apician Cookbook, a collection of first through fifth century recipes

attributed to gastrophiles associated with Apicius, the famous Roman gourmet. [479]

F.P. Retief calculated that lead production in the Graeco-Roman era in Europe and the Mediterranean area during the 2nd millennium BC increased tenfold, reaching a peak in the 1st millennium BC and the period up to AD 500, after which it dropped dramatically until AD 1 000 to levels com- parable with those of the 3rd millennium BC.

"Lead contamination in the ice layers of Greenland dating from the period 500 BC to AD 300 must have been caused by atmospheric pollution from the ore furnaces of ancient Rome (and Greece).

The burden of lead in the ice is equivalent to 15% of the 20th century's ice pollution due to leaded petrol." [480]

Other than cognitive decline, fatigue and sterility, the main deteriorating effect of the aristocrats' lead poisoning seems to have been lack of resolve and hormonal confusion, enhancing oikophobia and anti- ethnocentrism.

As we see, according to their lifestyle, the aristocracy would have received a much higher steady dose than the lower classes, which could have contributed to the circumstance that these upper classes were more affected by the reluctance to have children, by low fertility, by low ethnocentrism and high levels of oikophobia.

"Ancient Rome featured a myriad of, what could be understood, both then and now, as experiences that transcended sex and gender norms." [481] Most famously, Elagabalus was a controversial teenage emperor who shook Roman society to its core with radical sexual promiscuity transforming from a boy to a woman, marrying once a sacred female priestess, them a man (he reigned from 218 - 222 AD). According to Dio Cassius, castration was one of Elagabalus' fondest desires, not out of religion but out of "effeminacy".

As for the endocrine disrupting effects of lead, extensive studies "presented direct interactions of lead with sex hormones and suggests a possible mechanism of lead induced reproductive toxicity at a molecular level." [482]

Chronic lead -poisoning causes hypogonadism in men. [483]

"In both men and women, lead has been associated with infertility and damaged in serum testosterone. Even In lead smelting workers without clinical symptoms of lead poisoning, a decrease in serum testosterone (T) is observed." [484] Reduced testosterone is most apparent in lead workers. [485]

Studies suggest that "lead poisoning may lead to a pituitary-hypo-thalamic defect in LH secretion and may also result in direct testicular seminiferous tubular injury." [486]

Accumulation of lead affects the majority of endocrine glands.

K. Doumouchtsis et al suggest that lead initially causes some sub-clinical testicular damage, followed by hypothalamic or pituitary disturbance when longer periods of exposure take place. Similarly, lead accumulates in granulosa cells of the ovary, causing delays in growth and pubertal development and reduced fertility in females. [487]

In terms of behavior, lead poisoning in our days is also apparent as a relation between hotspots of crime and hotspots of lead exposure. The association between lead and crime appears particularly robust with respect to rates of violent index crime, but less so for rates of property index crime. [488]

"The brain of adults who were exposed to increased lead levels during their childhood also shows a decreased volume, especially in the prefrontal cortex." [489] The prefrontal cortex plays an important role in impulse control and thus deficits are associated to anti-social behavior.

Today, in young adults with low levels of lead exposure, higher blood lead levels are associated with increased odds of major depression, panic disorders and other psychological alterations. [490] "Exposure to lead even at levels generally considered safe could result in adverse mental health outcomes." [491] And lead removal from the body has been used in many cases to completely resolve such symptoms. Lead-exposed workers in foundries, battery plants, or lead smelter are reported to suffer from cognitive and neuromotor deficits, as well as mood disorders such as anxiety, hostility, and depressive states. [492]

Many young children with elevated blood lead levels will have iron insufficiency or iron deficiency anemia. Thus, iron deficiency is an important comorbidity of lead toxicity; pica behavior has sometimes been associated with iron-deficient status (pica behavior is a tendency or craving to eat substances other than normal food, such as clay, plaster, or ashes, occurring during childhood or pregnancy, or as a symptom of disease). [493] The Roman elite was known for gluttony, not only drinking and eating large quantities, but also weird things.

Roman writers did note that "*Indeed, those who eat the least expensive foods are the strongest. Thus, slaves are generally stronger than their masters, country folk are stronger than city folk, and the poor are stronger than the rich. Furthermore, those who eat inexpensive food can work harder, are less fatigued by working, and are sick less often than those who eat expensive food. Also, they are better able to tolerate cold, heat, lack of sleep, and so forth."* (trans. King, 2010) [494]

Apart from the lead poisoning via wine cauldrons, alcohol itself disrupts testosterone (see above). [495]

Beyond the well documented lead poisoning of the Roman elite, mercury (Hg) concentration was on average 3.5-fold greater in ancient Roman compare to post-Roman inhabitants, even on the edge of the Roman Empire. [496]

Mercury poisoning can cause anxiety, depression, insomnia and other symptoms. [497]

And mercury is also a strong endocrine disruptor, of course. [498]

Further, it has recently been suggested that another heavy metal, antimony, may have done the main job of dissolving the empire. [499]

If true, it is noteworthy that antimony from drinking water is a neurotoxin more effective than lead, and it also acts as an endocrine disruptor, of course.

Today, antimony can be responsible for estrogenic effects. "Leaching of antimony from PET containers may lead to endocrine-disrupting effects." [500] Shotyk et al. (2006) found antimony in up to 30 times higher concentrations in mineral water from PET compared to glass bottles and confirmed its leaching from PET. [501]

Pornography addiction: a proxy for male testosterone deterioration?

These days, pornography is very prevalent in our society, and porn addiction (as by self-diagnosis) affects about 5-8% of adults. [502]

With a common number of unrecorded cases for self-reported addiction, this can amount rather to 30% in reality.

The pornography market has grown exorbitantly from 1975 to today.

The numbers for total annual revenue are disputed. The consensus values for the late 1970s range between $5–10 million [503] on the lower end; and $100 million a year (for gross retail volume in Los Angeles alone (1979 Revision of the Federal Criminal Code).

The Guardian claims *"Current [adult content] revenue estimates for the US range from $9bn to $97bn a year. The latter figure looks excessive, a conservative estimate is $15bn."* [504] In 2007, The Observer newspaper gave a figure of $13 billion. [505] 100,000 websites offer illegal child pornography (U.S. Customs Service estimate, 2001). [506]

Taken together, today's estimates for annual pornography revenues range from 13 to 90 billion.

While the sales increases are obviously related to the invention of the internet and thus to availability, it is nevertheless astonishing to see that in less than 50 years between the late 1970s and today, the pornography market increased 1300 times or possibly 10,000 times, roughly inversely proportional to gonad hormone levels.

Pornography consumption can also lead to further 'undermining of self- confidence in men'. Even though the actual condition of micro-penis is affecting more and more men - about 0.6 % of young men in 2016 and possibly approaching 1 % today - it is still relatively rare. Nevertheless, most men believe their penis is "smaller than the average." [507] A 2019 research article notes that most males believe the average length for an erect penis is around 15.2 centimeters (cm) or 6 inches. [508] According to analysis published in the British Journal of Urology International, the average flaccid, pendulous penis is 9.16 cm (3.61 inches) in length; the average erect penis is 13.12 cm (5.16 inches) long. [509] In a 2005 study, 37 percent of respondents said that their problems concerning Small Penis Syndrome began in adolescence after they had seen erotic images for the first time. *"Because of the growing availability of pornography on the Internet, this could become even more of a problem in the future."* [510] Actual penis size is difficult to determine statistically. More conclusive is that even in the 1990s, according to surveys, 70 % of men already believed theirs was smaller than average. This number must now be well over 90 %.

For the survival of society, things as penis size are obviously trivial, but the subject is somewhat exemplary in these decisive moments of history: low self-confidence but high narcissism, hormonal confusion, sex obsession but high Viagra consumption.

The 'speedo index' as a proxy of testosterone levels and positive life outlooks?

While women's swimwear fashion trends fluctuate since the 1960s - sometimes more revealing, then less so - men's swimwear (even in Italy) is continually moving back to 1940 'prudery'. Since the late 1950s till the 1990s, men who went to the beach tried to look like athletes, as if they were there for some serious swimming or board diving. James Deen, Elvis, Burt Lancaster and the rest wore tight shorts, even on US beaches, where larger board shorts were more practical for surfing. In Europe, it was mostly teenage boys in puberty and men who were perceived as 'creepy' who wore baggy shorts at a swimming location.

And now, are all men at the beach afraid women could tell that they belong to the presumed ' below average 90 %'?

Fig. 6 the 'Speedo index' men's swimwear 1950s to 2000s vs. sperm morphology value 1968 to 2008 (white curve). Sperm morphology declined from 63% from normal to 4 % from normal. An alleged correlation between sperm count, testosterone levels, pornography consumption, male self-confidence and swimwear fashion?

Chapter 16
Remedies and prevention

As a generalized rule, what disturbs sperm production and fertility also disturbs testosterone production and function in men and even estrogen in women. Thus, reducing Endocrine Disrupting Chemicals that disrupt fertility, will generally be favorable for testosterone or estrogen regulation. More detailed advice on how to prevent EDC intake in everyday life is again provided in S. Swan's "Countdown", Chapter 11.

Below is a short list of the most prevalent sources of EDCs and measures for prevention that are relatively easy to implement. For reduction of endocrine disrupting non-ionizing radiation (EDNR), see paragraph at the end of this chapter.

16.1. Minerals and vitamins

Deficiency in **Magnesium, Selenium** [511]**, Zinc, Vitamin C** [512]**, Vitamin D, Vitamin E** [513] [514], are all associated with testosterone/ estrogen disfunction and deficiency. Deficiency of some of these minerals and vitamins can also be induced by wireless- EMF.

Zinc and vitamin D were not only successfully used in animal studies to alleviate the harmful effects of mobile/ wireless EMF, but it was shown that zinc deficiency can actually be induced by EMF exposure.

As it happens, deficiency of zinc and vitamin C, D, E is also implicated in the treatment and prevention of severe cases of COVID 19.

"One of the risk factors du jour for cor0navirus disease 2019 (COVID -19) has been vitamin D deficiency." Even Dr. Faucl recommends Vitamin D supplements to improve severe COVID outcomes (see below). [515]

Testosterone and COVID

First a disclaimer: COVID-19 is an infectious virus disease, take measures to protect yourself and others.

Early on in the pandemic it was shown that "For men, low testosterone means a high risk of severe COVID-19.

Scientists presented new clues on why more men than women develop severe disease outcomes." [516]

The connection was corroborated by this case-control study: Severely low testosterone in males with COVID-19, "significantly lower levels of LH and tT were found in patients with COVID-19 compared to healthy controls."

"Testosterone levels suggestive for hypogonadism were observed in 89.8% of patients at hospital admission. In as many as 85% of cases, hypogonadism was secondary." [517]

"Abhinav Diwan, MD, professor of medicine, lead author of a recent Covid study, supported by the National Institutes of Health (NIH), found if a man had low testosterone when he first came to the hospital, his risk of having severe COVID-19 -- meaning his risk of requiring intensive care or dying -- was much higher compared with men who had more circulating testosterone. And if testosterone levels dropped further during hospitalization, the risk increased. It was found that *"Lower testosterone levels seemed to predict which patients were likely to become very ill over the next few days."* [518]

Similarly, in Sept 2020, Aneela N. Hussain et al concluded: *"Low testosterone levels in males [with Covid 19] have a direct correlation with the high probability of Intensive Care Unit admission and the worse disease outcome (Acute respiratory distress syndrome (ARDS), duration of ICU stay and mortality)."* [519]

Then it turned out Covid deaths were associated with areas of 5G high mmW exposure in the United States. Stephanie McCarter, MD, 2020 revealed a *"statistically significant increase in the rates of COVID-19 cases and deaths in the areas of the US with 5G high mmW (millimeter Wave) exposure. 5G mmW index was a statistically significant factor for the higher cases and rates in all three analyses in all 50 states, the country's largest counties, and the largest counties in California."*

"Covid death per million were 94% higher and deaths per test were 81% higher in 5G high mmW areas."

McCarter summarized: *«the potential for 5G and even lower RF frequencies to contribute to increased infection by COVID-19 and the severity of infection has clear evidence in multiple peer-reviewed studies. The mechanisms of RF causing increased infection and its severity include oxidative stress with depletion of key nutrients like **Vitamin D** and glutathione."* [520]

In January, 2022, Zhang et al confirmed:

"Decline in testosterone levels has been observed in male patients hospitalized for acute illness, and low testosterone levels are associated with the need for admission to the ICU. In this study, we also found that the serum testosterone level of COVID-19 patients was significantly lower than that of healthy males, and the serum testosterone level of COVID-19 patients in the ICU group was lower than that of the non-ICU group. Schroeder et al. also found that low testosterone levels were significantly associated with admission to the respiratory intensive care unit for COVID-19 patients. When testosterone was < 5 nmol/L, the energy efficiency of patients who need to be admitted to the respiratory intensive care unit is higher." [521]

EMFs cause mineral and vitamin deficiency

Dr. Trevor Marshall demonstrated that very low radiofrequencies, much lower than 5G frequencies, affect the human Vitamin-D receptor (VDR) in the cell by changing its shape. This change in the receptor affects its ability to bind with vitamin D. The binding of VDR with vitamin D is important in regulating cellular metabolic pathways. [522]

See more on the effects of vitamin D deficiency below.

To add to the problem, Wi-Fi router radiation has caused lung tissue changes in rats. [523] As we saw on page 82, a Wi-Fi router increased antibiotic resistance and motility of E Coli and increased metabolic activity and biofilm production in Staphylococcus Aureus and Staphylococcus Epidermis.

It should be carefully considered in a pandemic with a virus that causes lung inflammation, whether it is the best idea to lock people in their homes, in home office, in front of their computers and TV screens, next to their Wi-Fi routers for years, without sunlight.

In addition to this, extensive hygiene mask wearing (with nanoparticles) can propagate the buildup of bacteria and fungi in the respiratory system.

Male albino rats who were exposed to a **950 MHz electromagnetic field (EMF),** showed significant increases in iron copper levels and copper/zinc ratio accompanied with a **decrease of zinc level in all studied organs.** [524] As we'll see shortly, exposure to an electromagnetic field (a 50-Hz frequency magnetic field for 5 minutes every other day over a period of 6 months) caused cellular damage in lung and liver tissues in rats and zinc supplementation inhibited the inflicted cellular damage. [525]

Vitamin D deficiency, wireless EMF and virus diseases: closing the circle to testosterone function

Extensive research exists documenting vitamin D's role in decreasing risk of infection from pathogens as well as strengthening immune function. *"Over a decade ago low vitamin D levels were identified as a pandemic. "* [526]
Vitamin D is an important factor in estrogen biosynthesis of both female and male gonads. [527]
"Taking vitamin D supplements might correct a deficiency and even contribute to increased testosterone levels." [528]
Likewise for women, there is a "positive correlation" between vitamin D and estradiol. In other words, women with lower levels of vitamin D tend also to have lower levels of estradiol, and women with higher levels of vitamin D tend also to have higher levels of estradiol. [529]

More recently, "one of the risk factors du jour for cor0navirus disease 2019 (COVID-19) has been vitamin D deficiency."
Even Anthony Fauci, MD, has said in 2020, he takes a vitamin D supplement. Vitamin D "does have an impact on your susceptibility to infection," Fauci, director of the National Institute of Allergy and Infectious Diseases, told actress Jennifer Garner in a September interview. *"I would not mind recommending—and I take it myself—taking vitamin D supplements."* [530]
Further studies have shown that "vitamin D levels are a critical factor in prevention of severe COVID 19 infections." [531]
"Vitamin D is critical for prevention as well as recovery, significantly lowering the risk of mortality in COVID-19." [532]
In addition, Daneshkhah et al presented evidence for an association of vitamin D status with cytokine storm and unregulated inflammation in COVID-19 patients. [533]

Update Dec 6 2021: A new study finds a theoretical COVID death rate of zero for those who take Vitamin D daily. [534]
In July 2022 the Jerusalem post titled:
"Vitamin D supplements can help protect patients with new COVID-19 strain." The probability of death was found to be higher by as much as 50% in COVID patients with severe vitamin D deficiency, while this probability fell to 5% in patients with good levels of the vitamin. [535]

Wireless EMF and vitamin D

In trials with male albino rats - who had lower testosterone values after mobile phone exposure with a harmful effect on testicular function - vitamin D resulted in a significant recovery of the hormonal deficits. [536]

EMF exposure to rats for 30 days, 1 h/day, resulted in significant decrease in immunoglobulin levels. Vitamin D supplementation reversed these results. It was concluded that exposure to mobile phone radiation compromises the immune system of rats, and vitamin D appears to have a protective effect. [537]

Sunlight and vitamin D3 can have a positive effect on some men fertility parameters. After the exposure to sunlight, there was a significant increase in count, activity and normal morphology of seminal fluid as well as elevation in LH, FSH and **testosterone and vitamin D3 level in the blood.** [538]

In another study, vitamin D showed protective effects against the harmful effects of cell phone radiation exposure on Albino rat testis. [539]

"For humans, vitamin D is not available in large enough quantities in food. The human body synthesizes the vitamin when exposed to sunlight, and this is the best source of vitamin D. " [540]

Vitamin C and E

"Vitamin E has been recognized as a requirement for normal testicular function for more than 50 years." [541]

"Exposure to 900-MHz radiation emitted by mobile phones to rats is associated with endometrial apoptosis and oxidative stress, but treatment with vitamins E and C can diminish these changes. " [542]

Further, vitamin E consumption has protective effects against 3 militesla electromagnetic field effects on oxidative parameters in rats. Vitamin E treatment significantly prevented the increase of the Malandialdehyde (MDA) levels and Glutathione peroxidise (GSHPx) activity and also prevented the decrease of superoxide dismutase (SOD) activity in tissue. [543]

In another study with rats exposed to 900 MHz EMF, vitamin E as well as silymarin has significantly reduced oxidative stress and ameliorated hormone levels, including free testosterone levels. [544]

Further, pumpkin seed oil and vitamin E have improved reproductive function of male rats who were inflicted by testicular injury. [545]

EMF and zinc (organic) supplementation

Extremely low-frequency magnetic field decreased calcium, zinc and magnesium levels in the costa of rats.

The rats were exposed to 100 and 500 µT ELF-MF, which are the safety standards of public and occupational exposure, for 2 h/day during 10 months. Levels of Calcium (Ca); Magnesium (Mg), and Zinc (Zn) were all significantly decreased in the ELF-500 exposure groups. It was concluded that long-term ELF-MF exposure can affect the chemical structure and metabolism of bone by changing the levels of some important elements such as Ca, Zn and Mg in rats. [546]

Zinc supplementation inhibits tissue damage caused by exposure to electromagnetic **field in rat lung and liver tissues.** Results of a study by A. K. Baltaci et al showed that exposure to an electromagnetic field caused cellular damage in lung and liver tissues. This EMF **exposure also led to a significant decrease in zinc levels in lung and liver tissues** (50 Hz). Zinc supplementation inhibited the inflicted cellular damage. [547]

*"A contributing factor to the ELF-EMF-induced oxidative stress may be **zinc deficiency**, as lipid peroxidation-induced in Sprague-Dawley rats by long term exposure to ELF-EMFs (50 Hz, 50 mG) can be ameliorated through systemic antioxidant zinc supplementation."* [548]

In corroboration, another study found zinc and vitamin E supplementation have preventative effects on oxidative stress induced by cellular phone radiation in brain tissues of rats and their fetuses. [549]

Zinc deficiency and testosterone

Dietary zinc restriction in normal young men is associated with a significant decrease in serum testosterone concentrations after 20 weeks of zinc restriction.

Zinc supplementation of marginally zinc-deficient normal elderly men for six months resulted in an increase in serum testosterone from 8.3 to 16.0 nmol/p. *"Zinc may play an important role in modulating serum testosterone levels in normal men."* [550] So, it doubled serum testosterone.

Androgen deficiency in adult male subjects with sickle cell anemia is correctable with zinc supplementation. [551]

Weight training in combination with zinc (6 weeks trial) supplementation improved testosterone and performance in athletes. [552]

Regarding non-athletes, M. Kilic, 2007 found: "exercise can decrease thyroid hormones and testosterone in sedentary men; however, zinc supplementation prevents this decrease." [553]

In corroboration of the above findings, zinc supplementation ameliorates electromagnetic field-induced lipid peroxidation in rat brains. (50Hz). [554] In breeding bulls, zinc supplements (organic) increase blood serum testosterone and sperm quality. [555]

Zinc deficiency and COVID 19

"Zinc not only balances immune responses but also has a proven direct antiviral action against some viruses. "

In a retrospective observational study with 249 COVID-19 patients admitted to Hospital del Mar in Barcelona, Spain, they found serum zinc levels lower than 50 µg/dl at admission correlated with worse clinical presentation, longer time to reach stability and higher mortality. [556] *"Serum zinc content is a novel biomarker to predict COVID-19 outcomes."*

In a prospective observational study in Chennai, India, patients with C0R0NAVIRUS disease 2019 had significantly low zinc levels in comparison to healthy controls. Zinc deficient patients developed more complications (70.4% vs 30.0%.). Further, zinc deficient COVID-19 patients had a prolonged hospital stay. [557]

J. S. Al-Awfi (2020) stated one of the symptoms in COVID-19 patients - loss of taste - has been associated with zinc deficiency. It is undetermined whether the virus is causative or those patients had zinc deficiency pre COVID-19.

"Approximately 57.4% COVID-19 patients have low zinc serum levels which may indicate an advantage to administer zinc therapeutically to those patients." [558]

Magnesium

A study on athletes and sedentary subjects showed taking supplements for at least 1 month might increase testosterone in men and women. People who exercise regularly see a more significant increase in testosterone levels than those who are not active. [559]

Note, high intensity (weight) training is more effective to naturally boost testosterone than endurance training.

Magnesium-rich foods include whole grains and dark leafy greens. Zinc is also contained in dark greens, flax seeds, and pumpkin seeds.

'Magnesium may also protect against EMF radiation'. Magnesium is a key nutrient important for a variety of functions in the body, 'including EMF radiation protection.' That's because magnesium is involved in over 300 chemical processes in the body, and acts as a cofactor for several antioxidant enzymes. *"This suggests magnesium has the ability to help decrease oxidative stress due to sustained EMF exposure. Furthermore, magnesium acts as a natural calcium channel blocker."* [560]

Date palm pollen (DPP)

As alluded to above, exposure of mice to 50 Hz EMF caused abnormalities in sperm and a significant decrease in testosterone levels. Administration of DPP before exposure improved the sperm count, viability, motility and testosterone level in experimental groups and prevented the sperm abnormality induced by EMF. [561] After serum testosterone levels in rats were decrease by EMF exposure, the effects were alleviated by administration of 5mg/kg Rosmarinic acid. Using Rosmarinic acid as food additive was suggested to be efficient for supporting people living in EMF environmental pollution. [562]

Physical Exercise

In maximal and submaximal physical short- and long-term exercise (800-m running, climbing, 36-km cross-country skiing), it turned out that in highly endurance-trained subjects, there was an increase and in less well-trained subjects a decrease of serum testosterone for equal distances and intensities of exercise. [563]

So, get well trained on a healthy level, and again, high Intensity strength training has a more beneficial effect on testosterone than endurance training.

Summery nutrients

As we have seen, mobile EMF can cause not only deficiency in gonadal hormones, but can be accompanied with a **decrease of zinc levels in various organs.** [564]

To optimize your gonad hormones, secure the minimum intake of the following nutrients to correct possible deficiencies: **Magnesium, Selenium, Zinc, Vitamin C, D and E.** Ideally, this is achieved by natural organic foods. Alternatively, high quality supplements can be used, it is important to make sure to not surpass the Upper Limit (UL) values for each mineral or vitamin.

As an example, for magnesium, the Upper Limit is the same as the daily value or recommended daily intake, so in theory, you should get it just right. For doses above the UL, in case of acute deficiencies or medical reasons, ask your doctor. For general health, make sure to get at least the daily amount of the essential 13 vitamins and 10 minerals. For an easy preliminary solution, there are supplements available sold as all-in-one combined tablets or powder.

Nutrient	The Daily Value, as in food labels; it is mostly the same as the Recommended Dietary Allowance (RDA)	UL (Tolerable Upper Intake Levels, USA) for food and suppl. combined.	Ratio Safe UL/ Daily Value
Zinc	15 mg	40 mg	2.6x
Magnesium	400 mg	350 mg/400 mg (SUL)	**1x**
Selenium	70 mcg	400 mcg	5.7x
Vitamin C	60 mg	2000 mg	33x
Vitamin D	10 mcg (400 IU)	100 mcg	10x
Vitamin E (alpha-tocopherol)	20 (30 IU) mg	1000 mg	50x

Table 1 The Daily Value is what is on food labels; it is mostly the same as the Recommended Dietary Allowance (RDA) USA. - UL = Tolerable Upper Intake Level (UUSA); Ratio Save UL/Daily Value = (an adult can take this many times the Daily Value without exceeding the UL; for instance: an adult should not take more than 5.7 times the recommended daily amount of selenium; Data and complete table by C. Alan Titchenal, PhD, CNS. Originally published in: NASM Certified Personal Trainer Course Manual, 2004, pp. 632-633; Copyright ©: National Academy of Sports Medicine - www.nasm.org http://www.nutritionatc.hawaii.edu/UL.htm

Table 1 compares the typical levels of US recommended daily nutrient intake to the United States Tolerable Upper Intake Levels (UL). The Daily Value amounts, which are currently used as reference values on food and supplement labels, are similar to the RDA (Recommended Dietary Allowance) values, but differ in some cases. UL values are the amounts that are considered to be the maximum safe level of intake from food and supplements combined.

For Vitamin D: "The type of vitamin D [D2 or D3] you get is less important than getting the right dose and making sure your levels are in the right range to avoid deficiency. Most experts recommend 600 to 800 IUs of vitamin D per day (so at least twice the Daily Value). The amount of vitamin D in foods and supplements is usually given in terms of International Units, or IUs. [565]

Further foods that can optimize gonad hormone regulation. Here especially testosterone boosters for men: Fatty fish (Salmon, sardines), dark leafy greens, cacao products, avocado, eggs, berries, cherries, and pomegranate, Shellfish like oysters and clams, parsley. [566]

16.2. Steps to reduce EDC exposure

Here is a very short overview of the easiest and cheapest ways to reduce your EDC intake from everyday sources.

EDCs are everywhere. You can't avoid them altogether. But the most common sources are from things we willingly but into our body. Remember, powerful and well-informed people live on the same planet and in the same city as you. They breathe the same air and use the same tab water (although, they probably don't drink it unfiltered).

Here is a short summery of those precautions which are easiest and free to implement:

- no excessive alcohol consumption. Heavy drinking is usually considered more than 15 drinks a week for men or more than eight drinks a week for women. [567]

- don't put plastic containers in the microwave (don't eat microwaved food in the first place. It kills rats and cats fast,[568] it will probably kill you in time).

- eat as little as possible from plastic containers or plastic food packaging.

- eat as much organic as you can afford.

- cook fresh food, with natural ingredients. No junk food. If there is a commercial for the thing you are eating, it probably contains EDCs and other harmful chemicals.

- Avoid soy products and MSG (monosodium glutamate).

- use no pesticides or as little as possible in your garden, (esp. atrazine or roundup).

- cook on cast iron pans instead of Teflon (non-stick) pans.

- find EDC-free and aluminum-free sun screen (nanoparticle- free zinc oxide sunscreen is one alternative) or avoid sunscreen and excessive sun exposure, if possible, but get moderate and regular sun, of course.

- get informed about substitutes for pharmaceutical drugs with endocrine disrupting effects. The list is on p. 61.

16.3. Steps to reduce wireless/ EMF exposure

The same here: You can't avoid wireless/ EMF exposure, if you don't want to live in a Russian monastery at the end of the world (Oh wait, they have wireless internet too, now: 'Russian monastery goes global with wireless, 2015'). [569]
Again, well-informed and well-connected people live among us, too, possibly in the apartment next to you. The main exposure probably comes from your own devices. Twice the distance = 1/4 of the radiation exposure; four times the distance =1/16 of the radiation. (Distance and the Inverse Square Law). [570]
The main Swiss phone company Swisscom had announced in 2019, that 5G antennas will emit a radiation cone of under 15° directly onto the individual phone and the user, this is in theory good to prevent the rest of the surroundings being radiated unnecessarily, but it also means the radiation cone follows your phone and aims at it. Wireless radiation in populated areas can't be avoided altogether, but you can avoid dosing yourself unnecessarily with Smart TVs, wireless routers, your phone, tablet, microwave ovens, etc.
"Smart TVs constantly send signals to connect to the Wi-Fi router. As it continues to search for the available router, it emits radio frequency (RF) signals. The TV will constantly transmit these signals since Wi-Fi is a built-in feature and you can't switch it off." LCD, LED and Plasma TVs emit EMF radiation and UV radiation from all directions to a distance of up to 12 feet (4 meters). [571] Children are more susceptible.

Let's go through a few things you can do to prevent unnecessary EMF exposure. Starting with remedies that are free and easy to implement, moving down to more advanced and then to costly ones.
- First, get your phone away from your crouch and your brain. (Men and women). This is easy enough, you can do it right now while you're reading this, even though caring it in your back pocket or in a backpack is not safe but it is much better (For men, protect the hypothalamic-pituitary-testes regulatory axis that controls testosterone production).
- even better, keep your phone away from your body as much as possible, especially from your crotch, your brain, and even from your kidneys (middle back), where the adrenal glands are, which also produce small amounts of testosterone.

- if you put your phone on airplane mode, it will keep connecting to the net and might keep emitting EMFs all the same.
- use the phone on speaker mode.
- If you use headphones, get airtubes - anti-radiation- earphones, which have the wires and the speakers a few inches away from your ear and transmit the sound by air tubes to the ear piece (5 + USD).
- stay a few feet or as far as conveniently possible away from your internet router and the flat screen TV, wi-fi connecting devices like printers etc.
- Set your screens to Night Shift to reduce blue light permanently, if you have no ambitions in computer graphics. Your iPhone, iPad, MacBook and Windows 10 devices have a feature called Night Shift for changing the color temperature of the screen. Many Android devices also offer a built-in 'Blue Light' or 'Night Light' feature and a variety of third-party utility apps get the job done, too.
- turn off wi-fi, connect your laptop with an ethernet cable. (for a MacBook and most thin laptops you need an ethernet adapter, c. 30 USD).
- if you turn off the Wi-Fi button of your router, it keeps emitting EMFs anyways, you can test this by putting it in a Faraday cage or wrap it in a metal mesh, it will build up a strong static field around itself and start crackling immediately. Keep it in another room or on the other side of your room.
- In the same way, your laptop might keep emitting EMFs after you turn off the airport or wireless network.
- So, for a more advanced measure, you can remove the wireless transmitter from your laptop. Disclaimer: you might lose your warranty for the device! Plus, I cannot assure you for all types of laptops that your internet connection will still work smoothly. But I have successfully disconnected and removed the Wi-Fi AirPort Blue Tooth Card (according to instructions for replacing the card and insolated the ends of the internal antenna cables with heat resistant tape) on two generations of MacBook Air and MacBook Pro; they run without problems, including fast internet connection. The procedure takes 30 minutes.
- Kindly enquire where your roommates, on-floor neighbors have their routers or emitting devices.
- You can't tell them what to do, it is perfectly legal to run as many routers and computers as they like, you can however adapt your own settings, don't place your bed on the other side of a wall behind their main router.

- And then depending on your budget and situation, you can move to the country side, away from high voltage power lines, 5G towers and close next-door neighbors. Or even have an electronics-free bedroom.

For the next generation:
This is the most important message of this book. The hormonal and behavioral degradation we are witnessing is a multigenerational problem. In adults, hormone levels can be rebalanced, but with limitations. hormonal glands which are underdeveloped from birth or puberty cannot be fully developed in adult life.
As we have seen, the crucial time for a human's balance of sex hormones throughout life is in pregnancy, more specifically the 8th-12th week of gestation. The best thing you can do for the happiness and well-being for the future life of a boy or girl, is to let them develop in the womb without toxins, without endocrine disrupting chemicals and radiation.
-No smoking or drinking or junk food for the future father three months before conception. The same for the mother lasting throughout pregnancy, of course. And what's with these smoker couples where she quits and he keeps on smoking right next to her, anyways?
- Then, for the future mother, all of the above, but strictly, no compromises, no phone near the belly, no microwave, no ED chemicals. Just keep yourself together for at least 9 months. That is the best you can do for your child. The next best thing is to protect them from EDCs throughout childhood, especially during puberty.
You can forget putting aside money for a college education or extra expensive health care, if a child develops to its full potential, it will need neither to be happy and successful. (Savings will be devalued anyways in the Great Reset by inflation and government confiscation in the coming years).

Sane, healthy and competent men and women will be highly sought after for the rebuilding of civilization.

The End

Notes

1 forbes.com: You're Not the Man Your Father Was; Oct 2, 2017,11:23am EDT forbes forbes.com. 2017;   https://www.forbes.com/sites/neilhowe/2017/10/02/youre-not-the-man-your-father-was/?sh=4a85d1b28b7f

2 Kahl Kristie L 2020: Testosterone levels show steady decrease among young US men; July 3, 2020; Urology Times Journal, Vol 48 No 7, Volume 48, Issue 07

3 Sartorius, G., Spasevska, S., Idan, A., Turner, L., Forbes, E., Zamojska, A., Allan, C.A., Ly, L.P., Conway, A.J., McLachlan, R.I. and Handelsman, D.J. (2012), Serum testosterone, dihydrotestos-terone and estradiol concentrations in older men self-reporting very good health: the healthy man study. Clin Endocrinol, 77: 755-763. https://doi.org/10.1111/j.1365-2265.2012.04432.x

4 Hagai Levine, Niels Jørgensen, Anderson Martino-Andrade, Jaime Mendiola, Dan Weksler-Derri, Irina Mindlis, Rachel Pinotti, Shanna H Swan, Temporal trends in sperm count: a systematic review and meta-regression analysis, Human Reproduction Update, Volume 23, Issue 6, November-December 2017, Pages 646–659, https://doi.org/10.1093/humupd/dmx022

5 Swan, Shanna, PhD, with Stacey Colino 2021: *Count Down, How Our Modern World Is Threatening Sperm Counts, Altering Male and Female Reproductive Development, and Imperiling the Future of the Human Race*; Scribner, February 2021

6 Parmigiani, Stefano, et al 2003; Exposure To Very Low Doses Of Endocrine Disrupting Chemicals (Edcs) During Fetal Life Permanently Alters Brain Development And Behavior In Animals And Humans; Jour Society and Structures. April 2003, 293-308; The Science and Culture Series — Nuclear Strategy and Peace Technology pp. 293-308 (2003)

7 Pete Myers; Jul 26, 2017: Science: Are we in a male fertility death spiral?; Male sterility is a growing problem. Here's why you should be worried—and your kids should be terrified.

8 The Guardian: 28 Mar 2021, Shanna Swan: 'Most couples may have to use assisted reproduction by 2045, https://www.theguardian.com/society/2021/mar/28/shanna-swan-fertility-reproduction-count-down

9 Stevenson, Betsey: 2009: The Paradox of Declining Female Happiness; NBER Working Paper No. 14969; May 2009; JEL No. D6,I32,J1,J7,K1

10 Rolland, M. Le Moal J, et al 2013: Decline in semen concentration and morphology in a sample of 26 609 men close to general population between 1989 and 2005 in France, Human Reproduction, Volume 28, Issue 2, February 2013, Pages 462–470, https://doi.org/10.1093/humrep/des415

11 Zak, Paul. Testosterone Administration Induces A Red Shift in Democrats. Ann Arbor, MI: Inter-university Consortium for Political and Social Research [distributor], 2021-11-24. https://doi.org/10.3886/E155441V1   https://www.openicpsr.org/openicpsr/project/155441/version/V1/view

12 Government funded feminists suggest banning heterosexual relationships
February 8, 2020, Simon Black, S; https://www.sgtreport.com/2020/02/government-funded-feminists-suggest-banning-heterosexual-relationships/

13 Sax, Leonard (August 2002). "How common is intersex? a response to Anne Fausto-Sterling". Journal of Sex Research. 39 (3): 174–178. doi:10.1080/00224490209552139. ISSN 0022-4499. PMID 12476264. S2CID 33795209. Archived from the original on 24 April 2021. Alt URL

14 California Decriminalized Shoplifting. The Results Were Completely Predictable.
BY RICK MORAN JUL 22, 2021; https://pjmedia.com/news-and-politics/rick-moran/2021/07/22/newsom-signs-law-designed-to-battle-organized-shoplifting-rings-n1463974

15 Geelmuyden, Niels Christian, 2019: Spermageddon Cappelen Damm 2019; Original title: ISBN: 9788202616014

16 Lead and Lead Poisoning from Antiquity to Modern Times; The Ohio Journal of Science. v88, n3 (June, 1988), 78-84; https://kb.osu.edu/handle/1811/23252

17 Zauner Gerhild, Girardi Guillermina; Potential causes of male and female infertility in Qatar; Journal of Reproductive Immunology; Volume 141; 2020; 103173; ISSN 0165-0378, https://doi.org/10.1016/j.jri.2020.103173.

18 WEIKART, RICHARD 1994: MARX, ENGELS, AND THE ABOLITION OF THE FAMILY History of European Ideas; Vol. 18, No. 5, pp. 657-672, 1994
0191-6599 (93) E0194-6 _ . Copyright c 1994 Elseyier Science Ltd Printed in Great Britain.

[19] Peer-Reviewed Publication; WASHINGTON UNIVERSITY SCHOOL OF MEDICINE NEWS RELEASE 25-MAY-2021; https://www.eurekalert.org/news-releases/608834

[20] Ibrahim, R., Ali, A., Khamis, N., Mohammed, H. (2019). Effect Of Exposure To Wi-Fi Router Radiation On The Lung Of Adult Male Albino Rats: Histological And Immunohistochemical Study. Egyptian Journal of Histology, 42(4), 1059-1069. doi: 10.21608/ejh.2019.7317.1070

[21] Rohr, Uwe D; 2002: The impact of testosterone imbalance on depression and women's health,; Maturitas,; Volume 41, Supplement 1,; 2002,; Pages 25-46,; ISSN 0378-5122,; https://doi.org/10.1016/S0378-5122(02)00013-0.

[22] Hammes , Stephen R; Levin, Ellis R. 2019: Impact of estrogens in males and androgens in females; Published May 1, 2019 ; J Clin Invest. 2019;129(5):1818-1826. https://doi.org/10.1172/JCI125755.

[23] Meo, S.A. et al (2010): Effects of mobile phone radiation on serum testosterone in Wistar albino rats. Saudi medical journal. 31. 869-73. https://www.wavewallcases.com/wp-content/uploads/2018/01/Effects_of_Mobile_Phone_Radiation_on_Serum_Testosterone.pdf

[24] Swiss Re SONAR Emerging risk insights; 2013; Sandra Burmeier, Reto Schneider, Philippe Brahin; ; https://www.jrseco.com/wp-content/uploads/electromagnetic_radiation_risk_assessment_swiss_re.pdf

[25] Swiss Re SONAR Emerging risk insights; 2013; Sandra Burmeier, Reto Schneider, Philippe Brahin; ; https://www.jrseco.com/wp-content/uploads/electromagnetic_radiation_risk_assessment_swiss_re.pdf

[26] Wikipedia; Gonad: updated 5 – 8- 2021; https://en.wikipedia.org/wiki/Gonad

[27] Wikipedia: Testosterone; up dated 5-4-2021

[28] Robert M. Sargis MD, PhD; Testes secrete the male hormone testosterone; 2021, Remedy Health Media; https://www.endocrineweb.com/endocrinology/overview-testes

[29] Ana Marcella Rivas, Zachary Mulkey, Joaquin Lado-Abeal & Shannon Yarbrough (2014) Diagnosing and Managing Low Serum Testosterone, Baylor University Medical Center Proceedings, 27:4, 321-324, DOI: 10.1080/08998280.2014.11929145

[30] Steinberger E, Smith KD, Tcholakian RK, Rodriguez-Rigau LJ. Testosterone levels in female partners of infertile couples. Relationship between androgen levels in the woman, the male factor, and the incidence of pregnancy. Am J Obstet Gynecol. 1979 Jan 15;133(2):133-8. doi: 10.1016/0002-9378(79)90463-0. PMID: 420268.

[31] Carcaillon L, Blanco C, Alonso-Bouzón C, Alfaro-Acha A, Garcia-García F-J, Rodriguez-Mañas L (2012) Sex Differences in the Association between Serum Levels of Testosterone and Frailty in an Elderly Population: The Toledo Study for Healthy Aging. PLoS ONE 7(3): e32401. https://doi.org/10.1371/journal.pone.0032401

[32] theguardian.com; Sarah Ditum; Wed 18 Jan 2017; Testosterone Rex by Cordelia Fine review – the question of men's and women's brains; https://www.theguardian.com/books/2017/jan/18/testosterone-rex-review-cordelia-fine

[33] Wikipedia: Estradiol; 6-14-2021; https://en.wikipedia.org/wiki/Estradiol

[34] Hammond J, Le Q, Goodyer C, Gelfand M, Trifiro M, LeBlanc A. Testosterone-mediated neuroprotection through the androgen receptor in human primary neurons. J Neurochem. 2001 Jun;77(5):1319-26. doi: 10.1046/j.1471-4159.2001.00345.x. PMID: 11389183.

[35] Frontiers. (2019, February 11). Oral contraceptives could impair women's recognition of complex emotions: Healthy women who use birth control pills are poorer judges of subtle facial expressions than non-users, according to new research. ScienceDaily. Retrieved July 20, 2022 from www.sciencedaily.com/releases/2019/02/190211083216.htm

[36] Scheele D, Plota J, Stoffel-Wagner B, Maier W, Hurlemann R. Hormonal contraceptives suppress oxytocin-induced brain reward responses to the partner's face. Soc Cogn Affect Neurosci. 2016 May;11(5):767-74. doi: 10.1093/scan/nsv157. Epub 2015 Dec 31. PMID: 26722017; PMCID: PMC4847696.

[37] Scientific America: Birth Control Pills Affect Women's Taste in Men; How synthetic hormones change desire in women—and their choice in a mate; By Melinda Wenner on December 1, 2008; https://www.scientificamerican.com/article/birth-control-pills-affect-womens-taste/

[38] The Truth About Birth Control Pills and Hormones; November 30, 2017; https://www.amenclinics.com/blog/the-truth-about-birth-control-pills-and-hormones/

[39] Rasmark Roepke E, Matthiesen L, Rylance R, Christiansen OB. Is the incidence of recurrent pregnancy loss increasing? A retrospective register-based study in Sweden. Acta Obstet Gynecol Scand. 2017 Nov;96(11):1365-1372. doi: 10.1111/aogs.13210. Epub 2017 Sep 25. PMID: 28832895.

[40] Covid Vaccines and Infertility; by KanekoaTheGreat; Jun 27 2022; https://abruptearthchanges.com/2022/08/03/covid-vaccines-and-infertility/

[41] 11 Symptoms of Low Estrogen and What You Can Do; DR: Uzzi Reiss MD; April 20, 2020; https://uzzireissmd.com/11-symptoms-of-low-estrogen-and-what-you-can-do/

[42] Taylor Beck; Harvard Correspondent; Estrogen and female anxiety; August 9, 2012; https://news.harvard.edu/gazette/story/2012/08/estrogen-and-female-anxiety/

[43] Riecher-Rössler, A. 2011: The estrogen hypothesis of schizophrenia; University of Basel, Switzerland: ttps://edoc.unibas.ch › Riecher-Rössler_Ch_11_fi...

[44] Kulkarni J, de Castella A, Fitzgerald PB, et al.2008: Estrogen in Severe Mental Illness: A Potential New Treatment Approach; Arch Gen Psychiatry. 2008;65(8):955–960. doi:10.1001/archpsyc.65.8.955

[45] Birge, Stanley J.1997: The role of estrogen in the treatment of Alzheimer's disease
Neurology May 1997, 48 (5 Suppl 7) 36S-41S; DOI: 10.1212/WNL.48.5_Suppl_7.36S

[46] Ting Ding, Jinjin Zhang, Tian Wang, et al 2020: A Multi-hospital Study in Wuhan, China: Protective Effects of Non-menopause and Female Hormones on SARS-CoV-2 infection
medRxiv 2020.03.26.20043943; doi: https://doi.org/10.1101/2020.03.26.20043943
https://www.medrxiv.org/content/10.1101/2020.03.26.20043943v1.full.pdf

[47] newscientist.com; 2 November 2005; By Gaia Vince: Hormone levels predict attractiveness of women; https://www.newscientist.com/article/dn8251-hormone-levels-predict-attractiveness-of-women/

[48] James R. Roney, Zachary L. Simmons 2008: Women's estradiol predicts preference for facial cues of men's testosterone; Hormones and Behavior; Volume 53, Issue 1, 2008; Pages 14-19, ISSN 0018-506X,: https://doi.org/10.1016/j.yhbeh.2007.09.008.

[49] Madison, G., Aasa, U., Wallert, J., & Woodley, M. A. (2014). Feminist activist women are masculinized in terms of digit-ratio and social dominance: a possible explanation for the feminist paradox. Frontiers in psychology, 5, 1011. https://doi.org/10.3389/fpsyg.2014.01011

[50] Stefanick Marcia L., PhD; 2005; Estrogens and progestins: background and history, trends in use, and guidelines and regimens approved by the US Food and Drug Administration; American Journal of Medicine; VOLUME 118, ISSUE 12, SUPPLEMENT 2, 64-73, DECEMBER 19, 2005 DOI:https://doi.org/10.1016/j.amjmed.2005.09.059

[51] Collaborative Group on Hormonal Factors in Breast Cancer (2019). Type and timing of menopausal hormone therapy and breast cancer risk: individual participant meta-analysis of the worldwide epidemiological evidence. Lancet (London, England), 394(10204), 1159–1168. https://doi.org/10.1016/S0140-6736(19)31709-X

[52] Yüksel M, Nazıroğlu M, Özkaya MO; 2016: Long-term exposure to electromagnetic radiation from mobile phones and Wi-Fi devices decreases plasma prolactin, progesterone, and estrogen levels but increases uterine oxidative stress in pregnant rats and their offspring. Endocrine. 2016 May;52(2):352-62. doi: 10.1007/s12020-015-0795-3. Epub 2015 Nov 14. PMID: 26578367.

[53] Mahmoud, E., Diab, A., Ibrahim, M., Bedeer, S. (2020). Effect Of Exposure To Electromagnetic Radiation On Sex Steroids And Systemic & Local Uterine Redox Status During Early And Late Pregnancy In Rats. Zagazig University Medical Journal, 26(1), 186-195. doi: 10.21608/zumj.2019.12044.1206

[54] Vahid, H. & Khatereh, D. & Esmaeal, F. & Maryam, N. & Mohammad, F.. (2012). The effects of mobile phone waves on the reproductive physiology in adult female rats. Advances in Environmental Biology. 6. 2735-2741.

[55] Washington Post; Too much happiness can make you unhappy, studies show; Marta Zaraska April 2, 2012; https://www.washingtonpost.com/national/health-science/too-much-happiness-can-make-you-unhappy-studies-show/2012/04/02/gIQACELLrS_story.html

[56] Estrogen and Women's Emotions; By Matthew Hoffman, MD; Medically Reviewed by Nivin Todd, MD on August 01, 2021; https://www.webmd.com/women/guide/estrogen-and-womens-emotions

[57] Hadine Joffe, Lee S. Cohen, Estrogen, serotonin, and mood disturbance: where is the therapeutic bridge?, Biological Psychiatry, Volume 44, Issue 9, 1998, Pages 798-811,, ISSN 0006-3223,, https://doi.org/10.1016/S0006-3223(98)00169-3.

[58] Andrée-Anne Hudon Thibeault, J. Thomas Sanderson, Cathy Vaillancourt,; Serotonin-estrogen interactions: What can we learn from pregnancy?,; Biochimie,; Volume 161,; 2019, Pages 88-108,; ISSN 0300-9084,; https://doi.org/10.1016/j.biochi.2019.03.023.
(https://www.sciencedirect.com/science/article/pii/S0300908419301002)

[59] Men's T Clinic® Blog Testosterone and Depression: What's the Connection?; https://www.menstclinic.com/blog/testosterone-and-depression-whats-the-connection;

[60] Araújo GCSd, Mourão NT, Pinheiro IN, Xavier AR, Gameiro VS (2015): Lead Toxicity Risks in Gunshot Victims. PLoS ONE 10(10): e0140220. https://doi.org/10.1371/journal.pone.0140220
https://journals.plos.org/plosone/article?id=10.1371/journal.pone.01402200

[61] Bouchard, M. F., Bellinger, D. C., Weuve, J., Matthews-Bellinger, J., Gilman, S. E., Wright, R. O., Schwartz, J., & Weisskopf, M. G. (2009). Blood lead levels and major depressive disorder, panic disorder, and generalized anxiety disorder in US young adults. Archives of general psychiatry, 66(12), 1313–1319. https://doi.org/10.1001/archgenpsychiatry.2009.164

[62] PEW RESEARCH CENTER; NOVEMBER 18, 2021; What Makes Life Meaningful? Views From 17 Advanced Economies; Family is preeminent for most publics but work, material well-being and health also play a key role; BY LAURA SILVER; https://www.pewresearch.org/global/2021/11/18/what-makes-life-meaningful-views-from-17-advanced-economies/

[63] Business Insider: These Maps Reveal What People Around The World Really Care About Christina Sterbenz Jul 25, 2014, https://www.businessinsider.com/what-do-people-find-important-in-life-2014-7?r=US&IR=T

[64] Loma Linda University Center for Fertility & IVF; 2015-2021; Low Testosterone & Fertility https://lomalindafertility.com/infertility/men/low-testosterone/

[65] Michigan Medicine - University of Michigan. (2018, April 19). Low total testosterone in men widespread, linked to chronic disease. ScienceDaily. Retrieved September 1, 2021 from www.sciencedaily.com/releases/2018/04/180419100119.htm

[66] Chodick, G., Epstein, S. & Shalev, V. Secular trends in testosterone- findings from a large state-mandate care provider. Reprod Biol Endocrinol 18, 19 (2020). https://doi.org/10.1186/s12958-020-00575-2

[67] Hagai Levine, Niels Jørgensen, Anderson Martino-Andrade, Jaime Mendiola, Dan Weksler-Derri, Irina Mindlis, Rachel Pinotti, Shanna H Swan, Temporal trends in sperm count: a systematic review and meta-regression analysis, Human Reproduction Update, Volume 23, Issue 6, November-December 2017, Pages 646–659, https://doi.org/10.1093/humupd/dmx022

[68] Swan, Shanna, PhD, with Stacey Colino 2021: *Count Down, How Our Modern World Is Threatening Sperm Counts, Altering Male and Female Reproductive Development, and Imperiling the Future of the Human Race*; Scribner, February 2021

[69] Travison, Thomas G, Andre B. Araujo, Amy B. O'Donnell, Varant Kupelian, John B. McKinlay 2007: A Population-Level Decline in Serum Testosterone Levels in American Men, The Journal of Clinical Endocrinology & Metabolism, Volume 92, Issue 1, January 2007, Pages 196–202, https://doi.org/10.1210/jc.2006-1375

[70] Perheentupa, A., Mäkinen, J., Laatikainen, T., Vierula, M., Skakkebaek, N. E., Andersson, A., & Toppari, J. (2013). A cohort effect on serum testosterone levels in Finnish men, European Journal of Endocrinology, 168(2), 227-233. Retrieved Jul 7, 2021, from https://eje.bioscientifica.com/view/journals/eje/168/2/227.xml

[71] Andersen, Dorthe Nørgaard; et al 2012: Exposure of pregnant consumers to suspected endocrine disruptors; Danish Environmental Protection Agency; Survey of chemical substances in consumer products no. 117; ISBN no.978-87-92903-02-0

[72] Lokeshwar SD, Patel P, Fantus RJ, Halpern J, Chang C, Kargi AY, Ramasamy R. Decline in Serum Testosterone Levels Among Adolescent and Young Adult Men in the USA. Eur Urol Focus. 2020 Feb 18:S2405-4569(20)30062-6. doi: 10.1016/j.euf.2020.02.006. Epub ahead of print. PMID: 32081788.

[73] Kahl, Kristie L .2020: Testosterone levels show steady decrease among young US men; July 3, 2020; Urology Times Journal, Vol 48 No 7, Volume 48, Issue 07 https://www.urologytimes.com/view/testosterone-levels-show-steady-decrease-among-young-us-men

[74] Article By: Dr. Laurie Blanscet, An Optimal You physician | Aug 03, 2015 What is a normal Testosterone level for a man? https://www.anoptimalyou.com/what-is-a-normal-testosterone-level-for-a-man/

[75] WSJ: Why Women Don't Want Macho Men; By Jena Pincott; Updated March 27, 2010 https://www.wsj.com/articles/SB10001424052748704100604575145810050665030

[76] Sundqvist, C., Lukola, A., & Valtonen, M. (1984). Relationship between serum testosterone concentrations and fertility in male mink (Mustela vison), Reproduction, 70(2), 409-412. Retrieved Jul 9, 2021, from https://rep.bioscientifica.com/view/journals/rep/70/2/jrf_70_2_007.xml

[77] GBD 2017 Population and Fertility Collaborators. Population and fertility by age and sex for 195 countries and territories, 1950-2017: a systematic analysis for the Global Burden of Disease Study 2017. Lancet. 2018 Nov 10;392(10159):1995-2051. doi: 10.1016/S0140-6736(18)32278-5. Epub 2018 Nov 8. Erratum in: Lancet. 2019 Jun 22;393(10190):e44. PMID: 30496106; PMCID: PMC6227915.

[78] Hagai Levine, Niels Jørgensen, Anderson Martino-Andrade, Jaime Mendiola, Dan Weksler-Derri, Irina Mindlis, Rachel Pinotti, Shanna H Swan, Temporal trends in sperm count: a systematic review and meta-regression analysis, Human Reproduction Update, Volume 23, Issue 6, November-December 2017, Pages 646–659, https://doi.org/10.1093/humupd/dmx022

[79] Cooper TG, Noonan E, von Eckardstein S, Auger J, Baker HW, Behre HM, Haugen TB, Kruger T, Wang C, Mbizvo MT, Vogelsong KM (May–Jun 2010). "World Health Organization reference values for human semen characteristics" (PDF). Human Reproduction Update. 16 (3): 231–45. doi:10.1093/humupd/dmp048. PMID 19934213.

[80] "Understanding Semen Analysis". Stonybrook, State University of New York. 1999. Archived from the original on October 17, 2007. Retrieved 2007-08-05.

[81] S H Swan, E P Elkin, and L Fenste2000: The question of declining sperm density revisited: an analysis of 101 studies published 1934-1996.
Environmental Health Perspectives 108:10 CID: https://doi.org/10.1289/ehp.00108961

[82] ,Men Have a Biological Clock, too. This Is the Age That Heightens High-Risk Pregnancies, Birth Defects'; Michael Charboneau; Men's journal; https://www.mensjournal.com/health-fitness/older-fathers-health-risks-study-2019/

[83] Dyer O. (2003). Babies born after fertility treatment run increased risk of genetic disorder. BMJ : British Medical Journal, 326(7382), 184.

[84] Alukal, J. P., & Lamb, D. J. (2008). Intracytoplasmic sperm injection (ICSI)--what are the risks?. The Urologic clinics of North America, 35(2), 277–x. https://doi.org/10.1016/j.ucl.2008.01.004

[85] Dyer O. (2003). Babies born after fertility treatment run increased risk of genetic disorder. BMJ : British Medical Journal, 326(7382), 184.

[86] Wen SW, Miao Q, Taljaard M, et al. Associations of Assisted Reproductive Technology and Twin Pregnancy With Risk of Congenital Heart Defects. JAMA Pediatr. 2020;174(5):446–454. doi:10.1001/jamapediatrics.2019.6096

[87] UCLA heath; Lorraine Kelley-Quon, 2007: In Vitro Fertilization Linked to Increased Risk of Birth Defects; https://www.uclahealth.org/u-magazine/in-vitro-fertilization-linked-to-increased-risk-of-birth-defects

[88] Luke B, Brown MB, Nichols HB, et al. Assessment of Birth Defects and Cancer Risk in Children Conceived via In Vitro Fertilization in the US. JAMA Netw Open. 2020;3(10):e2022927. doi:10.1001/jamanetworkopen.2020.22927

[89] The macho sperm myth; Robert D Martin https://aeon.co/essays/the-idea-that-sperm-race-to-the-egg-is-just-another-macho-myth;

[90] Luke B, Brown MB, Nichols HB, et al. Assessment of Birth Defects and Cancer Risk in Children Conceived via In Vitro Fertilization in the US. JAMA Netw Open. 2020;3(10):e2022927. doi:10.1001/jamanetworkopen.2020.22927

[91] Lu, Y. H., Wang, N., & Jin, F. (2013). Long-term follow-up of children conceived through assisted reproductive technology. Journal of Zhejiang University. Science. B, 14(5), 359–371. https://doi.org/10.1631/jzus.B1200348

[92] Dobler, Sacha, 2017: Black Death and Abrupt Earth Changes in the 14th century https://abruptearthchanges.files.wordpress.com/2018/02/01-02-2018-updated-black-death-and-abrupt-earth-changes.pdf

[93] Peter Beaumont and Amanda Holpuch; How The Handmaid's Tale dressed protests across the world; Fri 3 Aug 2018 05.00 BST; https://www.theguardian.com/world/2018/aug/03/how-the-handmaids-tale-dressed-protests-across-the-world

[94] Ana Marcella Rivas, Zachary Mulkey, Joaquin Lado-Abeal & Shannon Yarbrough (2014) Diagnosing and Managing Low Serum Testosterone, Baylor University Medical Center Proceedings, 27:4, 321-324, DOI: 10.1080/08998280.2014.11929145

[95] What is Low Testosterone? Urology Care Foundation; ©2021; https://www.urology-health.org/urology-a-z/l/low-testosterone

[96] Sartorius, G., Spasevska, S., Idan, A., Turner, L., Forbes, E., Zamojska, A., Allan, C.A., Ly, L.P., Conway, A.J., McLachlan, R.I. and Handelsman, D.J. (2012), Serum testosterone, dihydrotestosterone and estradiol concentrations in older men self-reporting very good health: the healthy man study. Clin Endocrinol, 77: 755-763. https://doi.org/10.1111/j.1365-2265.2012.04432.x

[97] The Endocrine Society. (2011, June 7). Older age does not cause testosterone levels to decline in healthy men. ScienceDaily. Retrieved July 7, 2021 from www.sciencedaily.com/releases/2011/06/110607121129.htm

[98] Endocrine Society.2012: "Declining testosterone levels in men not part of normal aging." ScienceDaily. ScienceDaily, 23 June 2012. <www.sciencedaily.com/releases/2012/06/120623144944.htm>.

[99] Dabbs, James M. Jr., PhD; Hargrove, Marian F. MS Age, Testosterone, and Behavior Among Female Prison Inmates, Psychosomatic Medicine: September/October 1997 - Volume 59 - Issue 5 - p 477-480

[100] University of Zurich. (2009, December 9). Testosterone does not induce aggression, study shows. ScienceDaily. Retrieved July 4, 2021 from www.sciencedaily.com/releases/2009/12/091208132241.htm

[101] Eisenegger, C., Naef, M., Snozzi, R. et a 2010: Prejudice and truth about the effect of testosterone on human bargaining behaviour. Nature 463, 356–359 (2010). https://doi.org/10.1038/nature08711

[102] The New York Times: Does Castration Stop Sex Crimes?
By Sandra G. Boodman; March 17, 1992; https://www.washingtonpost.com/archive/lifestyle/wellness/1992/03/17/does-castration-stop-sex-crimes/34bf63ee-840c-41e4-9c5f-5ac1bcf95b15/

[103] Simpson, K. (2020). The Role of Testosterone in Aggression. McGill Journal of Medicine, 6(1). https://doi.org/10.26443/mjm.v6i1.559

[104] Cueva, Carlos et al 2017: Testosterone administration does not affect men's rejections of low ultimatum game offers or aggressive mood; Hormones and Behavior; Volume 87, 2017; Pages 1-7; ISSN 0018-506X; https://doi.org/10.1016/j.yhbeh.2016.09.012

[105] Inge Volman, Ivan Toni, Lennart Verhagen, Karin Roelofs, Endogenous Testosterone Modulates Prefrontal–Amygdala Connectivity during Social Emotional Behavior, Cerebral Cortex, Volume 21, Issue 10, October 2011, Pages 2282–2290, https://doi.org/10.1093/cercor/bhr001

[106] George MJ. 1997: Into the Eye of the Medusa: Beyond Testosterone, Men, and Violence. The Journal of Men's Studies. 1997;5(4):295-313. doi:10.1177/106082659700500403

[107] Duca, Y., Aversa, A., Condorelli, R. A., Calogero, A. E., & La Vignera, S. (2019). Substance Abuse and Male Hypogonadism. Journal of clinical medicine, 8(5), 732. https://doi.org/10.3390/jcm8050732

[108] Jessica Bursztynsky; 2018-07-20; Large scale study links status and testosterone Psychologist: Link differs for men and women; College of Liberal Arts & Sciences; https://las.illinois.edu/news/2018-07-20/large-scale-study-links-status-and-testosterone

[109] TED talk; The surprising science of alpha males; Frans de Waal; 09.07.2018; https://www.youtube.com/watch?v=BPsSKKL8N0s

[110] Mazur, Allan & Booth, Alan (1997 in press). Testosterone and Dominance in Men. Behavioural and Brain Sciences. : Cambridge University Press). http://cogprints.org/663/

[111] Logan, Cheryl A, ; Wingfield, John C, 1990: Autumnal territorial aggression is independent of plasma testosterone in mockingbirds,; Hormones and Behavior, Volume 24, Issue 4, 1990, Pages 568-581, ISSN 0018-506X, https://doi.org/10.1016/0018-506X(90)90042-V.

[112] Duke University. (2009, October 21). Presidential Election Outcome Changed Voters' Testosterone. ScienceDaily. Retrieved July 12, 2022 from www.sciencedaily.com/releases/2009/10/091020181257.htm

[113] Colleen Williams and Jenni Glenn Gingery 2015: Most Men with Borderline Testosterone Levels May Have Depression; Endocrine Society: March 06, 2015 https://www.endocrine.org/news-and-advocacy/news-room/2015/most-men-with-borderline-testosterone-levels-may-have-depression

[114] Aydoganet, Umit et al 2012: Increased frequency of anxiety, depression, quality of life and sexual life in young hypogonadotropic hypogonadal males and impacts of testosterone replacement therapy on these conditions; Endocrine Journal; 2012 Volume 59 Issue 12 Pages 1099-1105; https://doi.org/10.1507/endocrj.EJ12-0134

[115] Low Testosterone – Could Your Cell Phone or Laptop Be to Blame?; ;Dr. Friedman's Health Blog; https://www.doctordavidfriedman.com/blog/low-testosterone-could-your-cell-phone-or-laptop-be-to-blame-1

[116] Colleen Williams and Jenni Glenn Gingery 2015: Most Men with Borderline Testosterone Levels May Have Depression; Endocrine Society: March 06, 2015 https://www.endocrine.org/news-and-advocacy/news-room/2015/most-men-with-borderline-testosterone-levels-may-have-depression

[117] Fui, M. N., Dupuis, P., & Grossmann, M. (2014). Lowered testosterone in male obesity: mechanisms, morbidity and management. Asian journal of andrology, 16(2), 223–231. https://doi.org/10.4103/1008-682X.122365

[118] Booth, A., Johnson, D., & Granger, D. (1999). Testosterone and Men's Depression: The Role of Social Behavior. Journal of Health and Social Behavior, 40(2), 130-140. doi:10.2307/2676369

[119] Zitzmann, Michael, 2020: Testosterone, mood, behaviour and quality of life; Andorlogy; Volume 8, Issue 6; Special Issue on: Late onset Hypogonadism; November 2020 Pages 1598-1605; First published: 13 July 2020; https://doi.org/10.1111/andr.12867

[120] Cornell, Robert, MD, PA; How Low Testosterone Affects Your Mental Health; https://www.urosurgeryhouston.com/blog/how-low-testosterone-affects-your-mental-health

[121] Tsujimura A. (2013). The Relationship between Testosterone Deficiency and Men's Health. The world journal of men's health, 31(2), 126–135. https://doi.org/10.5534/wjmh.2013.31.2.126

[122] Can prescription medications affect testosterone levels?; Reviewed by the medical professionals of the ISSM's Communication Committee; International Society of Sexual Medicine; https://www.issm.info/sexual-health-qa/can-prescription-medications-affect-testosterone-levels/

[123] Bennett A. E. 1990: Adrenocortical function, social rank, and personality among wild baboons. Award paper. Sapolsky RM; Biol Psychiatry. 1990 Nov 15; 28(10):862-78.

[124] medium.com: Good posture and testosterone; Good Posture; Nov 14, 2017; https://medium.com/@goodposturecom/good-posture-and-testosterone-8e412abda2e5

[125] 12 Signs of Low Testosterone; Medically reviewed by Alana Biggers, M.D., MPH — Written by Ryan Wallace — Updated on April 25, 2019
https://www.healthline.com/health/low-testosterone/warning-signs#_noHeaderPrefixedContent

[126] Hahn, Andreas, et al 2016: Testosterone Affects Language Areas of the Adult Human Brain; Human Brain Mapping 37:1738–1748 (2016); https://www.ncbi.nlm.nih.gov/pmc/articles/PMC4949561/pdf/HBM-37-1738.pdf

[127] Hammond J, Le Q, Goodyer C, Gelfand M, Trifiro M, LeBlanc A. Testosterone-mediated neuroprotection through the androgen receptor in human primary neurons. J Neurochem. 2001 Jun;77(5):1319-26. PubMed.

[128] Beauchet Olivier, 2006: Testosterone and cognitive function: current clinical evidence of a relationship in European Journal of Endocrinology; Volume 155: Issue 6; Pp.773–781 DOI: https://doi.org/10.1530/eje.1.02306

[129] What is Low Testosterone? Urology Care Foundation; ©2021; https://www.urology-health.org/urology-a-z/l/low-testosterone

[130] Tsujimura A. (2013). The Relationship between Testosterone Deficiency and Men's Health. The world journal of men's health, 31(2), 126–135. https://doi.org/10.5534/wjmh.2013.31.2.126

[131] Cherrier MM, Matsumoto AM, Amory JK, et al 2007: Characterization of verbal and spatial memory changes from moderate to supraphysiological increases in serum testosterone in healthy older men. Psychoneuroendocrinology. 2007 Jan;32(1):72-79. DOI: 10.1016/j.psyneuen.2006.10.008

[132] Falter, C.M, Arroyo, M., Davis, G.J 2006: Testosterone: Activation or organization of spatial cognition?,; Biological Psychology,; Volume 73, Issue 2; 2006, Pages 132-140,; ISSN 0301-0511,; https://doi.org/10.1016/j.biopsycho.2006.01.011.

[133] Üner Tan & Meliha Tan; The Curvelinear Correlations Between the Total Testosterone Levels and Fluid Intelligence in Men and Women; International Journal of Neuroscience
Volume 94, 1998 - Issue 1-2

[134] Low Testosterone – Could Your Cell Phone or Laptop Be to Blame?; ;Dr. Friedman's Health Blog; https://www.doctordavidfriedman.com/blog/low-testosterone-could-your-cell-phone-or-laptop-be-to-blame-1

[135] Newhouse, Paul et al 2010: Estrogen Treatment Impairs Cognitive Performance following Psychosocial Stress and Monoamine Depletion in Postmenopausal Women;
July 2010; Menopause (New York, N.Y.) 17(4):860-73; DOI:10.1097/gme.0b013e3181e15df4

[136] Tuiten A, Van Honk J, Koppeschaar H, Bernaards C, Thijssen J, Verbaten R. Time Course of Effects of Testosterone Administration on Sexual Arousal in Women. Arch Gen Psychiatry. 2000;57(2):149–153. doi:10.1001/archpsyc.57.2.149

[137] Cleveland Clinic; https://my.clevelandclinic.org/health/articles/22572-serotonin

[138] American Psychological Association; By the numbers: Antidepressant use on the rise; By Lea Winerman; November 2017, Vol 48, No. 10; https://www.apa.org/monitor/2017/11/numbers

[139] NIDA. 2021, April 13. What are MDMA's effects on the brain?. Retrieved from https://nida.nih.gov/publications/research-reports/mdma-ecstasy-abuse/what-are-mdmas-effects-on-brain on 2022, August 23

[140] Mustafa NS, Bakar NHA, Mohamad N, Adnan LHM, Fauzi NFAM, Thoarlim A, Omar SHS, Hamzah MS, Yusoff Z, Jufri M, Ahmad R. MDMA and the Brain: A Short Review on the Role of Neurotransmitters in Neurotoxicity. Basic Clin Neurosci. 2020 Jul-Aug;11(4):381-388. doi: 10.32598/bcn.9.10.485. Epub 2020 Jul 1. PMID: 33613876; PMCID: PMC7878040.

[141] US Pharmacist; Drug-Induced Serotonin Syndrome; Charles H. Brown, MS Pharm, RPh, CACP; Us pharmacist; NOVEMBER 17, 2010; https://www.uspharmacist.com/article/drug-induced-serotonin-syndrome

[142] Krysiak R, Okopien B. Potentiation of Endocrine Adverse Effects of Lithium by Enalapril and Verapamil. West Indian Med J. 2014 Dec;63(7):803-6. doi: 10.7727/wimj.2013.192. Epub 2014 Aug 29. PMID: 25867572; PMCID: PMC4668978.

[143] Jared Ng, Manne Sjöstrand & Nir Eyal, 2011: Adding Lithium to Drinking Water for Suicide Prevention—The Ethics; Public Health Ethics 12 (3):274-286 (2019); DOI 10.1093/phe/phz002

[144] The conversation: How testosterone and oxytocin hormones interact in male work and parenting effort; Adrian Jaeggi; March 20, 2015 8.43pm GMT •Updated: June 12, 2018 ; https://theconversation.com/how-testosterone-and-oxytocin-hormones-interact-in-male-work-and-parenting-effort-38953

[145] Aydoganet, Umit et al 2012: Increased frequency of anxiety, depression, quality of life and sexual life in young hypogonadotropic hypogonadal males and impacts of testosterone replacement therapy on these conditions; Endocrine Journal; 2012 Volume 59 Issue 12 Pages 1099-1105; https://doi.org/10.1507/endocrj.EJ12-0134

[146] Zarrouf, Fahd Aziz MD*; Artz, Steven MD†; Griffith, James MD†; Sirbu, Cristian MD, PhD‡; Kommor, Martin MD† Testosterone and Depression, Journal of Psychiatric Practice: July 2009 - Volume 15 - Issue 4 - p 289-305 doi: 10.1097/01.pra.0000358315.88931.fc

[147] CATIE Canada's source for HIV and Hepatitis b information; https://www.catie.ca/a-practical-guide-to-a-healthy-body-for-people-living-with-hiv/hormone-changes

[148] Kassotis, C. D., Vandenberg, L. N., Demeneix, B. A., Porta, M., Slama, R., & Trasande, L. (2020). Endocrine-disrupting chemicals: economic, regulatory, and policy implications. The lancet. Diabetes & endocrinology, 8(8), 719–730. https://doi.org/10.1016/S2213-8587(20)30128-5

[149] Andersen, Dorthe Nørgaard; et al 2012: Exposure of pregnant consumers to suspected endocrine disruptors; Danish Environmental Protection Agency; Survey of chemical substances in consumer products no. 117; ISBN no.978-87-92903-02-0

[150] Pete Myers; Jul 26, 2017: Science: Are we in a male fertility death spiral?; Male sterility is a growing problem. Here's why you should be worried—and your kids should be terrified.

[151] Pete Myers; Jul 26, 2017: Science: Are we in a male fertility death spiral?; Male sterility is a growing problem. Here's why you should be worried—and your kids should be terrified.

[152] Carreno, J; Rivas, A; Granada, A; Lopez-Espinosa, MJ; Mariscal, M; Olea, N; Olea-Serrano, F. Exposure of young men to organochlorine pesticides in Southern Spain. Environ Res 2007, 103, 55–61.

[153] Pete Myers; Jul 26, 2017: Science: Are we in a male fertility death spiral?; Male sterility is a growing problem. Here's why you should be worried—and your kids should be terrified.

[154] Horan TS, Marre A, Hassold T, Lawson C, Hunt PA (2017) Correction: Germline and reproductive tract effects intensify in male mice with successive generations of estrogenic exposure. PLOS Genetics 13(8): e1006980. https://doi.org/10.1371/journal.pgen.1006980 View correction

[155] Horan TS, Marre A, Hassold T, Lawson C, Hunt PA (2017) Correction: Germline and reproductive tract effects intensify in male mice with successive generations of estrogenic exposure. PLOS Genetics 13(8): e1006980. https://doi.org/10.1371/journal.pgen.1006980 View correction

[156] Gaspari, Laura et al 2011: Prenatal environmental risk factors for genital malformations in a population of 1442 French male newborns: a nested case-control study: Hum Reprod. 2011 Nov; 26(11):3155-62. doi: 10.1093/humrep/der283. Epub 2011 Aug 25. PMID: 21868402 DOI: 10.1093/ humrep/der283

[157] Fleisch AF, Wright RO, Baccarelli AA. Environmental epigenetics: a role in endocrine disease? J Mol Endocrinol. 2012 Aug 30;49(2):R61-7. doi: 10.1530/JME-12-0066. PMID: 22798698; PMCID: PMC3752847.

[158] UL.com; Grimes, Eleanor MA: EU Proposes to add Two New Hazard Classes to the EU CLP Regulation to Cover Endocrine Disruptors; April 8, 2021; https://www.ul.com/news/eu-proposes-add-two-new-hazard-classes-eu-clp-regulation-cover-endocrine-disruptors

[159] Andersen, Dorthe Nørgaard; et al 2012: Exposure of pregnant consumers to suspected endocrine disruptors; Danish Environmental Protection Agency; Survey of chemical substances in consumer products no. 117; ISBN no.978-87-92903-02-0

[160] Nelson CP, Park JM, Wan J, Bloom DA, Dunn RL, Wei JT. The increasing incidence of congenital penile anomalies in the United States. J Urol. 2005;174:1573–1576.

[161] Paris, F., De Ferran, K., Bhangoo, A., Ten, S., Lahlou, N., Audran, F., Servant, N., Poulat, F., Philibert, P. and Sultan, C. (2011), Isolated 'idiopathic' micropenis: hidden genetic defects?. International Journal of Andrology, 34: e518-e525. https://doi.org/10.1111/j.1365-2605.2010.01135.x

[162] Cleveland Clinic; 2018. How common is micropenis?; Cleveland Clinic medical professional on 09/14/2018.; https://my.clevelandclinic.org/health/diseases/17955-micropenis

[163] Ahmed S.F., Dobbie R., Finlayson A.R.. Prevalence of hypospadias and other genital anomalies among singleton births, 1988-1997, in Scotland. Arch Dis Child Fetal Neonatal Ed. 2004; 89: F149–51.

[164] Garcia, Jessica, et al 2017: Association of reproductive disorders and male congenital anomalies with environmental exposure to endocrine active pesticides; Reproductive Toxicology; Volume 71, 2017; Pages 95-100, ISSN 0890-6238, https://doi.org/10.1016/j.reprotox.2017.04.011. (https://www.sciencedirect.com/science/article/pii/S0890623817302241)

[165] Gaspari L. et al 2012: High prevalence of micropenis in 2710 male newborns from an intensive-use pesticide area of Northeastern Brazil; Volume35, Issue3; June 2012; Pages 253-264

[166] Gaspari, Laura et al 2011: Prenatal environmental risk factors for genital malformations in a population of 1442 French male newborns: a nested case-control study: Hum Reprod. 2011 Nov; 26(11):3155-62. doi: 10.1093/humrep/der283. Epub 2011 Aug 25. PMID: 21868402 DOI: 10.1093/ humrep/der283

[167] El Kholy, Mohamed, et al 2013: Penile length and genital anomalies in Egyptian male newborns: epidemiology and influence of endocrine disruptors; J Pediatr Endocr Met 2013; 26(5-6): pp. 509–513 DOI 10.1515/jpem-2012-0350

[168] Mnif, Wissem, Aziza Ibn Hadj Hassine, Aicha Bouaziz, Aghleb Bartegi, Olivier Thomas, and Benoit Roig. 2011. "Effect of Endocrine Disruptor Pesticides: A Review" International Journal of Environmental Research and Public Health 8, no. 6: 2265-2303. https://doi.org/10.3390/ijerph8062265

[169] Parinya Panuwet, Chandresh Ladva, Dana Boyd Barr, Tippawan Prapamontol, John D. Meeker, Priya Esilda D'Souza, Héctor Maldonado, P. Barry Ryan & Mark G. Robson (2018) Investigation of associations between exposures to pesticides and testosterone levels in Thai farmers, Archives of Environmental & Occupational Health, 73:4, 205-218, DOI: 10.1080/19338244.2017.1378606

[170] Freire, Carmen, et al 2014: Association between serum levels of organochlorine pesticides and sex hormones in adults living in a heavily contaminated area in Brazil, International Journal of Hygiene and Environmental Health, Volume 217, Issues 2–3,
2014, Pages 370-378, ISSN 1438-4639, https://doi.org/10.1016/j.ijheh.2013.07.012.

[171] Goncharov Alexey, Rej Robert, et al 2009: Lower Serum Testosterone Associated with Elevated Polychlorinated Biphenyl Concentrations in Native American Men; Environmental Health Perspectives 117:9 CID: https://doi.org/10.1289/ehp.0800134

[172] D Gunnell, R Fernando, M Hewagama, W D D Priyangika, F Konradsen, M Eddleston, The impact of pesticide regulations on suicide in Sri Lanka, International Journal of Epidemiology, Volume 36, Issue 6, December 2007, Pages 1235–1242, https://doi.org/10.1093/ije/dym164

[173] Parron, T; Alarcon, R; Requena, MDM; Hernandez, A. Increased breast cancer risk in women with environmental exposure to pesticides. Toxicol. Lett 2010, 196, S180.

[174] Romano, R.M., Romano, M.A., Bernardi, M.M. et al. 2010: Prepubertal exposure to commercial formulation of the herbicide glyphosate alters testosterone levels and testicular morphology. Arch Toxicol 84, 309–317 (2010). https://doi.org/10.1007/s00204-009-0494-z

[175] Clair E, Mesnage R, Travert C, Séralini GÉ. A glyphosate-based herbicide induces necrosis and apoptosis in mature rat testicular cells in vitro, and testosterone decrease at lower levels. Toxicol In Vitro. 2012 Mar;26(2):269-79. doi: 10.1016/j.tiv.2011.12.009. Epub 2011 Dec 19. PMID: 22200534.

[176] Bethsass, Jennifer & Colangelo, Aaron (2006) European Union Bans Atrazine, While the United States Negotiates Continued Use, International Journal of Occupational and Environmental Health, 12:3, 260-267, DOI: 10.1179/oeh.2006.12.3.260

[177] EPA,gow; Atrazine: https://www.epa.gov/teach/chem_summ/Atrazine_summary.pdf

[178] Sanders Robert, Berkley News, Media relations| MARCH 1, 2010
https://news.berkeley.edu/2010/03/01/frogs/

[179] Hayes Tyrone B., Khoury, Vicky 2010: Atrazine induces complete feminization and chemical castration in male African clawed frogs (Xenopus laevis); Proceedings of the National Academy of Sciences Mar 2010, 107 (10) 4612-4617; DOI: 10.1073/pnas.0909519107

[180] Friedmann, Andrew S 2002: Atrazine inhibition of testosterone production in rat males following peripubertal exposure, Reproductive Toxicology, Volume 16, Issue 3, 2002, Pages 275-279, ISSN 0890-6238, https://doi.org/10.1016/S0890-6238(02)00019-9.

[181] Rey, F., González, M., Zayas, M.A. 2009: Prenatal exposure to pesticides disrupts testicular histoarchitecture and alters testosterone levels in male Caiman latirostris. Gen Comp Endocrinol. 2009; 162(3): 286–92.

[182] ACKERMAN FRANK, PHD,2007: The Economics of Atrazine; INT J OCCUP ENVIRON HEALTH 2007;13:441–449 VOL 13/NO 4, OCT/DEC 2007 • www.ijoeh.com
http://www.panna.org/sites/default/files/EconAtrazine.pdf

[183] European Commission: 2004/248/EC: Commission Decision of 10 March, 2004 concerning the non-inclusion of atrazine in Annex I to Council Directive 91/414/EEC and the withdrawal of authorisations for plant protection products containing this active substance (Text with EEA relevance) (notified under document number C(2004) 731).

[184] Publicey.ch: Banned in Europe: How the EU exports pesticides too dangerous for use in Europe; Laurent Gaberell and Géraldine Viret; data visualisation: Martin Grandjean, 10 September 2020; https://www.publiceye.ch/en/topics/pesticides/banned-in-europe

[185] Swissinfo.ch; Swiss ban export of highly dangerous pesticides; October 15, 2020 - 14:21; Keystone-SDA/jdp; https://www.swissinfo.ch/eng/swiss-ban-export-of-highly-dangerous-pesticides/46099090

[186] Hauck S. J. et. Al ; Antioxidant Enzymes, Free-Radical Damage, and Response to Paraquat in Liver and Kidney of Long-Living Growth Hormone Receptor/Binding Protein Gene-Disrupted Mice; Horm Metab Res 2002; 34(9): 481-486; DOI: 10.1055/s-2002-34787

[187] Jim West; Pesticides and Polio: A Critique of Scientific Literature; 8/13/2018 https://www.westonaprice.org/health-topics/environmental-toxins/...

[188] Krause W 1977: Influence of DDT, DDVP and malathion on FSH, LH and testosterone serum levels and testosterone concentration in testis. Bull Environ Contam Toxicol. 1977 Aug;18(2):231-42. doi: 10.1007/BF01686072. PMID: 890160.

[189] ABC news: More polio cases now caused by vaccine than by wild virus as 4 African countries report them; The Associated Press; 25 November 2019; https://abcnews.go.com/Health/wireStory/polio-cases-now-caused-vaccine-wild-virus-67287290

[190] Endocrine (Hormone) Disruptors". United States Fish and Wildlife Service. Retrieved April 8, 2015.

[191] Jurewicz J, Hanke W, Radwan M, Bonde JP (January 2010). "Environmental factors and semen quality". International Journal of Occupational Medicine and Environmental Health. 22 (4): 305–329. doi:10.2478/v10001-009-0036-1. PMID 20053623. S2CID 6681999.

[192] Martins R, Carruthers M. Testosterone as the Missing Link Between Pesticides, Alzheimer Disease, and Parkinson Disease. JAMA Neurol. 2014;71(9):1189–1190. doi:10.1001/jamaneurol.2014.795

[193] Mnif, Wissem, Aziza Ibn Hadj Hassine, Aicha Bouaziz, Aghleb Bartegi, Olivier Thomas, and Benoit Roig. 2011. "Effect of Endocrine Disruptor Pesticides: A Review" International Journal of Environmental Research and Public Health 8, no. 6: 2265-2303. https://doi.org/10.3390/ijerph8062265

[194] Rogan WJ, Chen A. 2005: Health risks and benefits of bis(4-chlorophenyl)-1,1,1-trichloroethane (DDT); Lancet. 366 (9487): 763–773. doi:10.1016/S0140-6736(05)67182-6. PMID 16125595. S2CID 3762435.

[195] Weidner IS, Moller H, Jensen TK, Skakkebæk NE. Cryptorchidism and hypospadias in sons of gardeners and farmers. Environ. Health Perspect. 1998;106:793–796.

[196] Clayton Sandell (Newsy), Scripps National; Posted at 9:36 AM, Oct 07, 2021; Bald eagles flying high after pesticides nearly wiped them out; https://www.turnto23.com/news/climate-change/bald-eagles-flying-high-after-pesticides-nearly-wiped-them-out

[197] Kumar, S. (2004): Occupational Exposure Associated with Reproductive Dysfunction. Journal of Occupational Health, 46: 1-19. https://doi.org/10.1539/joh.46.1

[198] Pan, Guowei, Hanaoka, Tomoyuki, et al 2006; Decreased Serum Free Testosterone in Workers Exposed to High Levels of Di-n-butyl Phthalate (DBP) and Di-2-ethylhexyl Phthalate (DEHP): A Cross-Sectional Study in China
Environmental Health Perspectives 114:11 CID: https://doi.org/10.1289/ehp.9016

[199] Swan, Shanna H. 2008: Environmental phthalate exposure in relation to reproductive outcomes and other health endpoints in humans, Environmental Research, Volume 108, Issue 2, 2008, Pages 177-184, ISSN 0013-9351, https://doi.org/10.1016/j.envres.2008.08.007.

[200] Howdeshell, Kembra L.;Wilson Vickie S., et al 2008: A Mixture of Five Phthalate Esters Inhibits Fetal Testicular Testosterone Production in the Sprague-Dawley Rat in a Cumulative, Dose-Additive Manner, Toxicological Sciences, Volume 105, Issue 1, September 2008, Pages 153–165, https://doi.org/10.1093/toxsci/kfn077

[201] Parks Louise G. Ostby Joe S. 2000: The Plasticizer Diethylhexyl Phthalate Induces Malformations by Decreasing Fetal Testosterone Synthesis during Sexual Differentiation in the Male Rat, Toxicological Sciences, Volume 58, Issue 2, December 2000, Pages 339–349, https://doi.org/10.1093/toxsci/58.2.339

[202] Chen, Xueping, Shisan Xu, Tianfeng Tan, Sin T. Lee, Shuk H. Cheng, Fred W.F. Lee, Steven J.L. Xu, and Kin C. Ho 2014. "Toxicity and Estrogenic Endocrine Disrupting Activity of Phthalates and Their Mixtures" International Journal of Environmental Research and Public Health 11, no. 3: 3156-3168. https://doi.org/10.3390/ijerph110303156

[203] Davis B.J. Maronpot R.R, Heindel, J.J. 1994: Di-(2-ethylhexyl) Phthalate Suppresses Estradiol and Ovulation in Cycling Rats, Toxicology and Applied Pharmacology, Volume 128, Issue 2, 1994, Pages 216-223, ISSN 0041-008X, https://doi.org/10.1006/taap.1994.1200.

[204] Perera, Frederica, et al 2016: Bisphenol A exposure and symptoms of anxiety and depression among inner city children at 10–12 years of age, Environmental Research, Volume 151, 2016, Pages 195-202, ISSN 0013-9351, https://doi.org/10.1016/j.envres.2016.07.028.

[205] Wiersielis, Kimberly R; et al 2020: Perinatal exposure to bisphenol A at the intersection of stress, anxiety, and depression, Neurotoxicology and Teratology, Volume 79, 2020, 106884, ISSN 0892-0362, https://doi.org/10.1016/j.ntt.2020.106884.

[206] Wang, J., Pan, L., Wu, S., Lu, L., Xu, Y., Zhu, Y., Guo, M., & Zhuang, S. (2016). Recent Advances on Endocrine Disrupting Effects of UV Filters. International journal of environmental research and public health, 13(8), 782. https://doi.org/10.3390/ijerph13080782

[207] Ivo Iavicoli , Luca Fontana & Antonio Bergamaschi; 2009: The Effects of Metals as Endocrine Disruptors; Pages 206-223 | Published online: 22 May 2009; https://doi.org/10.1080/10937400902902062

[208] Laks DR. Luteinizing hormone provides a causal mechanism for mercury associated disease. Med Hypotheses. 2010 Apr;74(4):698-701. doi: 10.1016/j.mehy.2009.10.036. Epub 2009 Nov 13. PMID: 19914008.

[209] De Craemer S, Croes K, van Larebeke N, et al. 2017: Metals, hormones and sexual maturation in Flemish adolescents in three cross-sectional studies (2002-2015). Environ Int. 2017 May;102:190-199. doi: 10.1016/j.envint.2017.02.014. Epub 2017 Mar 18. PMID: 28318602.

[210] Smithsonian: Leaded Gas Was a Known Poison the Day It Was Invented; Kat Eschner; December 9, 2016; https://www.smithsonianmag.com/smart-news/leaded-gas-poison-invented-180961368 /

[211] Davey JC, Nomikos AP, Wungjiranirun M, Sherman JR, Ingram L, Batki C, Lariviere JP, Hamilton JW. Arsenic as an endocrine disruptor: arsenic disrupts retinoic acid receptor-and thyroid hormone receptor-mediated gene regulation and thyroid hormone-mediated amphibian tail metamorphosis. Environ Health Perspect. 2008 Feb;116(2):165-72. doi: 10.1289/ehp.10131. PMID: 18288313; PMCID: PMC2235215.

[212] Kold Jensen, Tina; Jørgensen, Niels et al ; 2004: Association of In Utero Exposure to Maternal Smoking with Reduced Semen Quality and Testis Size in Adulthood: A Cross-Sectional Study of 1,770 Young Men from the General Population in Five European Countries, American Journal of Epidemiology, Volume 159, Issue 1, 1 January 2004, Pages 49–58, https://doi.org/10.1093/aje/kwh002

[213] Swan, S. 2021: Coutdown chapter 5

[214] Thorup J.; Cortes D, and Petersen B.L.: 2006: The Incidence of Bilateral Cryptorchidism is Increased and the Fertility Potential is Reduced in Sons Born to Mothers who Have Smoked During Pregnancy; Volume 176; Issue 2; August 2006; Page: 734-737

[215] Kandel, D B, and Udry, J R 1999: "Prenatal effects of maternal smoking on daughters' smoking: nicotine or testosterone exposure?", American Journal of Public Health 89, no. 9 (September 1, 1999): pp. 1377-1383.

[216] Ernst A., Kristensen S.L. et al 2012: Maternal smoking during pregnancy and reproductive health of daughters: a follow-up study spanning two decades, Human Reproduction, Volume 27, Issue 12, December 2012, Pages 3593–3600, https://doi.org/10.1093/humrep/des337

[217] Swan, S. 2021: Coutdown chapter 6

[218] Jack H. Mendelson, Michelle B. et al 2003: Effects of Intravenous Cocaine and Cigarette Smoking on Luteinizing Hormone, Testosterone, and Prolactin in Men; Journal of Pharmacology and Experimental Therapeutics October 2003, 307 (1) 339-348; DOI: https://doi.org/10.1124/jpet.103.052928

[219] Bouchard, M. F., Bellinger, D. C., Weuve, J., Matthews-Bellinger, J., Gilman, S. E., Wright, R. O., Schwartz, J., & Weisskopf, M. G. (2009). Blood lead levels and major depressive disorder, panic disorder, and generalized anxiety disorder in US young adults. Archives of general psychiatry, 66(12), 1313–1319. https://doi.org/10.1001/archgenpsychiatry.2009.164

[220] William H. James, Smoking, sperm quality and testosterone level, Human Reproduction, Volume 17, Issue 12, December 2002, Pages 3275–3276, https://doi.org/10.1093/humrep/17.12.3275

[221] Talwar GP, Singh O, Pal R, Chatterjee N. Vaccines for control of fertility and hormone dependent cancers. Int J Immunopharmacol. 1992 Apr;14(3):511-4. doi: 10.1016/0192-0561(92)90183-I. PMID: 1618603.

[222] Talwar GP. 2013: Making of a vaccine preventing pregnancy without impairment of ovulation and derangement of menstrual regularity and bleeding profiles. Contraception. 2013 Mar;87(3):280-7. doi: 10.1016/j.contraception.2012.08.033. Epub 2012 Oct 4. PMID: 23040138.

[223] Junco JA, Rodríguez R, et al 2019: Safety and Therapeutic Profile of a GnRH-Based Vaccine Candidate Directed to Prostate Cancer. A 10-Year Follow-Up of Patients Vaccinated With Heberprovac. Front Oncol. 2019 Feb 25;9:49. doi: 10.3389/fonc.2019.00049. PMID: 30859088; PMCID: PMC6397853.

[224] Caldeira J, Bustos J, Peabody J, Chackerian B, Peabody DS (2015) Epitope-Specific Anti-hCG Vaccines on a Virus Like Particle Platform. PLoS ONE 10(10): e0141407. https://doi.org/10.1371/journal.pone.0141407

[225] Tetanus vaccine may be laced with anti-fertility drug. International / developing countries. Vaccine Wkly. 1995 May 29 - Jun 5:9-10. PMID: 12346214. https://pubmed.ncbi.nlm.nih.gov/12346214/

[226] Dean W. Arnold; When The U.N. Used "Vaccinations" To Secretly Sterilize 3 Million Kenyan Women; March 26, 2021; http://dean-w-arnold.com/articles-blogs/kenya

[227] Steve Weatherbe, "'A mass sterilization exercise': Kenyan doctors find anti-fertility agent in U.N. tetanus vaccine," Life Site News, Nov. 6, 2014, https://web.archive.org/web/20080413151205/http://www.ad2000.com.au/articles/2003/jul2003p6_1370.html (Retrieved April 24, 2019).

[228] evidencebasedtribalism; Stasiu , May 5, 2021

https://evidencebasedtribalism.wordpress.com/2021/05/05/byproduct-of-common-covid-19-vaccine-ingredient-linked-to-reduced-testosterone-study/

[229] thegatewaypundit By Michael Robison Published June 19, 2022; https://www.thegatewaypundit.com/2022/06/confirmed-pfizers-covid-vaccine-reduces-sperm-count-men-another-adverse-affect-forced-vaccine-tyranny/

[230] Covid Vaccines and Infertility; by KanekoaTheGreat; Jun 27 2022; https://abruptearthchanges.com/2022/08/03/covid-vaccines-and-infertility/

[231] https://abruptearthchanges.com/2022/02/18/the-nanoparticle-pandemic-covid-how-the-global-bio-tech-and-insurance-industry-predicted-a-nanotech-disaster/

[232] Tara Copp; SENIOR PENTAGON REPORTER, DEFENSE ONE: US Army Creates Single Vaccine Against All COVID & SARS Variants, Researchers Say; Decemper 21, 2021 https://www.defenseone.com/technology/2021/12/us-army-creates-single-vaccine-effective-against-all-covid-sars-variants/360089/

[233] Myocarditis (Inflammation of the Heart Muscle) and Pericarditis reported in the United States; 2010- 2021; BY SACHA DOBLER ON 20. NOVEMBER 2021; https://abruptearthchanges.com/2021/11/20/myocarditis-inflammation-of-the-heart-muscle-and-pericarditis-reported-in-the-united-states-2010-2021/

[234] VAERS COVID Vaccine; Myo/Pericarditis Reports; Through June 10, 2022 https://openvaers.com/covid-data/myo-pericarditis

[235] science.org 21 DEC 2020 BYJOP DE VRIEZE https://www.science.org/content/article/suspicions-grow-nanoparticles-pfizer-s-covid-19-vaccine-trigger-rare-allergic-reactions

[236] CDC confirms Covid Vaccines cause Heart Inflammation.; BY SACHA DOBLER ON 15. FEBRUARY 2022; https://abruptearthchanges.com/2022/02/15/cdc-confirms-covid-vaccines-cause-heart-inflammation/

[237] ADAC: Impfschäden sind nicht versichert; JANUAR 22, 2022; https://www.anderweltonline.com/klartext/klartext-20221/adac-impfschaeden-sind-nicht-versichert/

[238] cas.org ; SEPTEMBER 2, 2020; Meet the mRNA vaccine rookies aiming to take down COVID-19; by YINGZHU LI; Updated: December 4, 2020 https://www.cas.org/resource/blog/covid-mrna-vaccine

[239] Der Nachrichtenspiegel; Dr. Wodargs Appell an Geimpfte: „Nehmen Sie auf keinen Fall noch eine Spritze!"; VON REGENBOGENBIEGER · 21. NOVEMBER 2021; https://www.nachrichtenspiegel.de/2021/11/21/dr-wodargs-appell-an-geimpfte-nehmen-sie-auf-keinen-fall-noch-eine-spritze/?fbclid=IwAR39W3LZOShdgeZSBGl1GIRu7vrexXSiRGY5Q2njtC7AzJ65jr2T59dANdU#:~:text=Wolfgang%20Wodargs%20Botschaft%20ist%20klar%3A%20Lassen%20Sie%20sich%20nicht%20mit%20diesen%20Covid%2DImpfstoffen%20impfen!%20Und%20wenn%20Sie%20bereits%20geimpft%20sind%3A%20Nehmen%20Sie%20auf%20keinen%20Fall%20noch%20eine%20Spritze!%20Seine%20Gesundheit%20bekommt%20man,%20wenn%20überhaupt,%20nur%20noch%20schwer%20zurück

[240] Sonia Ndeupen, et al 2021: The mRNA-LNP platform's lipid nanoparticle component used in preclinical vaccine studies is highly inflammatory; bioRxiv 2021.03.04.430128; doi: https://doi.org/10.1101/2021.03.04.430128
Now published in iScience doi: 10.1016/j.isci.2021.103479

[241] Tara Copp; SENIOR PENTAGON REPORTER, DEFENSE ONE: US Army Creates Single Vaccine Against All COVID & SARS Variants, Researchers Say; Decemper 21, 2021 https://www.defenseone.com/technology/2021/12/us-army-creates-single-vaccine-effective-against-all-covid-sars-variants/360089/

[242] Cao W, He L, Cao W, Huang X, Jia K, Dai J. Recent progress of graphene oxide as a potential vaccine carrier and adjuvant. Acta Biomater. 2020 Aug;112:14-28. doi: 10.1016/j.actbio.2020.06.009. Epub 2020 Jun 10. PMID: 32531395.

[243] Application CN202011031367.1A events ; 2020-09-27; Application filed by Shanghai National Engineering Research Center for Nanotechnology Co Ltd; 2020-09-27; Priority to CN202011031367.1A; 2021-01-15; Publication of CN112220919A; Nano coronavirus recombinant vaccine taking graphene oxide as carrier; https://patents.google.com/patent/CN112220919A/en

[244] Graphene-Info; Graphene-Info's top 10 graphene applications of 2020; https://www.graphene-info.com/graphene-infos-top-10-graphene-applications-2020

[245] THE EXPOSÉ, By Rhoda Wilson; The real pandemic – Covid-19 or Graphene Oxide? Poisonous Nano-Material found in Covid Vaccines and Face Masks ON JULY 10, 2021

[246] Ou, L., Song, B., Liang, H. et al. Toxicity of graphene-family nanoparticles: a general review of the origins and mechanisms. Part Fibre Toxicol 13, 57 (2016). https://doi.org/10.1186/s12989-016-0168-y

[247] Detection Of Graphene In Covid19 Vaccines By Micro - Raman Spectromtry; Technical; REPORT Almeria, Spain, November 2, 2021; Prof. Dr. Pablo Campra Madrid; ASSOCIATE UNIVERSITY Professor;

https://www.drop-box.com/s/tnnq4ftw818chmx/FINAL_VERSIÓN_CAMPRA_REPORT_DETECTION_GRAPHENE_IN_COVID19_VACCINES.pdf?dl=0

[248] Scanning & Transmission Electron Microscopy Reveals Graphene Oxide in CoV-19 Vaccines; Updated: Dec 16, 20212021, February 5th, Updated October 1st, 2021; Author: Robert O Young CPC, MSc, DSc, PhD, Naturopathic Practitioner; http://www.drrobertyoung.com; https://www.drrobertyoung.com/post/transmission-electron-microscopy-reveals-graphene-oxide-in-cov-19-vaccines

[249] Iavicoli, I., Fontana, L., Leso, V., & Bergamaschi, A. (2013). The effects of nanomaterials as endocrine disruptors. International journal of molecular sciences, 14(8), 16732–16801. https://doi.org/10.3390/ijms140816732

[250] A method for non-surgical sterilization of mammals using an antibody-guided nanoparticle carrying cytotoxin to kill gonadal cells exhibiting anti-Mullerian hormone II receptors." Published: 29/4/2020; Sandra Ayres; Qiaobing Xu; Non-surgical, species agnostic animal sterilization.; Applications Animal Sterilization; PCT Publication No. WO 2018-022292 (February 1, 2018) https://viceprovost.tufts.edu/method-non-surgical-sterilization-mammals-using-antibody-guided-nanoparticle-carrying-cytotoxin

[251] Wang R, Song B, Wu J, Zhang Y, Chen A, Shao LQ. 2018: Potential adverse effects of nanoparticles on the reproductive system. Int J Nanomedicine. 2018;13:8487-8506 https://doi.org/10.2147/IJN.S170723; https://www.dovepress.com/potential-adverse-effects-of-nanoparticles-on-the-reproductive-system-peer-reviewed-fulltext-article-IJN

[252] Graphene-based nanomaterials: biological and medical applications and toxicity Fernanda MP Tonelli, Vânia AM Goulart, Katia N Gomes, Marina S Ladeira, Anderson K Santos, Eudes Lorençon, Luiz O Ladeira, and Rodrigo R Resende; Nanomedicine 2015 10:15, 2423-2450

[253] Dziewięcka, Marta, et al 2017: Short-term in vivo exposure to graphene oxide can cause damage to the gut and testis, Journal of Hazardous Materials, Volume 328, 2017, Pages 80-89, ISSN 0304-3894, https://doi.org/10.1016/j.jhazmat.2017.01.012. (https://www.sciencedirect.com/science/article/pii/S0304389417300171)

[254] Bhabra G, Sood A, Fisher B, Cartwright L,et al . Nanoparticles can cause DNA damage across a cellular barrier. Nat Nanotechnol. 2009 Dec;4(12):876-83. doi: 10.1038/nnano.2009.313. PMID: 19893513.

[255] Yoosefi Mahdieh et al 2015: The effects of titanium dioxide nanoparticles on pituitary-gonad axis in male mice; J. Chem. Pharm. Res., 2015, 7(10):720-723 Research Article; ISSN: 0975-7384 CODEN(USA): JCPRC5

[256] Gasem Mohammad Abu-Taweel, et al, 2021: Alleviation of silver nanoparticle-induced sexual behavior and testicular parameters dysfunction in male mice by yttrium oxide nanoparticles, Toxicology Reports, Volume 8, 2021, Pages 1121-1130, ISSN 2214-7500, https://doi.org/10.1016/j.toxrep.2021.05.014.

[257] Benjamin Zablotsky, Ph.D et a 2017: Estimated Prevalence of Children With Diagnosed Developmental Disabilities in the United States, 2014–2016; NCHS Data Brief; No. 291; November 2017; https://www.cdc.gov/nchs/data/databriefs/db291.pdf

[258] Datenbank mit Verdachtsfällen von Impfkomplikationen (DB-UAW); Paul-Ehrlich-Institut gemeldeten Verdachtsfälle von Impfkomplikationen und Impfnebenwirkungen; https://www.pei.de/DE/arzneimittelsicherheit/pharmakovigilanz/uaw-datenbank/uaw-datenbank-node.html

[259] Healthline; Written by Moira McCarthy on March 9, 2021 — Here's Why Women Experience Stronger Side Effects to COVID-19 Vaccines; https://www.healthline.com/health-news/why-women-experience-stronger-side-effects-to-covid-19-vaccines

[260] Ben Maamar, M., Lesné, L., Hennig, K. et al. Ibuprofen results in alterations of human fetal testis development. Sci Rep 7, 44184 (2017). https://doi.org/10.1038/srep44184

[261] Kristensen, David Møbjerg; Christèle Desdoits-Lethimonier, et al 2018: Ibuprofen alters human testicular physiology to produce a state of compensated hypogonadism; PNAS January 23, 2018 115 (4) E715-E724; first published January 8, 2018; https://doi.org/10.1073/pnas.1715035115

[262] Can prescription medications affect testosterone levels?; Reviewed by the medical professionals of the ISSM's Communication Committee; International Society of Sexual Medicine; https://www.issm.info/sexual-health-qa/can-prescription-medications-affect-testosterone-levels/

[263] Cui, Ruirui 2013 et al ; Influences of fluoride exposure in drinking water on serum androgen binding protein and testosterone of adult males: JOURNAL OF ZHENGZHOU UNIVERSITY (MEDICAL SCIENCES) (ISSN 1671-6825) Nov. 2013, Vol. 48, No. 6, Pages 750-753. doi: 10.3969/j.issn. 1671-6825.2013.06.010

[264] CHEN, Peizhong, et al 1997: Effects of High Fluoride on Reproductive Endocrine of Male Adults; Endemic Diseases Bulletin Volume 12 | Issue 2 | 1997 | pp. 57-58

[265] Dushyant Singh Chauhan et al 2013: Influence of Fluoride Exposure on Hypothalamic Pituitary Gonadal Axis Hormones and Semen Quality; Asian Journal of Biological and Life Sciences, December 2013; Research Article; 2013,2,3,201-206.

[266] Duan L. Zhu J. et al 2016: Does Fluoride Affect Serum Testosterone and Androgen Binding Protein with Age-Specificity? A Population-Based Cross-Sectional Study in Chinese Male Farmers. Biol Trace Elem Res. 2016 Dec;174(2):294-299. doi: 10.1007/s12011-016-0726-z. Epub 2016 May 6. PMID: 27154732.

[267] Patisaul, H. (2017). Endocrine disruption by dietary phyto-oestrogens: Impact on dimorphic sexual systems and behaviours. Proceedings of the Nutrition Society, 76(2), 130-144. doi:10.1017/S0029665116000677

[268] Adgent, M. A., Daniels, J. L., Edwards, L. J., Siega-Riz, A. M., & Rogan, W. J. (2011). Early-life soy exposure and gender-role play behavior in children. Environmental health perspectives, 119(12), 1811–1816. https://doi.org/10.1289/ehp.1103579

[269] Holland, Daniel, 2018: Does Ibuprofen Disrupt Testosterone Production? Pharmacytimes; https://www.pharmacytimes.com/view/does-ibuprofen-disrupt-testosterone-production

[270] Wikipedia , Herbivore men; 8-4-2021: https://en.wikipedia.org/wiki/Herbivore_men

[271] Glaser, Z.R., PhD., 1971. Naval Medical Research Institute Research Report, June 1971. Bibliography of Reported Biological Phenomena ("Effects") and Clinical Manifestations Attributed to Microwave and Radio-Frequency Radiation. Report No. 2 Revised. ⟨ https://scholar.google.com/scholar?Q=Glaser+naval+medical +microwave+radio-frequency+1972&btnG=&hl=en&as_sdt=0%2C38⟩

[272] Gamze Altun, Ömür Gülsüm Deniz, Kıymet Kübra Yurt, Devra Davis, Süleyman Kaplan,2018: Effects of mobile phone exposure on metabolomics in the male and female reproductive systems, Environmental Research, Volume 167, 2018, Pages 700-707, ISSN 0013-9351, https://doi.org/10.1016/j.envres.2018.02.031.

[273] CELL TOWER RADIATION HEALTH EFFECTS; INTERNATIONAL ASSOCIATION OF FIRE FIGHTERS; https://www.iaff.org/cell-tower-radiation/

[274] Wavewall; Testosterone: The Effects of Mobile Phones on Testosterone Levels rats, https://www.wavewallcases.com/the-effects-of-mobile-phones-on-testosterone-levels/

[275] NOAA: Solar Radio Data; https://www.ngdc.noaa.gov/stp/solar/solarradio.html

[276] Al-Akhras, Moh'd-Ali et al, 2006: Influence of 50 Hz magnetic field on sex hormones and other fertility parameters of adult male rats; Bioelectromagnetics 27:127–131, 2006; First published: 22 November 2005; https://doi.org/10.1002/bem.20186

[277] Baharara, J. et al 2015: Protective effect of date palm pollen (Phoenix dactylifera) on sperm parameters and sexual hormones in male NMRI mice exposed to low frequency electromagnetic field (50 Hz); J Herbmed Pharmacol. 2015;4(3): 75-80.

[278] Hamdi BA, Soleimanirad J, Khiki AA, Roshangar L.2011: Developmentel exposure to emf and its effect on spermatogenesis in adulthood in mice. International journal of reproductive biomedicine. 2011;9(1):67.

[279] Gharamaleki H., H. et al 2014: Effects of electromagnetic field exposure during the prenatal period on biomarkers of oxidative stress and pathology of testis and testosterone level Of Adult Rats in f1 generation; General Endocrinology; Science and Research Branch, Islamic Azad University - Dep. of Biology, Fars doi: 10.4183/aeb.2014.577

[280] Khaki AA, Zarrintan S, Khaki A, Zahedi A. The effects of EMF on the microstructure of seminal vesicles in rat: a light and transmission electron microscope study. Pak J Biol Sci. 2008;11(5):692–701. doi: 10.3923/pjbs.2008.692.701.

[281] Bahaodini, Aminollah et al, 2015: Low frequency electromagnetic fields long-term exposure effects on testicular histology, sperm quality and testosterone levels of male rats; Asian Pacific Journal of Reproduction; Volume 4, Issue 3, 2015, Pages 195-200, ISSN 2305-0500, https://doi.org/10.1016/j.apjr.2015.06.001.
(https://www.sciencedirect.com/science/article/pii/S2305050015000044)

[282] Al-Akhras MA. 2008: Influence of 50 Hz magnetic field on sex hormones and body, uterine, and ovarian weights of adult female rats. Electromagn Biol Med. 2008;27(2):155-63. doi: 10.1080/15368370802072125. PMID: 18568933.

[283] Khaki AA, Soleimanirad J, Arjani H, Mohadjel Shoja MA, Zarrintan S, Khalili A, et al 2006: Study of effects of electromagnetic fields on men infertility and the ways for decrease of its harmful effects. Medical Journal of Tabriz University of medical sciences. 2006;28(4):41–7.

[284] Baharara, Javad et al 2015: Protective effect of date palm pollen on sperm parameters and sexual hormones in male NMRI mice exposed to low frequency electromagnetic field (50 Hz); JOURNAL ARTICLE; 2015/7/1; J Herbmed Pharmacol; 75-8043 J Herbmed Pharmacol 2015/7/1;4(3):75-80; http://herbmedpharmacol.com/Article/JHP_20150629145934

[285] Arezoo, Farsi; et al 2013: Improvement effect of rosmarinic acid on serum testosterone level after exposing with electromagnetic fields; international journal of women's health and reproduction SCIENCES SUMMER 2013 , Volume 1 , Number 2; Page(s) 45 To 50.

[286] Iorio R, Scrimaglio R, Rantucci E, DelleMonache S, Di Gaetano A, Finetti N, et al. A preliminary study of oscillating electromagnetic field effects on human spermatozoon motility. Bio electromagnetic. 2007;28(1):72–5. doi: 10.1002/bem.20278

[287] Wang Zhaopin Z.et al, 2016: Effects of electromagnetic fields exposure on plasma hormonal and inflammatory pathway biomarkers in male workers of a power plant;
International Archives of Occupational and Environmental Health volume 89, pages 33–42 (2016)

[288] Morgan, Lloyd L., Kesari, Santosh; Lee Davis, Devra; 2014: Why children absorb more microwave radiation than adults: The consequences,; Journal of Microscopy and Ultrastructure,; Volume 2, Issue 4,; 2014,; Pages 197-204,; ISSN 2213-879X,
https://doi.org/10.1016/j.jmau.2014.06.005.

[289] Pall, Martin L. 2016: Microwave frequency electromagnetic fields (EMFs) produce widespread neuropsychiatric effects including depression, Journal of Chemical Neuroanatomy, Volume 75, Part B, 2016, Pages 43-51, ISSN 0891-0618, https://doi.org/10.1016/j.jchemneu.2015.08.001.

[290] Jaffar et al 2019: Adverse Effects of Wi-Fi Radiation on Male Reproductive System: A Systematic Review; 2019; The Tohoku Journal of Experimental Medicine; Volume 248 Issue 3 Pages 169-179; DOI https://doi.org/10.1620/tjem.248.169

[291] Ali, BMH (2020) Study the electromagnetic radiation effects on testicular function of male rats by biochemical and histopathological. Eurasia J Biosci 14: 3869-3873.

[292] Shahin, S, Singh, SP, Chaturvedi, CM. 2018: 1800 MHz mobile phone irradiation induced oxidative and nitrosative stress leads to p53 dependent Bax mediated testicular apoptosis in mice, Mus musculus. J Cell Physiol. 2018; 233: 7253– 7267. https://doi.org/10.1002/jcp.26558

[293] Lin, Y. Y et al. (2017). 1950MHz Radio Frequency Electromagnetic Radiation Inhibits Testosterone Secretion of Mouse Leydig Cells. International journal of environmental research and public health, 15(1), 17. https://doi.org/10.3390/ijerph15010017

[294] Cetkin, M, Kızılkan, N, Demirel, C, et al. Quantitative changes in testicular structure and function in rat exposed to mobile phone radiation. Andrologia. 2017; 49:e12761. https://doi.org/10.1111/and.12761

[295] Diab, YAA et al 2021: Protective Effect of Vitamin D against Harmful Effect of Cell Phone Radiation Exposure on Albino Rat Testis; Annals of R.S.C.B., ISSN:1583-6258, Vol. 25, Issue 6, 2021, Pages. 5119 - 5128 Received 25 April 2021; Accepted 08 May 2021

[296] Ozguner M, Koyu A, Cesur G, et a 2005: Biological and morphological effects on the reproductive organ of rats after exposure to electromagnetic field. Saudi Medical Journal. 2005 Mar;26(3):405-410. https://europepmc.org/article/med/15806208

[297] Meo, S.A. et al (2010): Effects of mobile phone radiation on serum testosterone in Wistar albino rats. Saudi medical journal. 31. 869-73. https://www.wavewallcases.com/wp-content/uploads/2018/01/Effects_of_Mobile_Phone_Radiation_on_Serum_Testosterone.pdf

[298] Yahyazadeh, A. &. Altunkaynak B. Z (2019) Protective effects of luteolin on rat testis following exposure to 900 MHz electromagnetic field, Biotechnic & Histochemistry, 94:4, 298-307, DOI: 10.1080/10520295.2019.1566568

[299] Sarookhani, M. R. et al 2010: The influence of 950 MHz magnetic field (mobile phone radiation) on sex organ and adrenal functions of male rabbits; School of Public Health, Qazvin University of Medical Sciences, Bahonar Blvd, Qazvin, Iran; Accepted 2 November, 2010

[300] Kamur, S. et al 2011: The therapeutic effect of a pulsed electromagnetic field on the reproductive patterns of male Wistar rats exposed to a 2.45-GHz microwave field; CLINICS 2011;66(7):1237-1245 DOI:10.1590/S1807-59322011000700020

[301] Kumar, Sanjay et al 2012 (Chapter 1): Influence of electromagnetic fields on reproductive system of male rats; International Journal of Radiation Biology; Volume 89, 2013 - Issue 3; Pages 147-154; https://doi.org/10.3109/09553002.2013.741282

[302] Sepehrimanesh, M., Saeb, M., Nazifi, S. et al.2014: Impact of 900 MHz electromagnetic field exposure on main male reproductive hormone levels: a Rattus norvegicus model. Int J Biometeorol 58, 1657–1663 (2014). https://doi.org/10.1007/s00484-013-0771-7

[303] Qin F, Zhang J, Cao H, Yi C, Li JX, Nie J, Chen LL, Wang J, Tong J. 2012: Effects of 1800-MHz radiofrequency fields on circadian rhythm of plasma melatonin and testosterone in male rats. J Toxicol Environ Health A. 2012;75(18):1120-8. doi: 10.1080/15287394.2012.699846. PMID: 22891885.

[304] Qin, F., Shen, T., Cao, H., Qian, J., Zou, D., Ye, M., & Pei, H. (2019): CeO2NPs relieve radiofrequency radiation, improve testosterone synthesis, and clock gene expression in Leydig cells by enhancing antioxidation. International journal of nanomedicine, 14, 4601–4611. https://doi.org/10.2147/IJN.S206561

[305] Jelodar G, Zare Y.2008: Effect of Radiation Leakage of Microwave Oven on Rat Serum Testosterone at Pre and Post Pubertal Stage. JSSU. 2008; 15 (4) :64-68
URL: http://jssu.ssu.ac.ir/article-1-624-en.html
[306] Lee, Sang-Kon et al 2014: Extremely Low Frequency Magnetic Fields Induce Spermatogenic Germ Cell Apoptosis: Possible Mechanism; BioMed Research International / 2014 / Article;; Volume 2014 |Article ID 567183 | https://doi.org/10.1155/2014/567183
[307] Chen L, Qin F, Chen Y, Sun J, Tong J. [Chronotoxicity of 1800 MHz microwave radiation on sex hormones and spermatogenesis in male mice]. Wei Sheng Yan Jiu. 2014 Jan;43(1):110-5. Chinese. PMID: 24564122.
[308] Salama, N., Kishimoto, T., Kanayama, Ho. et al. Effects of exposure to a mobile phone on sexual behavior in adult male rabbit: an observational study. Int J Impot Res 22, 127–133 (2010). https://doi.org/10.1038/ijir.2009.57
[309] Qin F, Cao H, Yuan H, et al. 2018: 1800 MHz radiofrequency fields inhibits testosterone production via CaMKI /RORα pathway. Reproductive Toxicology (Elmsford, N.Y.). 2018 Oct;81:229-236. DOI: 10.1016/j.reprotox.2018.08.014. PMID: 30125682.
[310] Eskander EF, Estefan SF, Abd-Rabou AA. How does long term exposure to base stations and mobile phones affect human hormone profiles? Clin Biochem. 2012 Jan;45(1-2):157-61. doi: 10.1016/j.clinbiochem.2011.11.006. Epub 2011 Nov 27. PMID: 22138021. https://www.sciencedirect.com/science/article/abs/pii/S0009912011027330
[311] Vangelova, Katya & Israel, Michel & Mihaylov, S. (2002). The effect of low level radiofrequency electromagnetic radiation on the excretion rates of stress hormones in operators during 24-hour shifts. Central European journal of public health. 10. 24-8.
[312] Shahabi, S., Hassanzadeh Taji, I., et al (2018). Exposure to cell phone radiofrequency changes corticotrophin hormone levels and histology of the brain and adrenal glands in male Wistar rat. Iranian journal of basic medical sciences, 21(12), 1269–1274. https://doi.org/10.22038/ijbms.2018.29567.7133
[313] Mortazavi, SMJ et al . (2009): Alterations in TSH and Thyroid Hormones following Mobile Phone Use. Oman medical journal, 24(4), 274–278. https://doi.org/10.5001/omj.2009.56
[314] Mahdavi, S. M., Sahraei, H., Yaghmaei, P., & Tavakoli, H. (2014). Effects of Electromagnetic Radiation Exposure on Stress-Related Behaviors and Stress Hormones in Male Wistar Rats. Biomolecules & Therapeutics, 22(6), 570–576. https://doi.org/10.4062/biomolther.2014.054
[315] Özorak, A. Nazıroğlu M., et al 2013: Wi-Fi (2.45 GHz) and mobile phone (900 and 1800 MHz)-induced risks on oxidative stress and elements in kidney and testis of rats during pregnancy and the development of newborns. Biol. Trace Elem. Res. 156(1-3), 221–229 (2013)
[316] Kesari K.K. et al. 2018: Radiations and male fertility; Reproductive Biology and Endocrinology (2018) 16:118 https://doi.org/10.1186/s12958-018-0431-1
[317] Pall, Martin L. 2018: Wi-Fi is an important threat to human health, Environmental Research, Volume 164, 2018, Pages 405-416, ISSN 0013-9351, https://doi.org/10.1016/j.envres.2018.01.035.
(https://www.sciencedirect.com/science/article/pii/S0013935118300355)
[318] Said-Salman, I H; et al 2019:. "Evaluation of Wi-Fi Radiation Effects on Antibiotic Susceptibility, Metabolic Activity and Biofilm Formation by Escherichia Coli 0157H7, Staphylococcus Aureus and Staphylococcus Epidermis." Journal of biomedical physics & engineering vol. 9,5 579-586. 1 Oct. 2019, doi:10.31661/jbpe.v0i0.1106
[319] Low Testosterone – Could Your Cell Phone or Laptop Be to Blame?; ;Dr. Friedman's Health Blog; https://www.doctordavidfriedman.com/blog/low-testosterone-could-your-cell-phone-or-laptop-be-to-blame-1
[320] Avendaño, Conrado; Mata, Ariela, etal 2012: Use of laptop computers connected to internet through Wi-Fi decreases human sperm motility and increases sperm DNA fragmentation, Fertility and Sterility, Volume 97, Issue 1, 2012, Pages 39-45.e2, ISSN 0015-0282, https://doi.org/10.1016/j.fertnstert.2011.10.012.
[321] LA VIGNERA, S. et 2012: Effects of the Exposure to Mobile Minireview Phones on Male Reproduction: A Review of the Literature; Journal of Andrology, Vol. 33, No. 3, May/June 2012 Copyright E American Society of Andrology
[322] Agarwal, Ashok; Deepinder, Fnu, et al 2008: Effect of cell phone usage on semen analysis in men attending infertility clinic: an observational study; Fertility and Sterility,; Volume 89, Issue 1; 2008; Pages 124-128; ISSN 0015-0282, https://doi.org/10.1016/j.fertnstert.2007.01.166.
[323] Tenorio BM, Jimenez GC, Morais RN, et al.2011: Testicular development evaluation in rats exposed to 60 Hz and 1 mT electromagnetic field. Journal of Applied Toxicology: JAT. 2011 Apr;31(3):223-230. DOI: 10.1002/jat.1584.
[324] Skokri S, Soltani A, Kazemi M, Sardari D, Babapoor Mofrad F. Effect of Wi-Fi (2.45 GHz) exposure on apoptosis, sperm parameters and testicular histomorphometry in rats. Cell J. 2015;17(2):322–

[325] Tenorio, Bruno Mendes et al 2012: Evaluation of testicular degeneration induced by low-frequency electromagnetic fields; Journal of Applied Toxicology; Volume 32, Issue 3; March 2012; Pages 210-218

[326] Kim YW, Kim HS, Lee JS, Kim YJ, Lee SK, Seo JN, et al. Effects of 60 Hz 14 micro T magnetic field on the apoptosis of testicular germ cell in mice. Bioelectromagnetics. 2009;30(1):66–72. doi: 10.1002/bem.20448.

[327] Sert, Cemil M. et al 2002; ELF Magnetic Field Effects On Fatty Acid Composition Of Phospholipid Fraction And Reproduction Of Rats' Testes; Electromagnetic Biology and Medicine; Volume 21, 2002 - Issue 1; Pages 19-29

[328] Kaydani M. et al 2020: Journal of Health; The Effect of Cellular Phone Microwave Radiation on Sperm Fertility Indices (Count, Motility, Viability and Morphology) in Mice; Vol. 11, No. 4, Autumn 2020, Pages 468-477

[329] Ibrahim, R., Ali, A., Khamis, N., Mohammed, H. (2019). Effect Of Exposure To Wi-Fi Router Radiation On The Lung Of Adult Male Albino Rats: Histological And Immunohistochemical Study. Egyptian Journal of Histology, 42(4), 1059-1069. doi: 10.21608/ejh.2019.7317.1070

[330] Jung, K. A., Ahn, H. S., Lee, Y. S., & Gye, M. C. (2007). Effect of a 20 kHz sawtooth magnetic field exposure on the estrous cycle in mice. Journal of microbiology and biotechnology, 17(3), 398-402.

[331] Nurbayatin, Anita; et al 2017: Radiation effect of wireless fidelity (wi-fi) on oocyte number of oocyte stimulation in mice (mus musculus); folia medica indonesiana vol. 53 no. 3 september 2017: 169-172

[332] Shahin, S., Singh, V.P., Shukla, R.K. 2013: et al. 2.45 GHz Microwave Irradiation-Induced Oxidative Stress Affects Implantation or Pregnancy in Mice, Mus musculus . Appl Biochem Biotechnol 169, 1727–1751 (2013). https://doi.org/10.1007/s12010-012-0079-9

[333] Tuor, M. et al 2005; Assessment of ELF Exposure from GSM Handsets and Development of an Optimized RF/ELF Exposure Setup for Studies of Human Volunteers; ITIS foundation, ETH Zurich; BAG Reg. No. 2.23.02.-18/02.001778

[334] Sun I. Kim, et al 2006: World Congress of Medical Physics and Biomedical Engineering 2006: August 27 - Septmber 1, 20006 COEX Seoul, Korea Springer Science & Business Media, 05.07.2007 - 586 Seiten p. 2709

[335] Beck, Robert C.: Copyright © 1978: Mood Modification With Elf Magnetic Fields: A Preliminary Exploration; ARCHAEUS Magazine; Issue 4 (1986) p. 47

[336] Beck, Robert, 1978: Mood Modification With Elf Magnetic Fields: A Preliminary Exploration; ARCHAEUS Magazine; Issue 4 (1986) p. 47

[337] CHICAGO TRIBUNE; Are you carrying your cellphone too close to your body?; By NARA SCHOENBERG; JAN 26, 2017; https://www.chicagotribune.com/lifestyles/sc-cell-phone-safety-family-0131-20170126-story.html

[338] CHICAGO TRIBUNE; We tested popular cellphones for radiofrequency radiation. Now the FCC is investigating; SAM ROE; AUG 21, 2019 https://www.chicagotribune.com/investigations/ct-cell-phone-radiation-testing-20190821-72qgu4nzlfda5kyuhteiieh4da-story.html

[339] Henshaw D. L, 2011: Use of mobile phones and risk of brain tumours: update of Danish cohort study: BMJ; 343 doi: https://doi.org/10.1136/bmj.d6387 (Published 20 October 2011); BMJ 2011;343:d6387

[340] Walonick, David S. 1990: Effects of 6-10 Hz ELF on Brain Waves; Minneapolis, MN; Borderland Sciences Research Foundation Journal of Borderland Research; Vol. 46; No. 03-4

[341] MIT News Office; Anne Trafton, March 30, 2010; Moral judgments can be altered ... by magnets; http://news.mit.edu/2010/moral-control-0330

[342] Young Liane et al, 2010: Disruption of the right temporoparietal junction with transcranial magnetic stimulation reduces the role of beliefs in moral judgments; PNAS first published March 29, 2010; Department of Brain and Cognitive Sciences, Massachusetts Institute of Technology, Cambridge

[343] Finlay, C. C. et al, December 2010: "International Geomagnetic Reference Field: the eleventh generation". Geophysical Journal International. 183 (3): 1216–1230. Bibcode:2010GeoJI.183.1216F.

[344] Hecht. Prof. Karl, 2018: Die Wirkung der 10-Hz-Pulsation der elektromagnetischen Strahlungen von WLAN auf den Menschen; Herausgeber: diagnose:funk; Quelle: www.diagnose-funk.org; 26.04.2018

[345] SRF: Pandemie schlägt auf Kinderaugen; Mehr am Bildschirm statt draussen: Die Zahl kurzsichtiger Kinder ist in der Pandemie auch in der Schweiz angestiegen. ; Karoline Thürkauf; Freitag, 09.04.2021, 11:28; https://www.srf.ch/news/panorama/gesundheit-pandemie-schlaegt-auf-kinderaugen

[346] Kim J, et al. Association between Exposure to Smartphones and Ocular Health in Adolescents. Ophthalmic Epidemiol. 2016 Aug;23(4):269-76.

[347] Digital Screen Time: Dry Eye, Cataracts, Computer Vision Syndrome;   Physicians for Safe Technology; Updated 6/9/20 https://mdsafetech.org/eye-effects/

[348] Gandhi, O. P., Lazzi, G., Furse, C. M. (1996). Electromagnetic absorption in the human head and neck for mobile telephones at 835 and 1900MHz. IEEE Trans. Microwave Theor. Techniq. 44(10):1884–1897.

[349] Gandhi, Om & Morgan, L Lloyd et al (2011). Exposure Limits: The underestimation of absorbed cell phone radiation, especially in children. Electromagnetic biology and medicine. 31. Pp.34-51. 10.3109/15368378.2011.622827. 14 Oct 2011

[350] Lipman RM, Tripathi BJ, Tripathi RC. 1988: Cataracts induced by microwave and ionizing radiation. Surv Ophthalmol. 1988 Nov-Dec;33(3):200-10. doi: 10.1016/0039-6257(88)90088-4. PMID: 3068822.

[351] Tök, L., Nazıroğlu, M., Doğan, S., Kahya, M. C., & Tök, O. (2014). Effects of melatonin on Wi-Fi-induced oxidative stress in lens of rats. Indian journal of ophthalmology, 62(1), 12–15. https://doi.org/10.4103/0301-4738.126166

[352] Yu K, Deng S-L, Sun T-C, Li Y-Y, Liu Y-X. Melatonin Regulates the Synthesis of Steroid Hormones on Male Reproduction: A Review. Molecules. 2018; 23(2):447. https://doi.org/10.3390/molecules23020447

[353] The Low Testosterone Epidemic; Sophia health institute; https://www.sophiahi.com/the-low-testosterone-epidemic/

[354] Robert J. Hedaya MD; The Dissolution of Gender; The role of hormones.; February 13, 2019; https://www.psychologytoday.com/us/blog/health-matters/201902/the-dissolution-gender

[355] Robert J. Hedaya MD; The Dissolution of Gender; The role of hormones.; February 13, 2019; https://www.psychologytoday.com/us/blog/health-matters/201902/the-dissolution-gender

[356] Rich AL, Phipps LM, Tiwari S, Rudraraju H, Dokpesi PO.2016: The Increasing Prevalence in Intersex Variation from Toxicological Dysregulation in Fetal Reproductive Tissue Differentiation and Development by Endocrine-Disrupting Chemicals. Environmental Health Insights. January 2016. doi:10.4137/EHI.S39825

[357] Health of people with intersex variations; health.vic, Victoria's hub for health services and business;   https://www2.health.vic.gov.au/about/populations/lgbti-health/health-of-people-with-intersex-variations

[358] Lilford R.J., Dear P.R. The intersex baby. Br J Hosp Med (Lond). 1987; 37(1): 28–30.

[359] Rich AL, Phipps LM, Tiwari S, Rudraraju H, Dokpesi PO.2016: The Increasing Prevalence in Intersex Variation from Toxicological Dysregulation in Fetal Reproductive Tissue Differentiation and Development by Endocrine-Disrupting Chemicals. Environmental Health Insights. January 2016. doi:10.4137/EHI.S39825

[360] Swan, Shanna, PhD, with Stacey Colino 2021: *Count Down, How Our Modern World Is Threatening Sperm Counts, Altering Male and Female Reproductive Development, and Imperiling the Future of the Human Race*; Scribner, February 2021 Chapter 4p.70

[361] Rich AL, Phipps LM, Tiwari S, Rudraraju H, Dokpesi PO.2016: The Increasing Prevalence in Intersex Variation from Toxicological Dysregulation in Fetal Reproductive Tissue Differentiation and Development by Endocrine-Disrupting Chemicals. Environmental Health Insights. January 2016. doi:10.4137/EHI.S39825

[362] Rich AL, Phipps LM, Tiwari S, Rudraraju H, Dokpesi PO. 2016: The Increasing Prevalence in Intersex Variation from Toxicological Dysregulation in Fetal Reproductive Tissue Differentiation and Development by Endocrine-Disrupting Chemicals. Environmental Health Insights. January 2016. doi:10.4137/EHI.S39825

[363] Heinrich Böll Stiftung: Human Rights Between the Sexes; A preliminary study on the life situations of inter* individuals; Volume 34; By Dan Christian Ghattas; Berlin : Heinrich-Böll-Stiftung, [2013]

[364] Behrens K. G. (2020). A principled ethical approach to intersex paediatric surgeries. BMC medical ethics, 21(1), 108. https://doi.org/10.1186/s12910-020-00550-x

[365] Babu R, Shah U. Gender identity disorder (GID) in adolescents and adults with differences of sex development (DSD): A systematic review and meta-analysis. J Pediatr Urol. 2021 Feb;17(1):39-47. doi: 10.1016/j.jpurol.2020.11.017. Epub 2020 Nov 12. PMID: 33246831.

[366] Sievert ED, Schweizer K, Barkmann C, Fahrenkrug S, Becker-Hebly I. Not social transition status, but peer relations and family functioning predict psychological functioning in a German clinical sample of children with Gender Dysphoria. Clinical Child Psychology and Psychiatry. 2021;26(1):79-95. doi:10.1177/1359104520964530

[367] Gooren, Louis 2006: The biology of human psychosexual differentiation, Hormones and Behavior, Volume 50, Issue 4, 2006, Pages 589-601, ISSN 0018-506X, https://doi.org/10.1016/j.yhbeh.2006.06.011.

[368] Swan, Shanna, PhD, with Stacey Colino 2021: *Count Down, How Our Modern World Is Threatening Sperm Counts, Altering Male and Female Reproductive Development, and Imperiling the Future of the Human Race*; Scribner, February 2021 Chapter 4p.70

[369369] Parmigiani, Stefano, et al 2003; Exposure To Very Low Doses Of Endocrine Disrupting Chemicals (Edcs) During Fetal Life Permanently Alters Brain Development And Behavior In Animals And Humans; Jour Society and Structures. April 2003, 293-308; The Science and Culture Series — Nuclear Strategy and Peace Technology pp. 293-308 (2003)

[370] Pol, H. E. H., Cohen-Kettenis, P. T., et al (2006). Changing your sex changes your brain: influences of testosterone and estrogen on adult human brain structure, European Journal of Endocrinology eur j endocrinol, 155(suppl_1), S107-S114. Retrieved Jul 16, 2021, from https://eje.bioscientifica.com/view/journals/eje/155/suppl_1/1550107.xml

[371] Swan, Shanna, PhD, with Stacey Colino 2021: *Count Down, How Our Modern World Is Threatening Sperm Counts, Altering Male and Female Reproductive Development, and Imperiling the Future of the Human Race*; Scribner, February 2021 Chapter 4p.70

[372] Vreugdenhil Hestien J I, Slijper Froukje M E, et al 2002; Effects of perinatal exposure to PCBs and dioxins on play behavior in Dutch children at school age.; Environmental Health Perspectives 110:10 CID: https://doi.org/10.1289/ehp.021100593

[373] Winneke, Gerhard; Ranft, Ulrich; Wittsiepe, Jürgen; Kasper-Sonnenberg, Monika; Fürst, Peter; et al. Environmental Health Perspectives (Online); Research Triangle Park Vol. 122, Iss. 3, (Mar 2014): 292. DOI:10.1289/ehp.1306533

[374] Hines M, Brook C, Conway GS. Androgen and psychosexual development: core gender identity, sexual orientation and recalled childhood gender role behavior in women and men with congenital adrenal hyperplasia (CAH). J Sex Res. 2004 Feb;41(1):75-81. doi: 10.1080/00224490409552215. PMID: 15216426.

[375] Nature Magazine, NEWS; 23 August 2021; Genetic patterns offer clues to evolution of homosexuality; https://www.nature.com/articles/d41586-021-02312-0

[376] van den Aardweg GJM. On the Psychogenesis of Homosexuality. Linacre Q. 2011 Aug;78(3):330-354. doi: 10.1179/002436311803888267. Epub 2011 Aug 1. PMID: 30082952; PMCID: PMC6026959.

[377] Lippa RA. Are 2D:4D finger-length ratios related to sexual orientation? Yes for men, no for women. J Pers Soc Psychol. 2003 Jul;85(1):179-88. doi: 10.1037/0022-3514.85.1.179. PMID: 12872893.

[378] Homosexuality may be caused by chemical modifications to DNA
A new study suggests that methylation patterns in DNA may influence sexual orientation; 8 OCT 2015 BY MICHAEL BALTER; https://www.science.org/content/article/homosexuality-may-be-caused-chemical-modifications-dna

[379] Ivanka Savic and Per Lindström; 2008: PET and MRI show differences in cerebral asymmetry and functional connectivity between homo - and heterosexual subjects PSNA; 2008 105 (27) 9403-9408; https://doi.org/10.1073/pnas.0801566105

[380] PEW RESEARCH CENTERMAY 14, 2019; Attitudes on Same-Sex Marriage; Public opinion on same-sex marriage; https://www.pewresearch.org/religion/fact-sheet/changing-attitudes-on-gay-marriage/

[381] Van Dongen, Stefan, 2009: Second to fourth digit ratio in relation to age, BMI and life history in a population of young adults: a set of unexpected results; Journal of Negative Results; Ecology & Evolutionary Biology; Vol. 6 (2009)

[382] Kobe Millet, Siegfried Dewitte,2005: Second to fourth digit ratio and cooperative behavior, Biological Psychology, Volume 71, Issue 1, 2006, Pages 111-115, ISSN 0301-0511, https://doi.org/10.1016/j.biopsycho.2005.06.001.

[383] Lippa RA. Are 2D:4D finger-length ratios related to sexual orientation? Yes for men, no for women. J Pers Soc Psychol. 2003 Jul;85(1):179-88. doi: 10.1037/0022-3514.85.1.179. PMID: 12872893.

[384] Wallien, Madeleine S.C.; Zucker, Kenneth J., et aal 2008: 2D:4D finger-length ratios in children and adults with gender identity disorder, Hormones and Behavior, Volume 54, Issue 3, 2008, Pages 450-454, ISSN 0018-506X, https://doi.org/10.1016/j.yhbeh.2008.05.002.

[385] Eklund E, Ekström L, Thörngren J-O, Ericsson M, Berglund B and Hirschberg AL (2020) Digit Ratio (2D:4D) and Physical Performance in Female Olympic Athletes. Front. Endocrinol. 11:292. doi: 10.3389/fendo.2020.00292

[386] Ziliang Wang, Yan Zhou, et al 2021: Prenatal exposure to bisphenol analogues and digit ratio in children at ages 4 and 6 years: A birth cohort study, Environmental Pollution, Volume 278, 2021, 116820, ISSN 0269-7491, https://doi.org/10.1016/j.envpol.2021.116820.

[387] Kirchengast, S, Dottolo, E, Praxmarer, E, Huber, J. Low digit ratio (2D:4D) is associated with early natural menopause. Am J Hum Biol. 2020; 32:e23374. https://doi.org/10.1002/ajhb.23374

388 Wu Xl, Yang Dy, Chai Wh, Jin Ml, Zhou Xc, Peng L, Zhao Ys. The Ratio of Second to Fourth Digit Length (2D:4D) and Coronary Artery Disease in a Han Chinese Population. Int J Med Sci 2013; 10(11):1584-1588. doi:10.7150/ijms.6360. Available from https://www.medsci.org/v10p1584.htm

389 Manning J. T Wood, S,2004: Second to fourth digit ratio (2D:4D) and testosterone in men: Asian J Androl 2004 Sep; 6: 211-215

390 theguardian.com: Does testosterone make you mean? Amy Fleming; Tue 20 Mar 2018 06.00 GMT; https://www.theguardian.com/science/2018/mar/20/testosterone-myth-male-hormone-be-haviour-risk-taking

391 tstos.com; Asbestos Cover; Up Michelle Whitmer; Last Modified June 7, 2021 https://www.asbestos.com/featured-stories/cover-up/

392 WEIKART, RICHARD 1994: MARX, ENGELS, AND THE ABOLITION OF THE FAMILY History of European Ideas; Vol. 18, No. 5, pp. 657-672, 1994
0191-6599 (93) E0194-6 _ . Copyright c 1994 Elseyier Science Ltd Printed in Great Britain.

393 Philosophy Pages; Garth Kemerling; http://www.philosophypages.com/index.htm

394 Usa today; China bans 'sissy men' from TV to encourage more masculinity in young men; Joe McDonald | The Associated Press; https://eu.usatoday.com/story/entertain-ment/tv/2021/09/02/china-bans-sissy-men-tv-encourages-more-masculinity/5694333001/

395 Christina E. Crawford; 2015; From the Old Family—to the New
; Harward design Magazine; No. 41 / Family Planning; ESSAY

396 Antonio, M.L, Gao, Z, et al 2019: Ancient Rome: A genetic crossroads of Europe and the Med-iterranean; Science. American Association for the Advancement of Science (published November 8, 2019). 366 (6466): 708–714.

397 Bacae, N. 2011: "A Short History of Mathematical Population Dynamics, 31 Springer-Verlag London Limited 2011, p. 31

398 George Getze; Los Angeles Times writer, Salt Lake City Tribune; Friday Nov. 17, 1967; https://www.newspapers.com/image/?clipping_id=36287902&fcfToken=eyJhbGciOi-JIUzI1NilsInR5cCl6IkpXVCJ9.eyJmcmVlLXZpZXctaWQiOjk4MTg5OTMsIm-lhdCl6MTU5MDY5NTA5NSwiZXhwIjoxNTkwNzgxNDk1fQ.GSQC9KZ00G_qo4Q56HKdawvamn zNL37MtAWGW3x95Vg

399 Ehrlich, Paul R. (1968). The Population Bomb. Ballantine Books. p. 135.

400 climatedepot.com: February 19, 2010 1:17 AM; Marc Morano; 1972 Article Unearthed: 'Worse than Hitler': 'Population Bomb' author Paul Ehrlich suggested adding a forced sterilization agent to 'staple food' and 'water supply';
https://www.climatedepot.com/2010/02/19/1972-article-unearthed-worse-than-hitler-population-bomb-author-paul-ehrlich-suggested-adding-a-forced-sterilization-agent-to-staple-food-and-wa-ter-supply/

401 "Ehrlich, Paul R. (1968). The Population Bomb. Ballantine Books. p. 136.

402 azquotes.com ; https://www.azquotes.com/quote/1314148

403 Weindling P. (2012). 'Julian Huxley and the Continuity of Eugenics in Twentieth-century Britain'. Journal of modern European history = Zeitschrift fur moderne europaische Geschichte = Revue d'histoire europeenne contemporaine, 10(4), 480–499. https://doi.org/10.17104/1611-8944_2012_4

404 Brown, Jasmine M; Bland, Roger; 2019.: A Brief History of Awareness of the Link Between Alcohol and Fetal Alcohol Spectrum Disorder. Canadian Journal of Psychiatry. 64 (3): 166.

405 Akison, L. K., Moritz, K. M., & Reid, N. (2019). Adverse reproductive outcomes associated with fetal alcohol exposure: a systematic review, Reproduction, 157(4), 329-343. Retrieved Sep 8, 2021, from https://rep.bioscientifica.com/view/journals/rep/157/4/REP-18-0607.xml

406 Kelly, Sandra J, 2009: GENDER & ALCOHOL; Sexually Dimorphic Effects of Alcohol Exposure during Development on the Processing of Social Cues Alcohol & Alcoholism Vol. 44, No. 6, pp. 555–560, 2009 doi: 10.1093/alcalc/agp061 Advance Access publication 19 September 2009

407 Russell B. 1949: Can A Scientific Society Be Stable? The British Medical Journal; Vol. 2, No. 4640 (Dec. 10, 1949), pp. 1307-1311
JSTORhttps://www.jstor.org › stable

408 Americamagazin; Nov, 27, 2017Margaret Sanger was a eugenicist. Why are we still celebrating her??; John J. Conley, S.J.; https://www.americamagazine.org/politics-society/2017/11/27/marga-ret-sanger-was-eugenicist-why-are-we-still-celebrating-her

409 United Nations: Convention on the Prevention and Punishment of the Crime of Genocide: Ap-proved and proposed for signature and ratification or accession by General Assembly resolution 260 A (III) of 9 December 1948; Entry into force: 12 January 1951, in accordance with article XIII; https://www.ohchr.org/EN/ProfessionalInterest/Pages/CrimeOfGenocide.aspx

410 Paul R Ehrlich; Anne H Ehrlich; John P Holdren, 1977: Ecoscience: population, resources, environment; San Francisco : W.H. Freeman, 1977.

[411] World Bank: Fertility rate, total (births per woman) ; United Nations Population Division. World Population Prospects: 2019; Revisionhttps://data.worldbank.org/indicator/SP.DYN.TFRT.IN

[412] BBC: Fertility rate: 'Jaw-dropping' global crash in children being born; By James Gallagher; Health and science correspondent; 15 July 2020; https://www.bbc.com/news/health-53409521

[413] Vollset S.E., DrPH et al, 2020: Fertility, mortality, migration, and population scenarios for 195 countries and territories from 2017 to 2100: a forecasting analysis for the Global Burden of Disease Study; The Lancet article; July 14, 2020: https://www.thelancet.com/journals/lancet/article/PIIS0140-6736(20)30677-2/fulltext

[414] Local authorities are scrambling to incentivize women to have more children, as the country's birth rate continues to drop; Peter Kotecki Aug 13, 2018, Businessinsider; https://www.businessinsider.com/china-demographic-time-bomb-one-child-limit-2018-8?r=US&IR=T

[415] Morning Consult: Millennials Were Already Putting Off Having Children. Then the Pandemic Hit. BY CLAIRE WILLIAMS; September 28, 2020 at 6:00 am ET crisishttps://morningconsult.com/2020/09/28/millennials-economy-children-poll/

[416] Harward Buisness review; Executive Women and the Myth of Having It All; by Sylvia Ann Hewlett; From the Magazine (April 2002); https://hbr.org/2002/04/executive-women-and-the-myth-of-having-it-all

[417] The Franchise; Elon Musk Says, Civilization will Perish if People Don't Have Enough Children https://thefranchiseuniverse.com/elon-musk-says-civilization-will-perish-if-people-dont-have-enough-children/

[418] Marsh, N, et al, 2017: Oxytocin-enforced norm compliance reduces xenophobic outgroup rejection; PNAS August 29, 2017 114 (35) 9314-9319; first published August 14, 2017

[419] Rockefeller University: Doping Western Cultures With Oxytocin Will Cure Hatred Of Refugees https://www.technocracy.news/doping-western-cultures-oxytocin-will-cure-hatred-refugees/

[420] Carsten K. W. De Dreu c.k.w.et al 2010: Oxytocin promotes human ethnocentrism; Edited by Douglas S. Massey, Princeton University, Princeton, NJ, and approved December 21, 2010 (received for review October 12, 2010); January 10, 2011; 108 (4) 1262-1266; https://doi.org/10.1073/pnas.1015316108

[421] Anti- Empire; Medical Ethics Professor Proposes Governments Add Psychoactive Drugs to Tap Water to Reduce Dissent From Lockdowns; Dr. Parker Crutchfield , 14 Dec 2020; https://anti-empire.com/medical-ethics-professor-proposes-government-adds-psychoactive-drugs-to-tap-water-to-reduce-dissent-from-lockdowns/

[422] Crutchfield, P. Compulsory moral bioenhancement should be covert. Bioethics. 2019; 33: 112–121. https://doi.org/10.1111/bioe.12496

[423] brainkart. Chapter: 11th 12th standard Class Physics science Higher secondary school College Notes https://www.brainkart.com/article/Cosmic-Rays--Latitude-effect--Altitude-effect--Cosmic-ray-showers_2972/

[424] NOAA: Solar Radio Data https://www.ngdc.noaa.gov/stp/solar/solarradio.html

[425] Canada solar weather monitoring services; https://www.nrc-cnrc.gc.ca/eng/solutions/advisory/solar_weather_monitori...

[426] Tanaka et al., 1973: Absolute calibration of solar radio flux density in the microwave region. Solar Phys. 29 (1973) p. 243-262; https://svalgaard.leif.org/research/Tanaka-Calibration-F107.pdf

[427] The Solar Radio Microwave Flux; The Solar Radio Microwave Flux; Guest Post by Leif Svalgaard, May 2009; 12 years ago https://wattsupwiththat.com/2009/05/14/the-solar-radio-microwave-flux/

[428] The Solar Radio Microwave Flux; The Solar Radio Microwave Flux; Guest Post by Leif Svalgaard, May 2009; 12 years ago https://wattsupwiththat.com/2009/05/14/the-solar-radio-microwave-flux/

[429] Popular Science; Do men have hormonal cycles? Short answer: Ever heard of man-struation?; BY DANIEL ENGBER | PUBLISHED OCT 30, 2015 6:38 PM https://www.popsci.com/do-men-have-hormonal-cycles/

[430] Ronca, A. E., Baker, E. S., Bavendam, T. G., Beck, K. D., Miller, V. M., Tash, J. S., & Jenkins, M. (2014). Effects of sex and gender on adaptations to space: reproductive health. Journal of women's health (2002), 23(11), 967–974. https://doi.org/10.1089/jwh.2014.4915

[431] Briggs Michael H. and Briggs Maxine 1972: STEROID HORMONE CONCENTRATIONS IN BLOOD PLASMA FROM RESIDENTS OF ZAMBIA, BELONGING TO DIFFERENT ETHNICAL GROUPS; European Journal of Endocrinology; Volume/Issue: Volume 70: Issue 3; Page Range: 619–624; DOI: https://doi.org/10.1530/acta.0.0700619; https://eje.bioscientifica.com/view/journals/eje/70/3/acta_70_3_017.xml

[432] everydayhealth.com ; Becky Upham: Where Men Spend Their Childhood Determines Testosterone Level, Study Says; Last Updated: June 28, 2018;

https://www.everydayhealth.com/mens-health/where-men-spend-their-childhood-determines-testosterone-level-study-says/

[433] European College of Neuropsychopharmacology (ECNP). (2016, September 18). Lack of interest in sex successfully treated by exposure to bright light. ScienceDaily. Retrieved July 19, 2021 from www.sciencedaily.com/releases/2016/09/160918214443.htm

[434] Szwed, Anita; Kosinska, Magdalena; Manning, John T. 2017: Digit ratio (2D:4D) and month of birth: A link to the solstitial-melatonin-testosterone effect; Early Human Development; Volume 104, 2017, Pages 23-26, ISSN 0378-3782,
https://doi.org/10.1016/j.earlhumdev.2016.11.005.
(https://www.sciencedirect.com/science/article/pii/S0378378216304662)

[435] Myerson, A. Influence of ultraviolet radiation on excretion of sex hormones in the male. Endocrinology 1939;25:7-12.

[436] Yu, Kun et al 2018: Melatonin Regulates the Synthesis of Steroid Hormones on Male Reproduction: A Review; Molecules 2018, 23(2), 447; https://doi.org/10.3390/molecules23020447

[437] Vartolomei, Mihai Dorin et al 2020: Systematic Review of the Impact of Testosterone Replacement Therapy on Depression in Patients with Late-onset Testosterone Deficiency; European Urology Focus; Volume 6, Issue 1, 15 January 2020, Pages 170-177

[438] Zitzmann, Michael, 2020: Testosterone, mood, behaviour and quality of life; Andorlogy; Volume 8, Issue 6; Special Issue on: Late onset Hypogonadism; November 2020
Pages 1598-1605; First published: 13 July 2020; https://doi.org/10.1111/andr.12867

[439] Layton JB, Kim Y, Alexander GC, Emery SL. Association Between Direct-to-Consumer Advertising and Testosterone Testing and Initiation in the United States, 2009-2013. JAMA. 2017;317(11):1159–1166. doi:10.1001/jama.2016.21041

[440] Gooren Louis J. & Behre Hermann M. 2012: Diagnosing and treating testosterone deficiency in different parts of the world: changes between 2006 and 2010;
The Aging Male; Volume 15, 2012 - Issue 1Pages 22-27 | Received 09 Sep 2011, Accepted 12 Dec 2011, Published online: 30 Jan 2012; https://doi.org/10.3109/13685538.2011.650246

[441] Low Testosterone – Could Your Cell Phone or Laptop Be to Blame?; ;Dr. Friedman's Health Blog; https://www.doctordavidfriedman.com/blog/low-testosterone-could-your-cell-phone-or-laptop-be-to-blame-1

[442] Dr. Puneet Masson, Penn Medicine: The Truth About Testosterone and Male Fertility; July 09, 2015; Male Fertility
https://www.pennmedicine.org/updates/blogs/fertility-blog/2015/july/the-truth-about-testosterone-and-male-fertility

[443] How to Live on Testosterone for the Rest of Your Life; Anabolic Doc; 23.02.2021; https://www.youtube.com/watch?v=GQ4jxJPkG98

[444] Elsevier. (2019, July 18). Testosterone replacement therapy (TRT) can increase men's risk of stroke and heart attack. ScienceDaily. Retrieved July 19, 2021 from www.sciencedaily.com/releases/2019/07/190718123258.htm

[445] Low Testosterone – Could Your Cell Phone or Laptop Be to Blame? ;Dr. Friedman's Health Blog; https://www.doctordavidfriedman.com/blog/low-testosterone-could-your-cell-phone-or-laptop-be-to-blame-1

[446] Sandblom, Robert E et al 1983: Obstructive Sleep Apnea Syndrome Induced by Testosterone Administration; March 3, 1983; New England Journal of Medicin; 1983; 308:508-510; DOI: 10.1056/NEJM198303033080908

[447] Ana Marcella Rivas, Zachary Mulkey, Joaquin Lado-Abeal & Shannon Yarbrough (2014) Diagnosing and Managing Low Serum Testosterone, Baylor University Medical Center Proceedings, 27:4, 321-324, DOI: 10.1080/08998280.2014.11929145

[448] Kapoor, D., Clarke, S., Channer, K.S. and Jones, T.H. (2007), Erectile dysfunction is associated with low bioactive testosterone levels and visceral adiposity in men with type 2 diabetes. International Journal of Andrology, 30: 500-507. https://doi.org/10.1111/j.1365-2605.2007.00744.x

[449] Glueck CJ, Richardson-Royer C, Schultz R, et al. Testosterone Therapy, Thrombophilia–Hypofibrinolysis, and Hospitalization for Deep Venous Thrombosis-Pulmonary Embolus: An Exploratory, Hypothesis-Generating Study. Clinical and Applied Thrombosis/Hemostasis. April 2014:244-249. doi:10.1177/1076029613499819

[450] Low Testosterone – Could Your Cell Phone or Laptop Be to Blame?; ;Dr. Friedman's Health Blog; https://www.doctordavidfriedman.com/blog/low-testosterone-could-your-cell-phone-or-laptop-be-to-blame-1

[451] Eisner, Manuel P, 2003: Long-Term Historical Trends in Violent Crime; Crime and Justice 30:83-142 · January 2003. p.88

[452] Lead and Lead Poisoning from Antiquity to Modern Times; The Ohio Journal of Science. v88, n3 (June, 1988), 78-84; https://kb.osu.edu/handle/1811/23252

[453] Trevor-Roper, Hugh, 1966: The Rise of Christian Europe (2nd. ed., London, 1966), p. 27)

454 Seeck, O.1921: Geschichte des Untergangs der antiken Welt. 6 Bände. Metzler, Stuttgart 1895–1920 (mehrere Neuauflagen; Nachdruck der Ausgabe von 1921 chapter I, the extinction oft he best.

455 The English review: Emmet Scott (October 2012) The Role of Infanticide and Abortion in Pagan Rome's Decline.

456 Seeck, O.1921: Geschichte des Untergangs der antiken Welt. 6 Bände. Metzler, Stuttgart 1895–1920 (mehrere Neuauflagen; Nachdruck der Ausgabe von 1921 chapter I, the extinction of the best. p. 372

457 Gilfillan S. C : Roman Culture And Dysgenic Lead Poisoning; Mankind Quarterly; p.132 https://www.unzcloud.net/PDF/PERIODICAL/MankindQuarterly-1965jan/13-31//

458 Arnold Hugh Martin Jones, A. H. M. 1986: The Later Roman Empire, 284-602: A Social Economic and Administrative Survey, Volume 2; Taylor & Francis, 1986; p. 1061

459 The Trumpet; The Roman Empire thrived When Its Citizens Valued Marriage And Family. It Fell When The Family Stopped Being Cherished; GERALD FLURRY, AUGUST 4, 2008;

460 Gibbon, Edward 1776:: History of the Roman Empire and Fall of the Western Roman Empire; Strahan & Cadell, London; Publication date; 1776–1789

461 Cahill Thomas, 1996: How the Irish saved civilization, Anchor Books, New York.p. 14

462 Cahill Thomas, 1996: How the Irish saved civilization, Anchor Books, New York.p. 59

463 Harris, William V., 1994: Child Exposure in the Roman Empire; The Journal of Roman Studies, Vol. 84

464 Gibbon, Edward 1776:: History of the Roman Empire and Fall of the Western Roman Empire; Strahan & Cadell, London; Publication date; 1776–1789

465 INCITE! Women of Color Against Violence INCITE! Women of Color Against Violence Duke University Press, 2 Sep 2016

466 Foundation for Economic education: The Ancient Suicide of the West; December 1, 198; https://fee.org/articles/the-ancient-suicide-of-the-west/

467 Dutton, E.: 2019: Race Differences in Ethnocentrism; Arctos Media, London. p 215

468 Murray, Charles, 2003: Human Accomplishment: The Pursuit of Excellence in the Arts and Sciences, 800 B.C. to 1950; New York: Harper Collins Publishers; p. 31

469 M. De Keersmaecker et al. A Short Historical Overview on the Use of Lead; Universiteit Gent; Academic Bibliography; https://biblio.ugent.be/publication/8558334/file/8558350.pdf

470 NDNR: METAL AND MINERAL TOXICITY PRESENTING AS NEUROLOGICAL COMPLAINTS; By Editor1 Posted December 28, 2008 https://ndnr.com/neurology/metal-and-mineral-toxicity-presenting-as-neurological-complaints-2/

471 ARCHIBALD ANNA; The Disturbingly Long History of Lead Toxicity in Winemaking BY https://www.winemag.com/2020/07/20/lead-toxicity-wine-history/

472 M. De Keersmaecker et al. A Short Historical Overview on the Use of Lead; Universiteit Gent; Academic Bibliography; https://biblio.ugent.be/publication/8558334/file/8558350.pdf

473 Dr. Herbert L. Needleman; HISTORY OF LEAD POISONING IN THE WORLD; http://103.24.47.157/history_of_lead_poisoning_in_the_world.htm

474 Doumouchtsis KK, Doumouchtsis SK, Doumouchtsis EK, Perrea DN. The effect of lead intoxication on endocrine functions. J Endocrinol Invest. 2009 Feb;32(2):175-83. doi: 10.1007/BF03345710. PMID: 19411819.

475 Lead poisoning in ancient Rome; Encyclopaedia Romana; http://penelope.uchicago.edu/~grout/encyclopaedia_romana/wine/leadpoisoning.html

476 Aneni, Monica. (2018). Lead Poisoning in Ancient Rome. Department of Classics, University of Ibadan;   https://www.researchgate.net/publication/325023100_Lead_Poisoning_in_Ancient_Rome

477 Aneni, Monica. (2018). Lead Poisoning in Ancient Rome. Department of Classics, University of Ibadan;   https://www.researchgate.net/publication/325023100_Lead_Poisoning_in_Ancient_Rome

478 By Joanna Moore, et al 2021: The Family in Past Perspective; Edition 1st Edition; First Published 2021; Imprint Routledge; P. 22

479 Sohn, Emily; Lead: Versatile Metal, Long Legacy; Dartmouth Toxic Metals Superfund Research Program; ; https://sites.dartmouth.edu/toxmetal/more-metals/lead-versatile-metal-long-legacy/

480 Retief, FP; Cilliers, L. 2005: LEAD POISONING IN ANCIENT ROME; Acta Theologica Supplementum 7 Vol. 26 No. 2 (2006): ; https://www.ajol.info/index.php/actat/article/view/52570

481 GVGK Tang ; Of Gods & Emperors: Trans Experiences in Ancient Rome; https://notchesblog.com/2017/11/14/of-gods-emperors-trans-experiences-in-ancient-rome/

482 Wani AL, Ara A, Usmani JA. Lead toxicity: a review. Interdiscip Toxicol. 2015 Jun;8(2):55-64. doi: 10.1515/intox-2015-0009. PMID: 27486361; PMCID: PMC4961898.

483 Dekker Marcel, 1978: Hypogonadism in Chronically Lead -Poisoned Men; UCLA School of Medicine, Los Angeles, California 90048 and Reproductive Research Branch National Institute of Child Health; Infertility, 1(1), 33-51 (1978)

484 Osmel La Llave León and José M. Salas Pacheco, 2020: Effects of Lead on Reproductive Health; Published: April 15th 2020; DOI: 10.5772/intechopen.91992

485 Yu T, Li Z, Wang X, Niu K, Xiao J, Li B. [Effect of lead exposure on male sexual hormone]. Wei Sheng Yan Jiu. 2010 Jul;39(4):413-5. Chinese. PMID: 20726225.

486 Braunstein GD, Dahlgren J, Loriaux DL. Hypogonadism in chronically lead-poisoned men. Infertility. 1978;1(1):33-51. PMID: 12265605.

487 Doumouchtsis KK, Doumouchtsis SK, Doumouchtsis EK, Perrea DN. The effect of lead intoxication on endocrine functions. J Endocrinol Invest. 2009 Feb;32(2):175-83. doi: 10.1007/BF03345710. PMID: 19411819.

488 Barrett, Kimberly L. ; January 2013; Assessing the Relationship Between Hotspots of Lead and Hotspots of Crime; University of South Florida, Criminology and Criminal Justice Commons.

489 Wani AL, Ara A, Usmani JA. Lead toxicity: a review. Interdiscip Toxicol. 2015 Jun;8(2):55-64. doi: 10.1515/intox-2015-0009. PMID: 27486361; PMCID: PMC4961898.

490 Araújo GCSd, Mourão NT, Pinheiro IN, Xavier AR, Gameiro VS (2015): Lead Toxicity Risks in Gunshot Victims. PLoS ONE 10(10): e0140220. https://doi.org/10.1371/journal.pone.0140220 https://journals.plos.org/plosone/article?id=10.1371/journal.pone.01402200

491 Bouchard, M. F., Bellinger, D. C., Weuve, J., Matthews-Bellinger, J., Gilman, S. E., Wright, R. O., Schwartz, J., & Weisskopf, M. G. (2009). Blood lead levels and major depressive disorder, panic disorder, and generalized anxiety disorder in US young adults. Archives of general psychiatry, 66(12), 1313–1319. https://doi.org/10.1001/archgenpsychiatry.2009.164

492 Bouchard MF, Bellinger DC, Weuve J, Matthews-Bellinger J, Gilman SE, Wright RO, Schwartz J, Weisskopf MG. Blood lead levels and major depressive disorder, panic disorder, and generalized anxiety disorder in US young adults. Arch Gen Psychiatry. 2009 Dec;66(12):1313-9. doi: 10.1001/archgenpsychiatry.2009.164. PMID: 19996036; PMCID: PMC2917196.

493 Edetanlen B, Saheeb B. Effect of bone fracture(s) on blood lead levels from retained lead pellets in craniomaxillofacial region. Human & Experimental Toxicology. 2019;38(12):1378-1383. doi:10.1177/0960327119862019

494 Lead poisoning in ancient Rome; Encyclopaedia Romana; http://penelope.uchicago.edu/~grout/encyclopaedia_romana/wine/leadpoisoning.html

495 Healthliine, How Alcohol Affects Testosterone; https://www.healthline.com/health/how-alcohol-affects-testosterone

496 Olalla López-Costas, Malin Kylander, Nadine Mattielli, Noemi Álvarez-Fernández, Marta Pérez-Rodríguez, Tim Mighall, Richard Bindler, Antonio Martínez Cortizas,; Human bones tell the story of atmospheric mercury and lead exposure at the edge of Roman World,; Science of The Total Environment,; Volume 710,; 2020,; 136319,; ISSN 0048-9697,; https://doi.org/10.1016/j.scitotenv.2019.136319.(https://www.sciencedirect.com/science/article/pii/S0048969719363156)

497 Siblerud RL, Motl J, Kienholz E. Psychometric evidence that mercury from silver dental fillings may be an etiological factor in depression, excessive anger, and anxiety. Psychol Rep. 1994 Feb;74(1):67-80. doi: 10.2466/pr0.1994.74.1.67. PMID: 8153237.[cited 2021 Sept 16]

498 Zhu X, Kusaka Y, Sato K, Zhang Q. The endocrine disruptive effects of mercury. Environ Health Prev Med. 2000 Jan;4(4):174-83. doi: 10.1007/BF02931255. PMID: 21432482; PMCID: PMC2723593.

499 Seeker; John Dyer; Antimony Poisoning — Not Lead — May Have Contributed to the Roman Empire's Fall; Analysis of a 2,000-year-old Roman pipe fragment from Pompeii revealed traces of antimony, a chemical that's even more toxic than lead. 8/17/2017

500 Sax L. Polyethylene terephthalate may yield endocrine disruptors. Environ Health Perspect. 2010 Apr;118(4):445-8. doi: 10.1289/ehp.0901253. PMID: 20368129; PMCID: PMC2854718.

501 Shotyk W, Krachler M (2007) Contamination of bottled waters with antimony leaching from polyethylene terephthalate (PET) increases upon storage. Environ Sci Technol 41:1560–1563

502 By The Recovery Village; Editor Megan Hull; Medically Reviewed By Dr. Anna; Pickering, PHD; Updated on 07/13/21 https://www.therecoveryvillage.com/process-addiction/porn-addiction/pornography-statistics/

503 Amis, Martin, 2001: A rough trade; London: guardian.co.uk. Retrieved April 10, 2009.

504 The guardian: The growth of internet porn tells us more about ourselves than technology; John Naughton; Sun 30 Dec 2018; https://www.theguardian.com/commentisfree/2018/dec/30/internet-porn-says-more-about-ourselves-than-technology

505 Helmore, Edward: 2009: Home porn gives industry the blues, guardian.co.uk, 16 December 2007. Retrieved 04 March 2009.

506 AP news: Web Site Closed, Child Porn Alleged; JEANNINE AVERSA; March 26, 2001; https://apnews.com/article/8c9fd469d8a563a8f8b23ca6b4f25489

[507] Wbur.org: "Am I Normal?' Check Biggest Study Yet Of Penis Size, Among 15,000 Men March 03, 2015; Carey Goldberg; https://www.wbur.org/news/2015/03/03/biggest-study-penis-size

[508] King BM. Average-Size Erect Penis: Fiction, Fact, and the Need for Counseling. J Sex Marital Ther. 2021;47(1):80-89. doi: 10.1080/0092623X.2020.1787279. Epub 2020 Jul 15. PMID: 32666897.

[509] Veale, D., Miles, S., Bramley, S., Muir, G. and Hodsoll, J. (2015), Nomograms for flaccid/erect penis length and circumference. BJU Int, 115: 978-986. https://doi.org/10.1111/bju.13010

[510] Spiegel international: Scientists Reassure Men Worried About Penis Size; Christian Stöcker; 06.06.2007; https://www.spiegel.de/international/zeitgeist/bigger-than-they-think-scientists-reassure-men-worried-about-penis-size-a-487102.html

[511] Türker, Y., Nazıroğlu, M., Gümral, N. et al. Selenium and L-Carnitine Reduce Oxidative Stress in the Heart of Rat Induced by 2.45-GHz Radiation from Wireless Devices. Biol Trace Elem Res 143, 1640–1650 (2011). https://doi.org/10.1007/s12011-011-8994-0

[512] Safaeian Layen, G., Davachi, S., Nemati, A., & Safaeian Laein, S. (2021). Effects of Low-frequency Electromagnetic Waves on the Spleen, Liver, and Kidney Weight and Therapeutic Role of Vitamin C in Mice. Journal of Nutrition, Fasting and Health, 9(1), 75-81.

[513] Anan, H. H., Gawish, M. F., Amer, M. G., & Ibrahim, N. E. (2012). Effects of low magnetic irradiation on morphology and ultrastructure of parotid glands in rats and amelioration by vitamin E. J Cytol Histol, 3, 139.

[514] Ding, Z., Li, J., Li, F., Mephryar, M. M., Wu, S., Zhang, C., & Zeng, Y. (2017). Vitamin C and Vitamin E Protected B95-8 and Balb/c-3T3 Cells from Apoptosis Induced by Intermittent 50Hz ELF-EMF Radiation. Iranian journal of public health, 46(1), 23–34.

[515] Rubin R MD; 2921: Sorting Out Whether Vitamin D Deficiency Raises COVID-19 Risk. JAMA. 2021;325(4):329–330. doi:10.1001/jama.2020.24127; https://jamanetwork.com/journals/jama/fullarticle/2775003

[516] Peer-Reviewed Publication; WASHINGTON UNIVERSITY SCHOOL OF MEDICINE NEWS RELEASE 25-MAY-2021; https://www.eurekalert.org/news-releases/608834

[517] Salonia, A., Pontillo, M.et al (2021), Severely low testosterone in males with COVID-19: A case-control study. Andrology, 9: 1043-1052. https://doi.org/10.1111/andr.12993

[518] Dhindsa S, Zhang N, McPhaul MJ, Wu Z, Ghoshal AK, Erlich EC, Mani K, Randolph GJ, Edwards JR, Mudd PA, Diwan A.2021: Relationship of circulating sex hormones with inflammation and disease severity in COVID19. JAMA Network Open. May 25, 2021

[519] Hussain, A. N., Hussain, F., & Hashmi, S. K. (2020). Role of testosterone in COVID-19 patients - A double-edged sword?. Medical hypotheses, 144, 110287. https://doi.org/10.1016/j.mehy.2020.110287

[520] McCarter Stephanie, MD 2020: Effects of EMF Radiation Related to COVID-19 Infection; EMF/EMR; National Association of Environmental Medicine ; https://envmedicine.com/effects-of-emf-radiation-related-to-covld-19-infection/

[521] Zheng, S., Zou, Q. et al. (2022). Serum level of testosterone predicts disease severity of male COVID-19 patients and is related to T-cell immune modulation by transcriptome analysis. Clinica chimica acta; international journal of clinical chemistry, 524, 132–138. https://doi.org/10.1016/j.cca.2021.11.006

[522] 21-Marshall TG, Heil TJR. Electrosmog and autoimmune disease. Immunol Res. 2017 Feb;65(1):129-135. doi: 10.1007/s12026-016-8825-7. PMID: 27412293; PMCID: PMC5406447: https://pubmed.ncbi.nlm.nih.gov/27412293/

[523] Ibrahim, R., Ali, A., Khamis, N., Mohammed, H. (2019). Effect Of Exposure To Wi-Fi Router Radiation On The Lung Of Adult Male Albino Rats: Histological And Immunohistochemical Study. Egyptian Journal of Histology, 42(4), 1059-1069. doi: 10.21608/ejh.2019.7317.1070

[524] Gharib, Ola A: Effect of kombucha on some trace element levels in different organs of electromagnetic field exposed rats, Journal of Radiation Research and Applied Sciences, Volume 7, Issue 1, 2014, Pages 18-22, ISSN 1687-8507, https://doi.org/10.1016/j.jrras.2013.11.002.

[525] Baltaci AK, Mogulkoc R, Salbacak A, Celik I, Sivrikaya A. The role of zinc supplementation in the inhibition of tissue damage caused by exposure to electromagnetic field in rat lung and liver tissues. Bratisl Lek Listy. 2012;113(7):400-3. doi: 10.4149/bll_2012_090. PMID: 22794512.

[526] Holick MF, Chen TC. 2008: Vitamin D deficiency: a worldwide problem with health consequences. OUP Academic. https://academic.oup.com/ajcn/article/87/4/1080S/4633477. Published April 1, 2008.

[527] Kinuta K, Tanaka H, Moriwake T, Aya K, Kato S, Seino Y. Vitamin D is an important factor in estrogen biosynthesis of both female and male gonads. Endocrinology. 2000 Apr;141(4):1317-24. doi: 10.1210/endo.141.4.7403. PMID: 10746634.

[528] Pilz S, Frisch S, Koertke H, Kuhn J, Dreier J, Obermayer-Pietsch B, Wehr E, Zittermann A. Effect of vitamin D supplementation on testosterone levels in men. Horm Metab Res. 2011 Mar;43(3):223-5. doi: 10.1055/s-0030-1269854. Epub 2010 Dec 10. PMID: 21154195.

[529] Huang, Hui MD1,*; Guo, Jing MD, PhD2,*; Chen, Qingyu MD, PhD3; Chen, Xiaotong MD3; Yang, Yabo MD, PhD1; Zhang, Wangjian PhD4; Liu, Yong MD5; Chen, Xiaoli MD, PhD1; Yang, Dongzi MD, PhD1 The synergistic effects of vitamin D and estradiol deficiency on metabolic syndrome in Chinese postmenopausal women, Menopause: October 2019 - Volume 26 - Issue 10 - p 1171-1177 doi: 10.1097/GME.0000000000001370

[530] Rubin R. Sorting Out Whether Vitamin D Deficiency Raises COVID-19 Risk. JAMA. 2021;325(4):329–330. doi:10.1001/jama.2020.24127; https://jamanetwork.com/journals/jama/fullarticle/2775003

[531] 20- José L Hernández, et. al. Vitamin D Status in Hospitalized Patients with SARS-CoV-2 Infection, The Journal of Clinical Endocrinology & Metabolism, 2020;, dgaa733, https://doi.org/10.1210/clinem/dgaa733

[532] Holloway, Pamela, et al 2020; Viral Pandemic: A Review of Integrative Medicine Treatment Considerations; Proceedings of ACIM Research; Vol 2 No 2 (2020): Vol 2 No 2 (2020).

[533] Daneshkhah, A., Agrawal, V., Eshein, A. et al. Evidence for possible association of vitamin D status with cytokine storm and unregulated inflammation in COVID -19 patients. Aging Clin Exp Res 32, 2141–2158 (2020). https://doi.org/10.1007/s40520-020-01677-y

[534] Borsche, Lorenz, Bernd Glauner, and Julian von Mendel. 2021. "COVID-19 Mortality Risk Correlates Inversely with Vitamin D3 Status, and a Mortality Rate Close to Zero Could Theoretically Be Achieved at 50 ng/mL 25(OH)D3: Results of a Systematic Review and Meta-Analysis" Nutrients 13, no. 10: 3596. https://doi.org/10.3390/nu13103596

[535] Jerusalem post ; Vitamin D supplements can help protect patients with new COVID-19 strain; By JUDY SIEGEL-ITZKOVICH; JULY 25, 2022; https://www.jpost.com/health-and-wellness/article-713006

[536] Diab, YAA et al 2021: Protective Effect of Vitamin D against Harmful Effect of Cell Phone Radiation Exposure on Albino Rat Testis; Annals of R.S.C.B., ISSN:1583-6258, Vol. 25, Issue 6, 2021, Pages. 5119 - 5128 Received 25 April 2021; Accepted 08 May 2021

[537] El-Gohary, Ola Ahmed and Abdel-Azeem, Said Mona. 2016: Effect of electromagnetic waves from mobile phone on immune status of male rats: possible protective role of vitamin D. Canadian Journal of Physiology and Pharmacology. 95(2): 151-156. https://doi.org/10.1139/cjpp-2016-0218

[538] Wally, Riyadh Hussein 2020: Indian Journal of Forensic Medicine & Toxicology . Apr-Jun 2020, Vol. 14 Issue 2, p2426-2431. 6p.

[539] Diab, YAA et al 2021: Protective Effect of Vitamin D against Harmful Effect of Cell Phone Radiation Exposure on Albino Rat Testis; Annals of R.S.C.B., ISSN:1583-6258, Vol. 25, Issue 6, 2021, Pages. 5119 - 5128 Received 25 April 2021; Accepted 08 May 2021

[540] Medicalnewstoday; What are vitamins, and how do they work?; Medically reviewed by Alexandra Perez, PharmD, MBA, BCGP — Written by Yvette Brazier — Updated on December 15, 2020https://www.medicalnewstoday.com/articles/195878#_noHeaderPrefixedContent

[541] DENISE R. COOPER, O. RAY KLING, MARY P. CARPENTER,1987: Effect of Vitamin E Deficiency on Serum Concentrations of Follicle-Stimulating Hormone and Testosterone during Testicular Maturation and Degeneration, Endocrinology, Volume 120, Issue 1, 1 January 1987, Pages 83–90, https://doi.org/10.1210/endo-120-1-83

[542] Oral, B., Guney, M., Ozguner, F. et al. Endometrial apoptosis induced by a 900-MHz mobile phone: Preventive effects of vitamins E and C. Adv Therapy 23, 957–973 (2006). https://doi.org/10.1007/BF02850217

[543] Ghanbari AA, Shabani K, Nejad DM.2015 Protective Effects of Vitamin E Consumption against 3MT Electromagnetic Field Effects on Oxidative Parameters in Substantia Nigra in Rats. Basic Clin Neurosci. 2016 Oct 7(4):315-22.

[544] El, Abd & Na, Rahman & Am, Hady & Eltahawy, Noaman. (2014). Silymarin and Vitamin E modulate 950MHz Electromagnetic Field-induced Oxidative Stress and Hormonal Changes in Male Albino Rats. Journal of American Science 2014;10(9). 10. 170-176.

[545] Hashemi, Jamilah M. et al 2013: Pumpkin Seed Oil and Vitamin E Improve Reproductive Function of Male Rats Inflicted by Testicular Injury; World Applied Sciences Journal 23 (10): 1351-1359, 2013 ISSN 1818-4952

[546] Ulku, R., Akdag, M.Z., Erdogan, S. et al. Extremely Low-Frequency Magnetic Field Decreased Calcium, Zinc and Magnesium Levels in Costa of Rat. Biol Trace Elem Res 143, 359–367 (2011). https://doi.org/10.1007/s12011-010-8855-2

[547] Baltaci AK, Mogulkoc R, Salbacak A, Celik I, Sivrikaya A. 2012: The role of zinc supplementation in the inhibition of tissue damage caused by exposure to electromagnetic field in rat lung and liver tissues. Bratisl Lek Listy. 2012;113(7):400-3. doi: 10.4149/bll_2012_090. PMID: 22794512.

[548] Claudia Consales, Caterina Merla, et al, Benassi , 2012: "Electromagnetic Fields, Oxidative Stress, and Neurodegeneration", International Journal of Cell Biology, vol. 2012, Article ID 683897, 16 pages, 2012. https://doi.org/10.1155/2012/683897

[549] An, Kang & Wang, Qiuli & Zhang, Yi & Guo, Dongmei & Cui, Xi. (2015). The preventative effects of zinc and vitamin E supplementation on cellular phone radiationinduced oxidative stress in brain tissues of rats and their fetuses. Trace Elements and Electrolytes. 32. 10.5414/TEX01377.

[550] Prasad, A. S, Chris S. Mantzoros, Frances W.J. Beck, Joseph W. Hess, George J. Brewer, 1996: Zinc status and serum testosterone levels of healthy adults; Nutrition; Volume 12, Issue 5, 1996; Pages 344-348; ISSN 0899-9007,; https://doi.org/10.1016/S0899-9007(96)80058-X.

[551] Prasad, A.S., Abbasi, A.A., Rabbani, P. and Dumouchelle, E. (1981), Effect of zinc supplementation on serum testosterone level in adult male sickle cell anemia subjects. Am. J. Hematol., 10: 119-127. https://doi.org/10.1002/ajh.2830100203

[552] Çınar V., et al M. 2021: The effects of the zinc supplementation and weight trainings on the testosterone levels // Человек. Спорт. Медицина. 2017. №4. URL: https://cyberleninka.ru/article/n/the-effects-of-the-zinc-supplementation-and-weight-trainings-on-the-testosterone-levels (дата обращения: 13.07.2021).

[553] Kilic M. Effect of fatiguing bicycle exercise on thyroid hormone and testosterone levels in sedentary males supplemented with oral zinc. Neuro Endocrinol Lett. 2007 Oct;28(5):681-5. PMID: 17984944.

[554] Bediz, Cem & Baltaci, Abdulkerim Kasim & Mogulkoc, Rasim & Oztekin, Esma. (2006). Zinc Supplementation Ameliorates Electromagnetic Field-Induced Lipid Peroxidation in the Rat Brain. The Tohoku journal of experimental medicine. 208. 133-40. 10.1620/tjem.208.133.

[555] Kumar N, Verma RP, Singh LP, Varshney VP, Dass RS. 2006: Effect of different levels and sources of zinc supplementation on quantitative and qualitative semen attributes and serum testosterone level in crossbred cattle (Bos indicus x Bos taurus) bulls. Reprod Nutr Dev. 2006 Nov-Dec;46(6):663-75. doi: 10.1051/rnd:2006041. Epub 2006 Dec 15. PMID: 17169313.

[556] Vogel-González, Marina et al 2020: Low zinc levels at clinical admission associates with poor outcomes in COVID-19; medRxiv 2020.10.07.20208645; doi: https://doi.org/10.1101/2020.10.07.20208645 ; October 11, 2020.

[557] Jothimani, Dinesh; Kailasam, Ezhilarasan; 2020: COVID-19: Poor outcomes in patients with zinc deficiency,; International Journal of Infectious Diseases,; Volume 100,; 2020,; Pages 343-349,; ISSN 1201-9712,; https://doi.org/10.1016/j.ijid.2020.09.014.

[558] Al-Awfi JS (2020) Zinc may have a potential role in taste malfunctions treatment for COVID-19 patients. Integr Food Nutr Metab 7: DOI: 10.15761/IFNM.1000296

[559] Cinar, V., Polat, Y., Baltaci, A.K. et al. Effects of Magnesium Supplementation on Testosterone Levels of Athletes and Sedentary Subjects at Rest and after Exhaustion. Biol Trace Elem Res 140, 18–23 (2011). https://doi.org/10.1007/s12011-010-8676-3

[560] Sturges, Missy. How magnesium may protect against EMF radiation. Go Integrative Health, 2020.https://gointegrativehealth.org/blogs/how-magnesium-may-protect-against-emf-radiation/

[561] Baharara, J. et al : Protective effect of date palm pollen (Phoenix dactylifera) on sperm parameters and sexual hormones in male NMRI mice exposed to low frequency electromagnetic field (50 Hz); J Herbmed Pharmacol. 2015;4(3): 75-80.

[562] Arezoo, Farsi; et al 2013: Improvement effect of rosmarinic acid on serum testosterone level after exposing with electromagnetic fields; international journal of women's health and reproduction SCIENCES SUMMER 2013 , Volume 1 , Number 2; Page(s) 45 To 50.

[563] Schmid, P. et al 1982: Serum FSH, LH, and Testosterone in Humans After Physical Exercise; Int J Sports Med 1982; 03(2): 84-89; DOI: 10.1055/s-2008-1026068

[564] Gharib, Ola A: Effect of kombucha on some trace element levels in different organs of electromagnetic field exposed rats, Journal of Radiation Research and Applied Sciences, Volume 7, Issue 1, 2014, Pages 18-22, ISSN 1687-8507, https://doi.org/10.1016/j.jrras.2013.11.002.

[565] Everlywell.com; Medically reviewed by Neka Miller, PhD on February 15, 2021. Vitamin D vs. D3: what's the difference? https://www.everlywell.com/blog/vitamin-d/vitamin-d-vs-d3-whats-the-difference/

[566] Healthline: 7 Foods That May Help Boost Testosterone https://www.healthline.com/nutrition/testosterone-boosting-food#frequently-asked-questions

[567] Healthliine, How Alcohol Affects Testosterone; https://www.healthline.com/health/how-alcohol-affects-testosterone

[568] Benedict C. Eke, Norbert N. Jibiri, Evelyn N. Bede, Bede C. Anusionwu, Chikwendu E. Orji, Chinwe S. Alisi,; 2017: Effect of ingestion of microwaved foods on serum anti-oxidant enzymes and vitamins of albino rats; Journal of Radiation Research and Applied Sciences; Volume 10, Issue 2, 2017, Pages 148-151, ISSN 1687-8507,

[569] Russian Monastery Goes Global With Wireless; Realwire.com; https://www.realwire.com/releases/Russian-Monastery-Goes-Global-With-Wireless 12 Jan 2015

[570] EMFWISEDistance and the Inverse Square Law; http://www.emfwise.com/distance.php
[571] Do TVs Emit EMF Radiation? By Roland; https://emfguardtips.com/do-tvs-emit-emf-radiation/

9 783033 088160